Gathering Disciples

Gathering Disciples

Essays in Honor of Christopher J. Ellis

Edited by
MYRA BLYTH
& ANDY GOODLIFF

Foreword by Neville Callam

◠PICKWICK *Publications* · Eugene, Oregon

GATHERING DISCIPLES
Essays in Honor of Christopher J. Ellis

Copyright © 2017 Wipf and Stock Publishers. All rights reserved. Except for brief quotations in critical publications or reviews, no part of this book may be reproduced in any manner without prior written permission from the publisher. Write: Permissions, Wipf and Stock Publishers, 199 W. 8th Ave., Suite 3, Eugene, OR 97401.

Pickwick Publications
An Imprint of Wipf and Stock Publishers
199 W. 8th Ave., Suite 3
Eugene, OR 97401

www.wipfandstock.com

PAPERBACK ISBN: 978-1-4982-3157-2
HARDCOVER ISBN: 978-1-5326-0440-9
EBOOK ISBN: 978-1-5326-0439-3

Cataloguing-in-Publication data:

Names: Blyth, Myra | Goodliff, Andy

Title: Gathering disciples : essays in honor of Christopher J. Ellis / edited by Myra Blyth and Andy Goodliff.

Description: Eugene, OR: Pickwick Publications, 2017 | Includes bibliographical references.

Identifiers: ISBN 978-1-4982-3157-2 (paperback) | ISBN 978-1-5326-0440-9 (hardcover) | ISBN 978-1-5326-0439-3 (ebook)

Subjects: LCSH: Baptists—History | Baptists—Doctrines | Public worship—Baptists | Ellis, Christopher John

Classification: BX6331.3 B49 2017 (paperback) | BX6331.3 (ebook)

Manufactured in the U.S.A.   02/03/17

The words to "The Best Way of All" and "God of Mission" by Christopher J. Ellis © Kevin Mayhew and are reproduced by permission of Kevin Mayhew Ltd, Licence no. KMAL160816/02.

The words to 'The Lord is here - he finds us as we seek' by Christopher Ellis © 1987 Oxford University Press from New Songs of Praise 3. Reproduced by permission. All rights reserved.

Contents

Contributors | vii
Foreword by Neville Callam | ix
Introduction | xiii

1 "Help Us to Search for Truth": Baptists and Doing Theology | 1
    —Robert Ellis

2 "The Lord Is Here": How Worship Confronts the Powers | 26
    —Craig Gardiner

3 "God of Love We Praise You": Baptist Worship
   and Congregational Song | 47
    —Shona Shaw

4 "In Obedient Living Find Your Home": Reflections on Baptists
   and Discipleship | 60
    —Paul Goodliff

5 "Your Will Be Always Done": Congregational Discernment
   as Contextual Discipleship | 74
    —Stuart Blythe

6 "That We Might See Ourselves as We Could Be": Baptist Interpretations of Scripture on the Complementarity of Male and Female | 90
    —Beth Allison-Glenny

7 "The Water Buries Like a Tomb": Baptists and Baptism | 112
    —Sally Nelson

8 "A Sign of Unity": The Changing Theology and Practice
   of Lord's Supper amongst British Baptists | 128
    —Myra Blyth

9 "To Become the Future Now": Baptists Being Shaped by the Table | 153
  —Ashley Lovett

10 "We are Gathered with the Millions": Celebrating the Communion of Saints | 173
  —Ruth Gouldbourne

11 "We Need Each Other": The Ecumenical Engagement of European Baptists | 185
  —Tony Peck

12 "Father, Son, and Holy Spirit": The Triune Creator in Hymn and Theology | 204
  —Paul S. Fiddes

13 "The Ground on Which we Dare to Build": Putting Calvinism to Work | 221
  —Nigel G. Wright

14 "Missionary God": The Place of Mission amongst British Baptists | 234
  —Andy Goodliff

Bibliography of the Writings of Christopher J. Ellis | 253
General Bibliography | 255

Contributors

Beth Allison-Glenny is Minister at John Bunyan Baptist Church, Cowley.

Myra Blyth is Chaplain and Tutorial Fellow in Pastoral Studies at Regent's Park College, Oxford.

Stuart Blythe is Rector at the International Baptist Theological Study Centre, Amsterdam.

Neville Callam is the General Secretary of the Baptist World Alliance.

Robert Ellis is Principal of Regent's Park College, Oxford.

Paul Fiddes is Professor of Systematic Theology at the University of Oxford and Senior Research Fellow at Regent's Park College, Oxford.

Craig Gardiner is Tutor in Christian Doctrine and Worship at South Wales Baptist College and the University of Cardiff.

Andy Goodliff is Minister at Belle Vue Baptist Church, Southend-on-Sea and a doctoral student at the University of St. Andrews.

Paul Goodliff is Minister at Abingdon Baptist Church and Associate Research Fellow at Spurgeon's College, London.

Ruth Gouldbourne is a Co-Minister at Bloomsbury Central Baptist Church, London.

Ashley Lovett is Minister at Socketts Heath Baptist Church, Grays.

Tony Peck is the General Secretary of the European Baptist Federation.

Sally Nelson is Baptist Tutor in doctrine and pastoral care at St Hild College, Yorkshire.

Shona Shaw is Co-minister at Moortown Baptist Church, Leeds.

Nigel Wright is Principal Emeritus of Spurgeon's College, London.

Foreword

Worship pertains to the whole life of the Christian community, which, for its vitality, needs the nourishment that comes from frequent communal gatherings whose primary concern rotates around the praise of God and the cultivation of communion involving God and God's people. In these gatherings, people confess the faith they believe and simultaneously are formed in their understanding of the faith of the church and their vocation as followers of Christ.

On July 12, 1905, when representative Baptists gathered in London, England, for the inauguration of the Baptist World Alliance (BWA), Alexander Maclaren, who presided over the congress, called on participants to mark their location within the wider church family by joyously giving an "audible and unanimous acknowledgement of [their] faith using the words of the Apostles' Creed." Asserting that this was "the first act of the Congress," Maclaren emphasized that the worshippers confessed their faith in this way "not as a piece of coercion or discipline, but as a simple acknowledgement of where [they] stand and what [they] believe." When Baptists celebrated BWA's centenary at their congress in Birmingham, England, they once again declared their faith by repeating the Apostles' Creed.

Yet, regular use of the historic creeds of the church or of the Statements of Faith that Baptists have formulated through the years has not been a feature of the corporate worship of many Baptist churches. Baptist ways of believing are more frequently reflected in the hymnody that marks Baptist congregational life. An analysis of the hymns and songs Baptists sing may open a window into understandings of the faith and the journey of discipleship that exist in the Baptist community.

Hymns and songs have been a feature of Baptist worship from the early years of the Baptist movement. This has been the case even where leading Baptists, such as John Smyth, frowned upon the use of fixed worship texts. In some places, Baptists have engaged in animated debate over the exact form hymn texts should take. In addition, both the appropriateness of musical accompaniment and the potentially negative impact of hymn singing on worshippers have also been hotly disputed. Yet, singing continues to be an essential feature of Baptist worship.

Not surprisingly, hymns play an important role in this Festschrift honoring Christopher Ellis, a much loved and highly respected Baptist scholar and pastor, whose outstanding contribution to the understanding of the corporate worship life of Baptist churches is widely recognized. Each of the fourteen chapters of this illuminating book begins with a brief and aptly-chosen selection from the corpus of Ellis's hymns. These excerpts help focus distinct understandings of the *lex orandi, lex credendi* and *lex vivendi* of Baptist communities.

Gathering Disciples: Essays in Honor of Christopher J. Ellis richly illustrates the rich tapestry of Ellis' contribution as a scholar who understands the service theologians can offer to the life of the church to the glory of God. By reflecting on the possible meanings of what churches do when they gather for worship and by exploring paths leading to the enrichment of the worship life of the people of God, liturgical theologians such as Ellis place the ecclesial community enormously in their debt.

Gathering Disciples provides insightful reflections that are located in a robust exposition of key aspects of the defining contribution of Ellis as a liturgical theologian. It reflects a salutary appreciation for the Baptist contribution while generously affirming the treasures that characterize the worship traditions of the wider ecumenical family.

In an address he presented at the International Conference on Baptists in Worship, which took place in Berlin, Germany, in 1998, Ellis identified the way churches "reflect the history and culture of their situation and respond to their local opportunities and needs" as part of the reason for the "great variety in Baptist life," including approaches to worship. When he served as chair of the Baptist World Alliance Commission on Worship and Spirituality from 2005–2010, Ellis characterized worship and spirituality as encompassing the "themes of identity, experience, faith and belief." The wide range of issues treated in this Festschrift does justice to the comprehensiveness of Ellis's own liturgical theology which is cast in the key of grace. Not surprisingly, a prayer that Ellis prepared for use in the observance of Baptist World Alliance Sunday 2016 states:

> We pray that our churches may truly be places
> in which grace is encountered,
> and from which grace overflows

for the sake of your world,
through Jesus Christ our Saviour.

Celebrating this grace, hundreds of Baptists assembled in the Singelkerk of the United Mennonite Congregation in Amsterdam, the Netherlands, on July 30, 2009, to mark the quadricentenary of the Baptist movement. Gathering as a community drawn from around the world, these Baptists participated in sung worship and Bible reading; they listened as the gospel was proclaimed. These acts of worship were complemented by a litany of thanksgiving, captioned "Cloud of Witnesses." The litany was a celebration of the gifts and contribution of Baptist women and men throughout the years who understood their calling to serve both church and world to the glory of God. Far from flagging up a wayward individualism, the gathering reflected the maturing of the instincts of Baptists as a people sharing a vibrant communal life, while affirming the *koinonia* that is shared with the wider ecclesial household.

This Festschrift does justice to the growing awareness among Baptists of the value of critical reflection on what Christians do when they gather for worship in communities of God's faithful people and how this expresses, informs and shapes their Christian stewardship in daily living.

Neville Callam
Baptist World Alliance

Introduction

THERE ARE NOT MANY roles in Baptist life that Chris has not held. He's been a pastor of five Baptist churches,[1] a Baptist college principal,[2] Baptist Union president,[3] as well as being moderator over the years of the Union's Doctrine & Worship Committee, Faith & Unity Executive,[4] and the Baptist Union Council. Chris has played a significant role within Baptist life. At the same time Chris has been a Baptist with strong ecumenical outlook. His first book offered a theology of ecumenism in the context of the attempts to re-start the ecumenical movement within Great Britain.[5] Chris himself was the first moderator of the Fellowship of Baptist Churches for Covenanting, a group of Baptists committed to the inter-church process in the late 1970s and early 1980s.[6] Later in the 1990s he was a Baptist representative in the Joint Liturgical Group and a member of the conversations between the Baptist Union and the Church of England.[7]

Beyond this, Chris has been our key thinker with regard to Baptist worship, seen most clearly in his important study of Baptist worship. This was the product of doctoral research completed in 2002[8] and published in

1. In various parts of the country — Brighton, Cardiff, Swindon, Sheffield, and Nottingham.

2. Chris was Principal of Bristol Baptist College, 2000–2006.

3. Between 2014 and 2015.

4. Since the changes in 2012 to the structures of the Baptist Union, sadly neither the Doctrine and Worship Committee or the Faith & Unity Executive exist.

5. Chris's book *Together on the Way: A Theology of Ecumenism* was published to coincide with the launch of the new ecumenical bodies, Churches Together in England and the Council for the Churches of Britain and Ireland.

6. Randall, *The English Baptists of the Twentieth Century*, 444.

7. The later conversations began in 1992 and finished in 2005, see the report of the conversations: *Pushing at the Boundaries of Unity*.

8. Chris studied for his doctorate at the University of Leeds, supervised by Haddon Wilmer (a Baptist) and Nigel Biggar. He began his research while he was the minister at Cemetery Road Baptist Church, Sheffield and completed it in his first two years as

2004 as *Gathering: A Theology and Spirituality of Free Church Worship*. In the twentieth century Baptist thinking about worship had been carried out by Neville Clark and Stephen Winward.[9] Like them, Chris was influenced by the liturgical movement, but Chris sets out in *Gathering* to offer a description of free church worship as liturgical theology in conversation with Alexander Schmemann and grounded in the results of a survey of the actual worship practices and patterns of churches in the Baptist Union of Great Britain.

Out of this theological work, in collaboration with Myra Blyth, Chris edited *Gathering for Worship*, which will perhaps be his most long-lasting legacy. He had also been one of a group of editors of the earlier book *Patterns and Prayers for Christian Worship* (OUP, 1991). *Gathering for Worship* has been widely received amongst Baptists, with the North American Baptist theologian Steven Harmon even suggesting that it is "the closest approximation of the Book of Common Prayer issued by any Baptist Union to date."[10] The book is shaped by what Chris learnt from his study of the history and practice of Baptist worship, what he called the core values of Baptist worship: attention to Scripture; devotion and openness to the Spirit; an understanding of church as community; concern for the kingdom of God; and the centrality of the Lordship of Jesus Christ.

A less well known role in Chris's ministry, but one which this book wants to highlight, is his writing of hymns.[11] Following an early Baptist (dissenting) tradition whereby ministers would write hymns to summarize their sermons and invite a response to its message, Chris has written around forty hymns, many during his period as minister of Central Church, Swindon. Thirteen of his hymns are included in this book. Here is a gift that we have not received perhaps as much as we might. With the prolific number of songs and hymns being produced year on year, as Baptists, it is notable that we have not—as Baptists—given sufficient attention to a Baptist-shaped corpus of songs and hymns. We hope in the use of some of Chris's hymns in this book, we might begin to redress that. What is wonderful about Chris's

---

Principal at Bristol Baptist College.

9. Clark, *A Call to Worship*; Winward, *The Reformation of Worship*.

10. Harmon, *Baptist Identity and the Ecumenical Future*, 184. In a similar fashion Curtis Freeman has said it is the 'finest worship resource for Baptists.'

11. Some of these have been published in different collections. Three can be found in *Baptist Praise and Worship*. These are "Open This Book" (no.103); "Passover God" (no.447); and "Made in God's Image" (no.663). Two other hymns can be found in *Complete Anglican: Hymns Old and New*: "Almighty God, we come to make confession" (27) and "What shall be bring" (no.730). "The Lord is Here," originally published in 1987, can be found in *Sing Praise* (no.222), along with "Lord of all Worlds" (no.248).

hymns are the way they offer a response to the breadth of Baptist life. Chris has written hymns for use in the hearing of the Word, the baptizing of believers, the sharing of the Lord's Supper, as well as hymns that summon us to mission and the work of justice, and even a hymn for councils and committees. With the loss of any kind of denominational hymn-book, we lose the opportunity of encountering hymns and songs that aid our way of being Baptist, with our focus on believers' baptism, congregational government, evangelism and more recently our rediscovery of covenant. One way in which we might continue to honor Chris's ministry—both its thinking and its practice—would be to nurture new hymnwriters and songwriters that might give meaning to our Baptist identity.

While Baptists (like many reformers) were initially hesitant (even resistant to) the singing of hymns, gradually it came to be seen as continuing the practices of the earliest worshipping communities. Long before Scripture was committed to text the gospel was passed on orally: stories and hymns were recited and sung to capture and pass on the life of Jesus (then) and the meaning of that life (now).[12] Singing Scripture and singing songs and hymns inspired by scripture was a way of forming disciples, and this remains true today. The eighteenth-century Baptist John Rippon, a distinguished collector of hymns, took this hymn writing tradition a stage further by skillfully arranging extensive collections of psalms and songs into a thematic celebration of the gospel.[13] In *Gathering* Chris succinctly traces the history of hymn singing in Baptist life, noting amongst the early advocates of congregational singing, Dan Taylor and Benjamin Keach.[14]

The eventual success of hymn singing was due in large part to figures beyond Baptist life such as the Wesley's and Isaac Watts. It was the latter whose hymns found a particular place in Baptist worship and it was by skillfully combining Watts with a generation of Baptist hymn writers that Rippon's collection paved the way to a denominational hymnbook. His collection not only widened Baptists access to a wide range of hymns (thereby locating Baptists within the church catholic), but incorporated a significant number of Baptist hymn writers including Anne Steele, Samuel Stennett, Daniel Turner, Benjamin Beddome, and John Fawcett. Most importantly Rippon organized this corpus of the material in a manner which reflected a distinctly Baptist understanding of the place of hymns within worship according to their themes and content.

12. See Lathrop, *The Four Gospels on Sunday*.

13. Rippon's Selection of Hymns went through 31 editions during his life-time. For more on Rippon see Ken Manley, *"Redeeming Love Proclaim": John Rippon and the Baptists*, esp. chapter four.

14. Ellis, *Gathering*, 153–57.

Ellis suggests that for over 200 years hymnbooks fulfilled three tasks: they unified Baptists with Christians past and present in the wider church; brought cohesion within the denomination between particular and general Baptists; and edified the spiritual life and mission endeavor of individuals and local congregations.[15] The significance of the demise of denominational hymnbooks in the twentieth century has not yet been fully analyzed, but Ellis's candid assessment of the role hymns have played hints at why it is important to deepen the reflection on what role songs, hymns and congregational singing might play today at a time when the denomination is looking for fresh streams of renewal and is needing to strengthen the bonds of unity across the Union.

The hymn texts by Chris which head each chapter of this book now take on a life of their own beyond the homily or special occasion which inspired him to write many of them. In the here and now, these texts invite further reflection on the gospel as it speaks into the present context and time. Through this evolving tradition of rehearsing the gospel through song, the reader is invited in ways similar to the earliest worshipping communities to celebrate salvation then and now.

Each of the contributors were given a hymn as a starting point. Some have chosen to give an exposition of the hymn, others have used it as a means to discuss the theme and its place within Baptist life. We offer this book, both as a means of honoring the life and ministry of Chris, but also as an example of Baptist theology at work. The chapters by Rob Ellis, Craig Gardiner, and Shona Shaw discuss how Baptist worship is, or can be, formative—intellectually, ethically, and spiritually. Paul Goodliff and Stuart Blythe offer explorations of discipleship, through the examples of monastic orders and the church meeting. These chapters are followed by Beth Allison-Glenny on Scripture, Sally Nelson on baptism, and Myra Blyth and Ashley Lovett on the Lord's Supper, each opening up how our practices shape our theology. Ruth Gouldbourne picks up a recent interest of some Baptists in the communion of saints and Tony Peck tells the story of how European Baptists are engaged in a variety of ecumenical discussions, projects and experiences. The final chapters engage with doctrine—Paul Fiddes on the Trinity, Nigel Wright on divine sovereignty, and Andy Goodliff on the language of "Missionary God." The book moves from the centrality of "gathering for worship" amongst Baptists into the importance of gifts of Scripture, baptism, and communion, and then into the role of doctrine. In this we

---

15. Ellis, *Gathering*, 158–59.

follow Chris, as he argues that Christian worship is "a way of learning more about God and our experience of God."[16]

Note: Through this book references to "Baptist Union" always mean the Baptist Union of Great Britain, unless otherwise indicated.

---

16. Ellis, *Gathering*, 3.

Learning and Life

Creator God, you make your world
So rich with things to do and know.
Widen our vision, raise our eyes
To see the wonder and to grow.

Jesus our teacher, friend and guide,
Challenge and shake false certainty;
Help us to search for truth in all
With courage and integrity.

Spirit of life, inspire and prompt
Our minds to question and to learn;
Fill us with love that all we know
May serve your world with your concern.

1

"Help Us to Search for Truth"
Baptists and Doing Theology

ROBERT ELLIS

INTRODUCTION

HOW DO BAPTISTS DO theology? In what follows I will pursue an answer to this question by examining the major written work of Christopher Ellis, in particular in dialogue with the systematics of James W. McClendon Jr.; then I will move to consider how these theological clues are reflected in Ellis's hymn "Learning and Life"; finally, again picking up a cue from McClendon, I will turn to a consideration of Ellis's life and the theological convictions and methods that may be implicit in it. First, however, it will be useful to consider the question more generally.

The lack of serious theological work by Baptists has been lamented widely. Brian Haymes recalls some gallows-like humor on the subject,[1] and when James McClendon reflects upon the dearth of Baptist[2] theology he offers a number of reasons, including the harshness of life for early communities, which often faced forms of persecution, and also a tendency to become preoccupied with particular theological issues.

---

1. Haymes, "Theology and Baptist Identity," 1.
2. McClendon insists on referring to "baptist" with a lower case "b," and reminds us of the considerable diversity that this term denotes.

Yet we may also suspect that there are other factors. The stress on inward experience in Baptist spirituality may downplay the significance of the kind of theological reflection that requires some attempt at critical distance between the individual, and the community, and their life of faith. Also, the importance of the Bible in Baptist life has sometimes seemed to render all further theological discourse unnecessary: all that is required is the locating of appropriate texts and their application to any given point at issue. This may seem to many an extraordinarily naïve way of understanding how Scripture functions theologically, but our Baptist communities are, after all, full of simple Bible believers (as Chris's former college principal, Barrie White, used to twinklingly describe himself). Harmon observes that Baptists, especially since the Enlightenment, have been suspicious of (and indeed antagonistic towards) "tradition."[3] This, we can say, reinforces the impulse always to go directly to the text of Scripture, without any intervening authority or interpreter—though we will see that McClendon has a more positive take on this. A third factor can probably be uncontroversially suggested: Baptist life appears to have a strong pragmatic leaning. With a characteristic emphasis on mission and evangelism, alongside personal experience of Christ, and actively discerning the will of Christ for the life and work of the church, Baptists are typically more comfortable in action than reflection.

These factors may combine to produce in some Baptist communities a certain kind of "anti-theological" disposition. We may speculate that it represents another manifestation of the typically Baptist refusal to concede to any kind of authority outside the self's conscience or the community's collective discernment?[4]

However, this volume is testimony to the fact that some Baptists, at least, are not anti-theological. Recent years have seen a significant number of important theologians and theological works emerge from Baptist communities. From the US, where the recent history of Baptist communities has been scarred by distressing and divisive disputes, we have been given two noteworthy attempts at systematics—by James McClendon[5] and Stanley Grenz.[6] Recent works by Steven R. Harmon and Curtis W. Freeman have located Baptist theological perspectives within the wider ("catholic") church with all its breadth and vigor. In the UK we might think of the corpus of Paul S. Fiddes' work, and also the writings of Stephen R. Holmes, John E.

---

3. Harmon, *Towards Baptist Catholicity*, 4, 41.
4. See the references later in this essay to "soul competency."
5. His three volume systematic theology was *Ethics*, *Doctrine* and *Witness*.
6. See Grenz, *Theology for the Community of God*.

Colwell, and Nigel G. Wright as exemplifying this development. What each of these writers have in common is a concern to address current theological issues generally, and ecclesiological issues in particular, and to do so—in part—through serious dialogue with the church's theological tradition in general *and* by engaging as conversation partners with more than four centuries of Baptist thinkers.

Ellis's *Gathering: Spirituality and Theology in Free Church Worship*,[7] both exemplifies and plays its part in deepening this trend of theological development. It is a work of "Liturgical Theology." Many Baptists think that "liturgy" is what other Christians do, rather than what we all do—well or less well, and in various forms and patterns. Ellis's work uses Baptist liturgies as a lens through which the faith of the community is focused and narrated—a clue about Baptists doing theology that we will return to presently.

From a British perspective one more initiative in Baptist theologizing is worth recalling. The collaborative working between a number of British Baptists that bore fruit in a series of "consultations" and volumes that used precisely the terminology deployed in this chapter heading: "doing theology together" or "in a Baptist way."[8] By their own assessment,[9] this group seems not at first to have had a great impact on the Baptist Union of Great Britain or upon the way theology is "done" in (British) circles, but a number of achievements might be identified. The first, and theologically most significant perhaps, was the foregrounding of the notion of covenant—understood not just as the voluntary commitment of church members to one another, but as a coinherence of divine and human covenants ("vertical" and "horizontal") described in terms of God's prevenient, gracious loving activity.[10] Covenant has become a key term in denominational discussions about ministry and associating, though its precise meaning in these discussions remains slippery. A second consequence was an emerging consensus amongst the participants on what "doing theology in a Baptist way" might involve, each of which connects with a key "moment" in Baptist life, the church meeting.

In different ways the participants affirm that when Baptists "do theology" this is a collaborative activity in which, as Fiddes puts it, there are

---

7. A full bibliography of Ellis's work is available at the end of this volume, but I am thinking here especially of his *Gathering*.

8. See Fiddes et al., "Doing Theology Together," 6–18 where the story is told in greater detail.

9. See ibid., 6.

10. This sense of the central and historical importance of "covenant" is not universally shared; and David Bebbington's magisterial history gives it marginal attention, see Bebbington, *Baptists*.

no "solo voices." Haymes cites as an example of this the production of the second volume of McClendon's *Systematic Theology*, for which there was an extensive process of consultation and discussion, drafting and redrafting. This characteristic appears to be a direct consequence of two key Baptist convictions: one is a lack of hierarchy in the Christian community, the other is the conviction that God's will is discerned when the community comes together. As Holmes puts it, authority resides in Christ alone, but the mind of Christ is known in the gathered community.[11]

The Baptist Union of Great Britain's "Declaration of Principle" affirms that "each Church has liberty, under the guidance of the Holy Spirit" to interpret Scripture and this corporate discernment is seen as "doing theology *in context*," and that also means a particular relationship of the Christian community to Scripture itself. We might say that Baptists will do theology *locally*, and in direct relationship to the biblical text. More recently, this type of language has come to be linked to the term "reflection upon practice," an expression in vogue in theological education and in the discipline of practical theology. Baptists ought to make natural practical theologians—and here our pragmatic leaning could serve us well.

My naming of these thinkers and movements is not by any means exhaustive–more could be added from the UK and the US, as well as from many other parts of the world. Considering we Baptists do not do much theology, we are blessed indeed to be heirs to this developing heritage.

ELLIS DOING "LITURGICAL THEOLOGY": A CLUE TO "BAPTISTS DOING THEOLOGY"

Speaking about Baptists *doing* theology may direct our attention away from the study or seminar and towards the concrete life of the Christian congregation. Such a method not only reflects a number of contemporary trajectories in theological method, with a desire to begin in practice of various kinds or in something "concrete" rather than "theoretical," but is also of a piece with Ellis's own major theological work, *Gathering*.

---

11. Holmes, "Introduction: Theology in Context?" 1. Holmes somewhat downplays the work of the scholar in the community. In a later essay, he talks about our necessary and shared "incompetence" in the church meeting, underlining that God's leading is as likely to be discerned in the most unlearned member of the community as in any with a pretence to knowledge or authority. See Holmes, "Knowing Together the Mind of Christ," 184: "My own preference would be for an insistence that all people are incompetent in things of God, without the aid of the Spirit . . . ."

In *Gathering*, he begins by asking how we find out what Christians believe.[12] A number of possible answers are enumerated, including the more typical "theoretical" answers: interrogating a theologian or other representative of the church; examining creeds or other statements; and so on. Beliefs discovered in such ways might then yield implications for behavior, service, or worship. Such a deductive process, however, has its counterpart in inductive methods—more familiar, Ellis points out, from mathematics and science,[13] but also now widely used in practical theology. When considered in relation to worship this inductive method directs our attention to practices—such as liturgical forms and content—which *embody* theology. Thus, when Ellis speaks of doing "Liturgical Theology" he commits to a process of "[exploring] the beliefs of the Christian community through a study of its worship practices."[14]

The Liturgical Theology that develops is not, and should be distinguished from, a "theology of worship." The latter involves the analysis of worship with theological tools and concepts developed elsewhere, away from the liturgy. By contrast, Liturgical Theology identifies and reflects upon the theology that is embodied in the worship—a subtle but significant distinction. Ellis cites the celebrated liturgical theologian Alexander Schmemann, who believed that worship precedes theology[15]—though as Ellis points out, this theological chicken-and-egg conundrum is not straightforward. This sentiment would seem an attractive one to Baptists given our relatively high view of heart-experience and relatively low estimation of theological discourse. The idea that worship precedes theology suggests that if we want to understand what we really believe it is to the liturgy that we might turn. This might seem a dispiriting proposal for any who lament some current trends in worship, but it will also resonate with those who have become familiar with Helen Cameron's distinction between the four theological voices: "espoused theology" is what *we* say we believe; "normative theology" is what the official documents of denomination and normative texts of our tradition say we believe; "formal theology" is what the theologians of the academy and the seminary say we believe; and "operant theology" is what our *practices* "say" we believe—an analysis of these practices discloses to us the theology embedded in what we actually do, when, as the modern saying goes, the rubber hits the road.[16] Liturgical Theology might be seen as a study

12. Ellis, *Gathering*, 1.
13. Ibid., 14.
14. Ibid., 7.
15. Ibid., 17.
16. Cameron et al., *Talking about God in Practice*, 53–56.

of the operant theology of the community at worship. The study of the worship of the Christian community in this way does not have, however, that worship as its primary focus—God is the primary focus of such an investigation: in Liturgical Theology the main emphasis is on the theology rather than the liturgy. The liturgy discloses to us what we believe about God (and, of course, therefore also about ourselves and the world, and so on).[17]

Ellis follows Roman Catholic scholar Kevin Irwin in suggesting that the church's worship is "always an act of the Church's self-understanding and self-expression."[18] According to Ellis, when Baptist worship is brought into focus we find four underlying core convictions, together with a "presiding conviction" which binds everything together. The four underlying core convictions are itemized by him as follows:

1. Attention to Scripture;
2. Personal devotion and openness to the Spirit;
3. A concern for the community of the church;
4. A missiological and eschatological dimension, focused on the Kingdom.[19]

None of these provides the capstone to Baptist worship, however. Without a further and more fundamental theme these observations lack focus. Here Ellis recalls the very earliest Christian confessions, such as 1 Cor 12:3—"Jesus is Lord." This central affirmation is more than a theological statement, important though that is, it has consequences for what Christians believe about "authority, behaviour, communal identity, and ways of viewing the world."[20] Christian worship is in the name of Jesus the Christ, and is directed to or through Jesus. Without this "presiding conviction"[21] the other core convictions look anaemic. And, similarly, without the four core convictions, simply stating that Baptist worship is shaped by the confession that Jesus is Lord is uninformative. The confession of the Lordship of Christ explains why and how Baptists attend to Scripture, express personal devotion and seek the Spirit's guidance, nurture concern for the community, and seek the kingdom. As McClendon remarks:

> Christian doctrine—and Christian theology in its doctrinal mode—begins and ends with the confession, *Iesous Kyrios*, Jesus

17. Ellis, *Gathering*, 17.
18. Ibid., 228.
19. Ibid., 228–29.
20. Ibid., 230.
21. Here he borrows a term from McClendon and Smith, *Convictions*, 96.

is Lord. But that confession by itself is a nonesuch, a word in an unknown tongue; uninterpreted it says nothing to us. To see its force we must see this ancient conviction tightly woven into a broad tapestry of other Christian convictions.[22]

The four core convictions here enumerated represent the thickest strands in this tapestry when we consider Baptist worship and Baptist life generally, for Ellis is clear that he seeks to identify the outlines of a spirituality *and* a theology, and that the line between them is blurred.[23]

BAPTISTS "DOING THEOLOGY": BUT WHICH BAPTISTS?

It is illuminating to place this analysis of Baptist Liturgical Theology alongside one of the most well-known and influential Baptist contribution in recent years, the work of the late James W. McClendon Jr., which has had a considerable impact on the way many Baptists "do" theology. He offers us a winsome definition of theology as the "discovery, understanding, and transformation of the convictions of a convictional community, including the discovery and critical revision of their relation to one another *and to whatever else there is.*"[24] Theology is, by such a definition, a narrative and historical activity as well as a systematic one, and it is of necessity plural—in an elasticated sense of a term we will use later, it is always "local." We might say, therefore, that there is a question prior to "how do Baptists do theology?" That prior question is: "which Baptists?" A brief diversion is in order.

In the United Kingdom we can take a rather parochial approach to Baptist identity at times, whereas a more global approach to Baptist identity, like that of David Bebbington in his *Baptists Through the Centuries*, is somewhat sobering. Bebbington notes that whereas until the end of the eighteenth century, British Baptist life shaped the tradition beyond these shores, including in the US, from the nineteenth century onwards that flow has been reversed.[25]

Bebbington outlines, in his concluding chapter on Baptist Identity, how Baptist communities came under strain as attitudes to the biblical text changed. He also highlights the Southern Baptist Edgar Y. Mullins's seminal

---

22. McClendon, *Doctrine*, 64 cited by Ellis, *Gathering*, 231.
23. Ellis, *Gathering*, 14.
24. McClendon, *Ethics*, 23, italics his.
25. Bebbington, *Baptists*, 281.

book *The Axioms of Religion*.[26] Mullins outlines six axioms of religion, but proposes that one overarching axiom makes sense of all the others—and that the others can be derived from this initial axiom. This initial axiom he calls "The souls' competency in religion."[27] This axiom "excludes at once all human interference, such as episcopacy and infant baptism, and every form of religion by proxy. Religion is a personal matter between the soul and God."[28] Mullins insists that "no human priest may claim to be mediator between the soul and God because no possible reason can be assigned for any competency on his part not common to all believers."[29] Bebbington remarks that Mullins fuses philosophical personalism with an evangelical stress on personal experience of Christ. This extraordinarily influential book is of its time and place, but it is possible to see its effects spreading across the Atlantic into Baptist life and convictions here in Britain.

> Although the American's phrase never gained widespread currency in the British Isles, it made its impact on Baptist leaders there. Mullins' views were responsible . . . for confirming a low estimate of the doctrine of the church, and . . . soul competency became the supreme Baptist value. Mullins drastically reoriented the way in which Baptist principles were presented.[30]

Bebbington traces developing global Baptist identities through the remainder of the twentieth century and finds no fewer than seven different strands of Baptist life emerging, each of which manifests local or regional variations.[31] All of this counts as some sort of disclaimer on any attempt to construe how "Baptists do theology," but it also serves to remind us of *our* place in a bigger, wider world—and perhaps reminds us why North America is so important for global Baptist life.

JAMES MCCLENDON: A "BAPTIST" VISION FOR DOING THEOLOGY

It is a daunting thing then, to attempt to identify key or constitutive elements in Baptist theolog*ies*. McClendon's stress is on "convictions" rather than "practices," but in beginning his Systematics with a volume on ethics

---

26. Mullins, *Axioms of Religion*.
27. Ibid., 53–58.
28. Ibid., 54.
29. Ibid., 56.
30. Bebbington, *Baptists*, 260.
31. Ibid., 265–72.

he gives a clue as to the importance he gives to the lived, practiced, life of faith. Scouring the meager library of Baptist theological contributions McClendon identifies a "short and perhaps incomplete... inventory of convictional features" of the Baptist vision.[32] There are five such convictional features.

In compiling this inventory McClendon has, so to speak, started in another place from Ellis. Rather than starting with "practice" of any kind, let alone the practice of liturgy and examining its embedded theology, McClendon has carried out what we might call a literature review of significant Baptist theological writing. This being the case it is interesting to compare McClendon's "short and perhaps incomplete inventory" with Ellis's four values, enumerated above.

1. *Biblicism*, a conviction that says less about particular forms of hermeneutics and more about "humble acceptance of the authority of Scripture."[33]

2. "*Liberty*, or soul competency, understood . . . as the God-given freedom to respond to God without the intervention of the state or other powers."[34] Mullins's axiom of soul competency is seen by McClendon as formed by a distinctively American individualism, and to downplay communal life—an assessment shared by Bebbington. We may add that militant congregational independence is rooted here too. For good or ill, this "localism" is an important feature in Baptist theological perspectives and in the way Baptists do theology.

3. *Discipleship*—not the special calling of a minority but the consequence of life transformed by the Lordship of Jesus Christ. McClendon regards the "presiding conviction" that brings coherence to others as the Lordship of Christ, and it is implied here. His stress on practices, beginning with ethics, and sympathy with Anabaptist perspectives, all support this sense that *following* is as important, as faith; perhaps *is* faith.

4. *A commitment to community*—seen not as the privileged access of the favored few, but as "sharing together in a storied life of witness to Christ.

---

32. McClendon, *Ethics*, 28.
33. Ibid., 27.
34. McClendon, *Ethics*, 27, italics mine.

5. *Mission* and/or evangelism: the responsibility to witness to Christ is a core part of who Baptists think they are, and this has involved a willingness to endure the difficulties that faithful witness involves."[35]

Do these five points map on to Ellis's four core convictions together with the presiding conviction of the lordship of Christ, assembled after a study of Baptist worship? McClendon's *biblicism* and Ellis's *attention to Scripture* have clear congruence. McClendon's *mission* resonates with Ellis's *eschatological* and *kingdom* emphases. McClendon's *liberty and soul competence* correspond with Ellis's *personal devotion and seeking the leading of the Spirit*—though neither would want to follow Mullins into an individualism which downplays the church. Hence, McClendon and Ellis both pick out a *concern for the Christian community* as core features. McClendon's other element, *discipleship*, bleeds into several of Ellis's, and points towards the cohering motif of the *Lordship of Christ*.

What are we to make of this correspondence? Without suggesting any quibble about Ellis's truly inductive approach, it is clear that he has read and admires McClendon's work. A direct influence cannot be ruled out. However, finding ourselves making similar observations about Baptist theological principles and the kind of theological arguments that Baptists are likely to propose and issues that Baptists are likely to address, even when starting from contrasting starting points, appears to suggest that in this common ground we may be confident that we have located some of the ways that many Baptists do theology—what concerns shape their discourse and establish trajectories towards their conclusions—even while recognizing our considerable plurality. We now zoom in a little closer on Ellis's Liturgical Theology.

DOING THEOLOGY BY SINGING IT: ELLIS'S HYMNS AND LITURGICAL THEOLOGY

Accessing and analyzing what we believe by studying our worship leads us felicitously back to the hymn with which this chapter is prefaced. Given Ellis's liturgical theology one might suppose that a consideration of the corpus of his hymns might give us a broad picture of core theological themes that he considers important for God's people to sing. A number of caveats must be offered immediately. Most of Ellis's hymns originate in one relatively short period of his ministry, at Swindon Central Church; they were, mostly, written for a particular congregation in a particular time and place,

35. Ibid., 28.

and generally to accompany the sermon written for that week following the Joint Liturgical Group's lectionary; finally, important though hymns are, we should be wary of assuming that they yield a comprehensive liturgical theology, instead of seeing them as one part (an important part, to be sure) of the texts used in liturgy, each of which discloses our beliefs.[36]

One corollary of these caveats is that liturgical theology in our tradition where the form and content of worship is not prescribed centrally, is, to a greater or lesser extent, a series of local theologies. This should come as neither a surprise nor a disappointment to Baptists who know the importance of the local. It also underlines McClendon's insistence that we are dealing with plurality. Perhaps we should speak of Baptists doing *theologies* rather than *theology*?

The title of the hymn "Learning and Life" gives us some hope that this hymn might offer us some help as we consider how Baptists do theology. However, we should no more expect one hymn to provide such a summary than we would expect one Scripture passage, or any other discrete moment of the liturgy to do so. We can, however, look for resonances within the hymn with the core themes we discussed earlier.

Recalling that Ellis believes that spirituality and theology should not be too quickly separated, what we might expect to see are some of the characteristics of what he calls "the Spirituality of Congregational Song."[37] In his chapter of that name he discusses the history of hymnody, the rise (and fall) of the hymnbook, the changing practice of singing, and the place of hymns and songs within the liturgy. But valuable though these accounts are, the analysis of and reflections upon the spirituality of hymn singing will be of most use to us and a few headlines can be picked out.

Sung worship is a communal activity and provides a key mode of participation in Baptist worship. Ellis recalls Manning's oft-quoted "Hymns are for us Dissenters what the liturgy is for the Anglican."[38] Singing usually provides Baptist worshippers with a "more obvious" form of active participation in worship than at any other point or by any other means. By singing together, the congregation expresses something of its nature as the

---

36. There is an interesting project for a research student somewhere: to analyze Ellis's Swindon hymn alongside other documents of the church, including its minutes and magazines, its other liturgical texts in so far as they are available, and the sermons preached by the ministry team during the period, in order to reconstruct the local liturgical theology operant in that church at that time—but such a prospect will not detain us here!

37. Ellis, *Gathering*, chapter 8.

38. Ibid., 151, quoting Manning, *The Hymns of Wesley and Watts*, 133.

community of the church, called out and gathered for worship by God.[39] This shared experience both expresses and nourishes the sense of communal identity.

But it also has a personal aspect to it. Early Baptist opponents of singing were cautious in part because they feared not only that the "set" words of a hymn (as opposed to extempore singing which some of them encouraged!) fettered the Spirit, but that singing hymns and songs asked people to identify with the words of others in ways that were not appropriate[40]—and which, perhaps, introduced an intermediary between them and God. Any of us who have felt manipulated in a service of worship will have some understanding of this. But what can sometimes be seen as a disadvantage can also be a boon. Hymns and songs allow worshippers to identify themselves with the events and realities celebrated in worship, with one another, and with the wider church (hymns and songs are, as Ellis observes,[41] remarkably ecumenical forms). Ellis notes how different sung forms, and worship-leading strategies, allow for the personal appropriation of the sentiments of song[42] thus allowing individuals to identify not only with the community of which they are (becoming) part, but also with the story narrated and celebrated in worship. For a worshipping community generally without creedal statements the songs *are* those statements. I recall my senior friend advising me early in ministry that at least one hymn or song in a service of worship ought to have a Trinitarian form or affirmation. Just as the Nicene Creed begins "We believe," so sung worship functions for Baptists as shared proclamation of the saving acts of God.[43] The identification with the story that singing allows extends to it being a converting ordinance.

Ellis speaks of the *ex*pressive and *im*pressive functions of sung worship: the expressive connotes this shared proclamation, but also the individual's standing with the community in faith and celebration; the impressive draws our attention to the way in which what we sing is internalized and makes an impression upon us. We express what is in our hearts, collectively and individually. But sung worship also impresses "on the singer a series of phrases, ideas and images which are then offered to God as the worship of the one

---

39. Ibid., 164.

40. Briggs, "English Baptists and their Hymnody," 155, quoted in Ellis, *Gathering*, 169.

41. Ellis, *Gathering*, 166.

42. Ibid., 163, 172.

43. Ibid., 165.

who has just read, but not written, them."[44] Worship is directed to God, but also *forms* those who worship.

A final point to note is the eschatological dimension of hymnody—what Ellis calls "singing in the Kingdom." With Isaac Watts, Ellis suggests that the congregation at praise is "in tune with heaven."[45] This is more than an affirmation of the communion of saints, because this praise "anticipates the eschatological completion in which all creation will acknowledge and praise God."[46] But there is a further important nuance: recalling Mowinckel and Brueggemann on the Psalms, we should understand that "to praise God *as* sovereign is to make a world in which God *is* sovereign."[47] The story with which singers identify themselves, communally and individually, is a story in which God is the present and coming Lord, known in Jesus Christ, ceaselessly at work by his Spirit.

When we turn to "Learning and Life," the first thing to strike us in the hymn is its Trinitarian structure. Here is that Trinitarian, Nicene, form for which my Senior Friend looked. Through this structure singers are drawn into the presence of God the Father, Son, and Holy Spirit, and implicitly (and in some respects, explicitly) both affirm and proclaim their faith. We might recall that the Trinity can be narrated, that it is not just some speculative doctrine but a way of telling the story of God and creation. This Trinitarian form therefore is also a means of identification with the Christian story. *Ex*pressively it allows Christians to affirm their faith, but *im*pressively singing these words allows worshippers to internalize affirmations about the Triune God—to learn to wonder at creation, and to relate to Jesus in particular ways, for instance.

An increased awareness of gendered language has led not only to greater flexibility in the use of personal pronouns more generally, but also in some quarters to a reluctance to use "Father" of the first person of the Trinity. Ellis shows just this qualm here: while I said above that the worshipper is drawn into the presence of God the Father, Son, and Holy Spirit—that is not quite the case; rather it is into the presence of Creator, Son, and Spirit. The reasons for this switch (very common in Iona material too, for example) are well understood. But it is not certain that it is theologically adequate: if we distinguish between the persons of the Trinity by their relation rather than by their function, as the early church fathers insisted, and is now a commonplace in the rediscovery of Trinitarian thought, we see more clearly

44. Ibid., 172.
45. Ibid., 167.
46. Ibid., 168.
47. Ibid., 168.

that each of the persons of the Trinity might be associated with the act of creation, and that naming the first person as Creator in contrast to the Son and the Spirit is problematic. In the great scheme of things this is a relatively minor quibble, but when we bear in mind both the *expressive* and *im*pressive processes at work here, it gives a short pause for thought.

The hymn has a Trinitarian form, but another formal feature comes into focus: the first two stanzas begin with an affirmation and conclude with a petition. We come into God's presence, affirm an aspect of our faith, and then seek God's help for Christian living—the affirmation of faith moves to faithful following. The final stanza is entirely petition, unless we count "Spirit of life" as an affirmation (which, I grant, it is of sorts): we could ask, mischievously, whether the lack of affirmation regarding the Spirit is another example of the downplaying of the Spirit; and we might wonder whether the hymn would have appeared both more finely balanced in structure, but also more theologically helpful, if its structure had been the same as the previous stanzas.[48]

The first verse, then, has the Creator God in focus. The hymn has a straightforward style, and God as Creator is affirmed simply and without unnecessary ornament ("you make your world"). Creation is God's world not ours, and the hymn begins and ends with attention away from us to God ("your world . . . your concern"). The creation is "rich with things to do and know," and the worshipper not only wonders at the fullness of creation with its range of beauty and complexity but also suggests that there is much delight in the exploring of this richness. But our horizons are cramped and the petition (recalling Paul's prayer for the Ephesians, perhaps) seeks to open them out with breadth ("widen our vision") and height ("raise our eyes"), to enlarge our appreciation of the creation—and our praise of the Creator. So we ask "to see the wonder and to grow," for we develop as persons and as a community of disciples when we more fully "comprehend, with all the saints, what is the breadth and length and height and depth, and to know the love of Christ that surpasses knowledge."[49]

The second verse addresses Jesus, "our teacher, friend and guide." This directs us clearly to Scripture, and to the Word in the word. The Lordship of Christ is the presiding conviction, and attention to Scripture (McClendon's "Biblicism") a core value in Baptist worship, and in the Liturgical Theology which may be derived therefrom. Here they are literally central in the hymn. Jesus is "teacher, friend and guide"—and we gain a clear sense

---

48. The suggested tune *Fulda*, also, I suggest, has this same two-part form—with the rising melody of lines three and four working well when affirmation turns to petition—and a little less well in the third verse.

49. Eph 3:18–19.

of dependence upon Christ for what we must learn as Christian people, but also that intimacy and heart relationship which is better described as friendship. Here Jesus is not simply one who stands over us but one who stands alongside us in the warp and weft of our living in and with the Christian story. Jesus is also one who goes out ahead of us, the leader and Lord, the disciples' guide. Identifying with the story of God's love in Christ means a complex and multi-layered relationship with the one called Lord, and at different times we (individuals and communities) will find these three terms resonating in different ways and with different weights.

But even as those who attend to Scripture and look to Christ, we can become complacent, become lulled into thinking that we know what is required of us and who Jesus is for us. Scripture may become domesticated and tame. That is why we go on to sing the prayer that our teacher, friend and guide will "challenge and shake false certainty." Even as "people of the book" we must understand that the God who speaks to us and the Lord who invites us to follow through it remains outside of our control, never at our beck and call. This sense of challenge is underlined in the next couplet. "Help us to search for truth *in all*,"[50] suggests that sometimes the God of all creation will speak to us in unexpected ways, and will challenge our self-satisfied and self-constructed biblical orthodoxy with unfamiliar voices. This appears an arresting move, but when we recall that personal experience of Christ and openness to the Spirit loom large in Ellis's account it should not surprise us. We are attentive to Scripture, but also to the Lord who speaks to us in other ways. This is a quest, like the journey of discipleship itself, which we must undertake "with courage and integrity." We may recall the opening sentence of McClendon's Systematics: "Theology means struggle."[51] Following with our minds, like any kind of following Christ the Lord, can be difficult. The "search for truth," and a life lived with Jesus as "teacher, friend and guide" requires of us both "courage and integrity."

Openness to the Spirit is central to the third stanza. "Spirit of life" has a multivalent feel, suggesting creative activity, the regenerative and sanctifying work ordinarily associated with a Christian account of the Holy Spirit, but also a broader experience of the Spirit's inspiring, equipping, and refreshing in the everyday. It resonates with the "search for truth in all" of which we have just sung: this is possible because of the Spirit's presence to all things and all people. While Jesus is our teacher, the Spirit ("inspire and prompt our minds") initiates our questions and our desire and need to learn. Questions may not be a sign of faithlessness but of the Spirit's work in us. The

---

50. Italics mine.
51. McClendon, *Ethics*, 17.

hymn as a whole implies a strongly positive view of the theological tasks of discipleship. But knowledge only takes us so far, and is never an end in itself. Love is the goal: the love with which individuals respond to God's love in Christ, that unites the community in the mutuality of Christian fellowship, and that then overflows outwards in mission to the world. The questioning and learning are penultimate, and so we sing "fill us with love that all we know may serve your world with your concern." The missiological aspect of Baptist worship and theology is near at hand here.

We approached this hymn asking whether we might hear in it echoes or hints of the major themes of the Liturgical Theology Ellis adumbrates in *Gathering*. This appears to be the case. We might pause to ask where in the narrative arc of worship such a hymn might be sung? The middle verse would appear to render it appropriately sung before or after the reading of Scripture; the opening verse might suggest it could be sung during opening praise; the final verse, with its outward orientation, has something of a closing hymn about it. Perhaps, more interestingly, the whole adheres to something like the narrative flow of worship as a whole—from praise, through Christ and the Word, to going out in the Spirit in love. When considered along with its Trinitarian structure we find a hymn that is versatile in its liturgical use, and which could be helpful in *ex*pressive and *im*pressive ways at various liturgical moments.

BIOGRAPHICAL THEOLOGY: CHRISTOPHER ELLIS AS THEOLOGIAN, PASTOR, ARTIST

So far we have attempted an account of Ellis's liturgical theology within a broader discussion of "Baptist theologies." However, McClendon, whose work we have already found helpful, offers us another possible line of enquiry as we consider the clues to "Baptists doing theology" in the work of Ellis: the use of biography as a tool for theology. Bearing some resemblance to narrative theology, McClendon explains that "the content of Christian faith, or for that matter any faith that must be lived out, is best expressed in the shared lives of its believers; without such lives, that faith is dead. These lives in their integrity and compelling power do not just illustrate, but test and verify (or their absence or failure falsify) the set of religious convictions that they embody."[52] To some this will sound alarmingly like a kind of hagiographic approach to theology—not something for which Baptists

---

52. McClendon, *Ethics*, 119–20.

have historically been known. But a reading of his use of the biographical method in *Ethics* should allay some fears: illuminating accounts of Jonathan and Sarah Edwards, Dorothy Day, and Dietrich Bonhoeffer, add flesh to the more conceptual chapters by which they are respectively preceded. They show how the issues debated can make sense in a lived-out way. Again, there may be something inherently appealing here to those whose shared life is marked by the appeal of the practical.

In his earlier and more extended treatment of biographical theology McClendon speaks about a "certain attention to compelling biographies" and to the presence of "dominant or controlling images which may be found in the lives of which they speak."[53] These central images both offer (to the extent that they serve as a cohering vision by which a life is lived out) a way of understanding what use may be made of "religious experience" as a theological datum,[54] but also relate in some way to significant biblical images.[55] Though he makes the case for those he studies in this book (including Martin Luther King Jr., Dag Hammarskjold, and Charles Ives) each drawing upon biblical images, he also says that there is no reason why the cohering images of a Christian life need to be drawn exclusively from Scripture:[56] instead the "vindication" for its use is the "quality of life which that vision evokes"[57] (more pragmatism, this time with a very Jamesian feel).

It should not, I think, be left to me to decide whether Chris Ellis's life presents a "compelling biography," and I will not assess his life and work in that way. Such an account should wait some time—and be done by someone else! However, I think we may be nudged by McClendon into considering Ellis as a "person in the round," not just as the producer of certain theological texts. Such a consideration will, I think, enrich our understanding of how *this* Baptist—and perhaps also many other Baptists—do theology.

Most people who know Chris and who have come under his influence during his working life, will know him as more than a theologian. Some will know him as a colleague and friend, including many outside and inside the churches and the councils he has served. They will know him, I suspect, as thoughtful (in both senses of the word) and witty company, and one whose attention and concern is engaged and sincere. Others know him as husband, father, grandfather, uncle, brother. These relationships tell us a great deal about who he is, before we consider his work and theological contributions.

53. McClendon, *Biography as Theology*, 89.
54. Ibid., 90.
55. Ibid., 93.
56. McClendon, *Biography as Theology*, 96.
57. Ibid., 110.

Might we find in even a superficial attempt at biography some indications of the same theological concerns that are found in Baptist worship—does he, so to speak, live a life that is harmonious with the account of Baptist Liturgical Theology he has offered?

This is not the moment to speculate on who someone is in their deepest self, or to assess which relationships are most constitutive of their identity, and so on. However, in theological terms we must certainly hazard the assertion that he is a disciple: one who has confessed Jesus as Lord and seeks to follow him. We are from time to time reminded that many of the great theologians of yore were first of all pastors—and Chris has been a pastor for more than forty years. But before they were pastors they were also disciples, followers of Jesus the Christ. Chris discovered his vocation for ministry very early: no ministry board would have considered meeting him when, still not in High School, he announced that he would be a pastor. But throughout his pastoral ministry, and even before it, he has modeled an earnest desire for growth. Leaving Regent's Park College and during a demanding pastorate he began a masters in doctrine; later, again in pastorate, he began doctoral work which would one day become *Gathering*. But growth is not merely a matter of the mind. Regular retreats and opportunities for reflection have been taken up, and his own spiritual experience enlarged and enlivened in various ways. He has remained open to the "light and truth" which is still to break forth. Never arriving and always journeying, this follower of Christ shows us something about the provisionality of our theological reflections but also how a living relationship with Jesus grows and develops. The personal devotion and openness to the Spirit that he offers as a hallmark of Baptist theology embedded in worship appears to have biographical reality for him.

Brought up in South Wales, he discovered his call to ministry in a very particular Christian culture, and the early preacher exhibited what the Welsh know as *hwyi*—a word indicating the passion and energy in address that has long been a distinctive of Welsh preaching. I recall listening to his preaching as a teenager, enthralled by its dynamism. A sermon on David and Absalom, well-travelled in the valleys while he was a student at Regent's, was particularly memorable. Later his sermon on Jonah would trigger my own call to ministry. Here was a preaching of the biblical text that placed the readers *in* it; the urgent demands of the gospel of Christ appeared inescapable and personal. This biblical text was directed to me, the listener. Earlier we had cause to consider the "attention to Scripture" that is characteristic of Baptist theologies and Baptist worship. We found this echoed in many places. When McClendon speaks of "biblicism" he is aware that this can degenerate into a stale and stultifying bibliolatry. However, when understood and lived correctly, it is a transformative attitude before the text (i.e., the text transforms us), which he summarizes as "the church now *is* the primitive church; *we* are Jesus' followers; the commands are addressed directly to *us*."[58] This sense of the immediacy of the text, of the biblical story as our story, seems to be a feature of Baptist theologies—as McClendon puts it "just such an awareness of the Bible and especially the New Testament setting in the present situation is characteristic of the baptist vision wherever we find it." This is the Bible of Chris's preaching—and in preaching, of course, Baptist pastors do theology with congregations every week. This immediacy of the text, of the text's story being our story, goes some way to explaining and even excusing the Baptist "suspicion" of tradition noted earlier. It may be naïve to think we can read the text without the layers of interpretation which have been laid down upon it over two millennia, but this sense of its immediacy accounts for the impression that this is what we do.

Chris's call to pastoral ministry, part of his sense of self from childhood, is inseparable from any biographical perspective on his life and work. It is underlined by his move back into local church ministry after his period as principal of Bristol Baptist College. Such a call to ministry is marked for him by a strong sense of the way Baptist ministry was understood by many during the second half of the twentieth century, as a call to the ministry of "Word, sacrament, and pastoral care." The first two of this triad find their most natural locus in worship—although that does not exhaust their range. Pastoral care also has a place in worship, of course, but we generally think of a broader exercise of ministry with regard to it. Though we often individualize pastoral care in the way in which we imagine it, it is fundamentally a ministry given (and received) in community.[59] The shepherd will know the individuals, but the shepherd leads the flock.[60] The call to pastoral ministry is the call to be a certain sort of person (often, nowadays, some say a certain sort of "leader") in a community: for the building up of that community, for the facilitating of worship and witness, to equip its members corporately and individually, and to "rejoice with those who rejoice and weep with those who weep."[61] The personal devotion and openness to the Spirit we have already highlighted in these biographical observations has at its heart, it may be recalled, not any sense of personal fulfillment but rather an other-facing nourishing of community. This tips into a concern for the Christian com-

---

58. McClendon, *Ethics*, 33, italics his.
59. See Goodliff, *Care in a Confused Climate*.
60. John 10:3–4.
61. Rom 12:15. Our problem-centered approaches to pastoral care often reverse the order of this text—or omit the rejoicing altogether.

munity *per se*, the third of the characteristics of Baptist theological concern. Chris's work as a pastor in Brighton, Cardiff, Swindon, Sheffield, and West Bridgford, yields much evidence for the internalizing of this theological core conviction. His writing of hymns, particularized by time and place and congregation as already noted, might be taken to be a very particular example of his concern to nurture a community and the individuals within it.

These biographical impressions have so far focused largely on the more public persona. I want now to turn briefly to the less public Christopher Ellis. Here is a person with a significant hinterland of interests. The slightly quaint term "hobbies" does not do justice to the significance of these interests. They are not diverting activities but an important part of who the person is. Where to begin?—perhaps in music. While he learnt the recorder and violin at school, and still occasionally plays both, his primary musical performance is vocal. His professionally trained bass-baritone voice led him to some solo appearances in oratorio early on, but is now generally exercised through choral singing. He currently sings in a small choir, where each singer is exposed and must be on their mettle. He is also a church musician. Beyond performance he is an eclectic and knowledgeable listener, demanding high standards of his audio kit. His taste encompasses vocal, chamber and orchestral music, especially baroque and classical, and also jazz. He has not (yet) come to find much to enjoy in more "popular" genres. The music he enjoys finds its way into other parts of his life—as those who have sat under his leadership in a retreat might testify. It forms a backdrop to his own reflection, but also fuels it.

He is a voracious reader. I recall our mother complaining that while reading he becomes oblivious to everything and anything else—it is still the case. In a typical year he will read millions of words. He generally eschews a newspaper these days, because he complains it restricts his book-time. He frequently has more than one book "on the go," and the lion's share of his reading is fiction, including detective writing, historical fiction, and literary novels. It is no accident that the second footnote in *Gathering* is a reference to a John Updike novel,[62] because while he enjoys this reading hugely and is entertained by it, it also feeds into a life of reflection. Reading fiction enriches us in various ways, but one of these ways is that a well-observed fictional account of the world often enables us to see that world in new ways and understand it and ourselves afresh. Not everything we read has the lacerating power of Shakespeare, but Updike is one of many who makes us think about ourselves, our relationships, our faith, and the way things are,

---

62. Ellis, *Gathering*, 2–3, the reference is to Updike, *Couples*, 41–42.

in helpful ways. As Nobel laureate Doris Lessing put it, "there is no doubt fiction makes a better job of the truth."[63]

Chris Ellis the preacher and pastor, the member of Baptist Union's Faith and Unity Executive and the BWA's Worship and Spirituality Commission, and so on, is a wordsmith—one who delights in well-chosen words of others but also is something of an artist in his own use of words. To my knowledge he has not written a novel to date, but as a teenager was writing poetry. Not the kind of soppy stuff of the clichéd joke about teenagers, but literary productions of some note which were published in his school magazine and one or two other places. While he did not develop this poetic career, we might guess that his gift for meter and cadence resurfaced again in Swindon in the writing of hymns. Poem and hymn texts alike compress meaning into few words, focus beliefs and aspirations that are difficult to pin down in prose, and then enable the reader or singer to be in touch with and express their own concerns.

But we look not to music, or to literature, but to visual arts to find what might be for our purposes his most illuminating passion. From early sketches, pen and ink drawings and the occasional painting, enriched by study and coaching, in his mature years Chris is now an amateur artist of some note. Here we may find what McClendon calls the cohering image that enables us to understand his "theological biography." Some decades ago Chris absorbed himself in artistic practices such as knitting and tapestry-making. In needlework he patiently learnt the basic techniques by working on the commercially sold kits before moving on to design his own work. One of the most ambitious of these was prepared for our parents' golden wedding in 1992—a large work depicting the homes in which they had grown up and the hill upon which they had courted in the years leading up to the outbreak of war in 1939. The names of their children and grandchildren were woven into this remarkable picture, indicating the importance of place and relationship.

After some years where his medium was wool and thread he began to turn again to fine art. Beginning with watercolors he came to experiment with acrylics and oils. Sometimes working from photographs and at other times making initial sketches in situ, he then works up his pictures—mainly landscapes. He studies technique and attends classes and courses, always seeking to extend his range and repertoire. A room in his home in Sheffield has been converted into a studio. A few of his paintings can be viewed on the website he created when a period of sabbatical leave during his pastorate

---

63. Lessing, *Under my Skin*, 314.

at West Bridgford took him to Italy in 2011[64] (a website that also allows him to indicate his love of poetry).[65]

When we turn to examine some of his reflections on painting on this website the cohering image comes into focus. He says: "It has been said that you never truly see something until you have tried to draw it. In my experience there is much truth in this—the regular practice of drawing from observation leads a person to see everything in a fresher, more lively way."[66] His words about drawing sound rather like the observations I have made about fiction. Drawing or painting is a way of enabling seeing; we might even call it a form of truth telling. He goes on to speak of the effect of light. It is in noticing what the light does, or does not do, to an object that we really begin to see it in its three-dimensionality. And then: "To see clearly—to be attentive to what is in front of us can be a cause of celebration as we respond to beauty and the wonder of creation. But good observational skills can also enable us to see horror and pain. Both should lead us to prayer." Seeing, then, and telling the truth about what we see, drives us to celebration or to prayer. Seeing the world in its variegated forms should produce in us wonder or supplication. Looking, and seeing truthfully, is a spiritual practice.

This act of seeing is the cohering image we have been seeking. We recall John 20:1–8. The passage is replete with acts of "seeing," though we often associate "seeing" with the story of Thomas later in the chapter. Here, though, Mary Magdalene "saw" that the stone had been removed. She goes, perplexed to Simon Peter. When Simon Peter and "the disciple whom Jesus loved," John, ran to the tomb, John ran fastest, lingered outside the tomb, peered in and "saw" the grave clothes. Then Simon Peter arrived and went *into* the tomb. He also sees these same grave clothes. So far, much has been seen but nothing has been grasped. Then John ventured inside the tomb alongside Peter. Now we are told that "he saw and believed." We may speculate on whether there is any significance that it is only when John enters the tomb *alongside Simon Peter* that he sees and believes, but our main point now is to notice that truly seeing is a spiritual activity, more than mere looking. Really seeing what is in front of us leads us to celebration or to prayer.

Just as prayer is a certain kind of "giving attention," Ellis argues on another website page,[67] so this looking at the world in and for the act of

---

64. One page is given over to his paintings—https://crammedwithheaven.org/art/—but others feature on other pages around the site. See the "forum sketch" on https://crammedwithheaven.org/italian-journey/2/

65. https://crammedwithheaven.org/poets/—though this page appears to have disappeared from the menus by which one navigates the site.

66. https://crammedwithheaven.org/art-of-seeing/.

67. https://crammedwithheaven.org/reflections/.

painting is sacramental in some way.[68] It allows us to see that, in the words of another of his favorite poems,

> Earth's crammed with heaven,
> And every common bush afire with God:
>
> But only he who sees, takes off his shoes,
> The rest sit round it, and pluck blackberries . . . .[69]

This seeing the world as God's, in its glory and its heartbreak, moves us to the final strands in the analysis of Baptist theology through worship. A world that belongs to God and to be committed to God is a world "waiting with eager longing"[70] for its final transformation. This is the "eschatological dimension" that gives orientation to the Christian community, turning it outward in prayer and mission.[71] The believer and the Church look outward and seek the Kingdom in prayer, service and proclamation.

This act of seeing, however, is not confined to its eschatological and missiological orientation. Christian community can only truly be nurtured when we learn to see and attend to the other; service of the world must truly see what the other needs, and what they can bring to us; openness to the Spirit and discernment of the "mind of Christ" requires an attending to the Other also.

CONCLUSION

Historically, Baptists have not done much theology. Unless, of course, we consider the theology that we have sung, prayed, and preached week by week—our liturgical theology. Ellis's analysis of this is congruent with one of the major systematic attempts to construct the "baptist vision" offered by James McClendon—the same major themes are found in each account, summarized by Ellis as attention to Scripture; a stress on personal experience of Christ and openness to the Spirit; a concern for the Christian community as a place where faith is nourished and celebrated; and an eschatological sense of God's coming transformation of all things and our calling within this. A brief glance at Ellis's own life, work, and consuming passions, has suggested that the notion of biographical theology has some traction here.

68. https://crammedwithheaven.org/art-of-seeing/.

69. Elizabeth Barrett Browning, *Aurora Leigh* (London: J. Miller, 1864), VII, quoted at https://crammedwithheaven.org/poets/.

70. Rom 8:19.

71. I make a similar point about prayer and mission in Ellis, "The Church as Praying Community".

In the Johannine image of "seeing" we find rich resources to unpack and develop these four major themes. This notion of "really seeing what is there" is present to us at the beginning of the hymn which acts as a focal point for this essay. In examining the life and work of Christopher Ellis we too may find that our vision has been broadened and our sense of wonder expanded. What remains is now that with the help of the Triune God we might

... see the wonder and ... grow ...
... search for truth in all
With courage and integrity.

And pray:

Fill us with love that all we know
May serve your world with your concern.

The Lord is Here

The Lord is here—he finds us as we seek
to learn his will and follow in his way.
He gives himself just as he gave his Word,
the God of promise greets us every day.

The Lord is here—he meets us as we share -
this is the life he calls us now to live;
in offered peace, in shared-out bread and wine
our God is gift and calls us now to give.

The Lord is here—inviting us to go
and share the news with people everywhere.
He waits outside in need and help alike,
the Spirit moves through deed as well as prayer.

So let us go, intent to seek and find,
living this hope that God is always near.
Sharing and trusting, let us live his love,
that all the world may say—"The Lord is here".

2

"The Lord Is Here"
How Worship Confronts the Powers

CRAIG GARDINER

THE CHRIS ELLIS HYMN "The Lord is here" is rooted in the earliest proclamation of the church at worship: the claim that "Jesus is Lord."[1] The lyrics affirm that as Christians gather for worship, "the Lord is here" and end with the community being sent, "living his love" so that "all the world" may make the same confession. If the uninitiated observer asked this hymn-singing congregation, "Who is this unnamed Lord whose presence you affirm?" the church surely would respond, "He is Jesus Christ." But for the early church this proclamation was more than a doxological response or a doctrinal affirmation: it was also a deeply subversive moral, political and missional act,[2] where, in its relationships with one another and the world, the church's ethical character was revealed. Worship provided the opportunity for early Christians to communally rehearse their Christ-like character and in time go on to perform the missional virtues of kin-dom[3] living in the world.

---

1. See for example, Rom 10:9; 1 Cor 8:16; 2 Cor 4:5.

2. Ruth A. Meyers has compelling argued that mission and worship belong together, not in a linear progression as worship in church prepared a congregation for mission in the world, but in interaction, like two sides of a Möbius strip, so that worship and mission flow in and out of one another. See *Missional Worship, Worshipful Mission*. A similar contention is made through the musical metaphor of polyphony in Gardiner, *How Can We Sing the Lord's Song?*

3. The phrase Kin-dom, with evocations of a more egalitarian "family of God's

This mission almost inevitably brought the early Christian "communities of character"[4] into conflict with the "powers and principalities of the age,"[5] those material and spiritual forces that oppose Christ's Lordship. Using the pattern suggested in Ellis's hymn, it will be suggested that the musical metaphors of practice and performance can help those charged with enabling worship to explicitly rehearse congregations in what is hoped has been happening implicitly, namely their formation in Christ-like ways of living, resisting the powers and performing within the world, the truth that Christ is Lord.

REHEARSING A METAPHOR FOR WORSHIP

Ellis's hymn echoes the ancient structure of worship found in the earliest accounts of Christian liturgy from Justin Martyr, written around 150 CE, and yet still seen in the deliberations of contemporary denominations.[6] This pattern follows a shape that roughly divides into four sections: Gathering, Word-Service, Table-Service, and the Dismissal of the People.[7] This pattern is important not just for providing consistent order, but because it enables communities to realize how worship might consciously rehearse them into the character of Christ.[8] As Stanley Hauerwas suggests:

> the regular, continual pattern of gathering for worship may be viewed as the church's rehearsal. Worship thus becomes a kind

---

people," is here preferred to that of "kingdom" with its sometimes problematic overtones of patriarchy and associated violence. See Isasi-Diaz, "Solidarity: Love of Neighbor in the 21st Century," 31–40. I am aware that the term "Lord" equally carries with it some similar associations of patriarchy but have decided, in dialogue with its use within the hymn, to retain it here.

4. See Hauerwas, *A Community of Character.*

5. Eph 6.12.

6. See Justin Martyr, 1 *Apology,* chapter 67, in Gordon Lathrop, *Holy Things,* 31–32. For a helpful comparison of Justin's liturgy to contemporary patterns of worship see Burns, *SCM Study Guide to Liturgy,* 18–23. Ellis himself discusses a variety of patterns of worship, including a number of Baptist variations in depth in Ellis, *Gathering* chapter 4.

7. Best and Heller, *Eucharist Worship in Ecumenical Contexts,* 35.

8. Dave White draws on the work of Simon Sheikh form the worlds of art to make the important point that in the "curating" of alternative worship, "Repetition could be transferred into continuity literally doing the same in order to produce something different not in the products but in the imagination . . . going into the depths of the matter rather than surfing the surface," Simon Sheikh in Paul O"Neill, ed., *Curating Subjects,* 184 as cited by White, "Depth a Close Friend But Not a Lover," 81.

of performance before the performance, a preparation beforehand for whatever witness the church might be called upon to give.[9]

This imagery of "performance before the performance" does not suggest any notion of "play acting." Rather it can be understood as the Christian community being caught up into God's "cosmic symphony"[10] and through Christ, being invited to "double the parts,"[11] along with what God is already doing in the world. This is not to presume that such kin-dom activity is restricted to the church, however sweet the name of Jesus sounds in a believer's ear, many non-believers still actively participate in resisting the powers and that this happens is not because "God so resented the Church, but because God so loved the world."[12] But the church is specifically called to proclaim in word and deed that Jesus is their Lord and in worship are invited to participate in a performance of Christ that names, unmasks and engages the surrounding and opposing powers. In this way, worship allows the church "to emerge in its true nature"[13] and become "a section of humanity in which Christ has really taken form."[14]

In the liturgical patterns of Orthodox worship, structure is, in and of itself, an important bearer of meaning. And while this will not always be true for other denominations in exactly the same way,[15] the deliberate patterning of Ellis's hymn suggests that such structure is purposefully selected to rehearse the people into Christ-like character. What remains important is not a slavish repetition of the structure, but the fact that the pattern deliberately rehearses the congregation in a rhythm of formation through which the domination of the powers is resisted and Christ is declared as Lord.

---

9. Hauerwas, *Performing the Faith*, 98.

10. Balthasar, *Truth is Symphonic*, 8.

11. See Jenson, *Systematic Theology*, Vol. 1, 235.

12. Wells, *God's Companions*, 34.

13. Allmen, *Worship: Its Theology and Practice*, cited in Ellis, "Duty and Delight," 329.

14. Bonhoeffer, *Ethics*, 85. While there is a danger that this imagery of rehearsal might lead to worship becoming routine and even stale, the fact that it is the performance of a relationship with the living Christ amidst a world of shifting powers should mitigate against this.

15. Ellis makes this point in, "Duty and Delight," 337.

REHEARSING OUR OPPOSITION TO THE POWERS

For the early church, this "presiding conviction"[16] of Christ as Lord offered a narrative for ethics and virtue that ran contrary to that of Caesar's Empire and the "powers and principalities" of the world. Similarly Ellis has noted how in the seventeenth century, early Baptist congregations spoke of "the Crown rights of the Redeemer" to explain "why Baptists found themselves in conflict with the civil authorities in a time of persecution, for Christ, as Lord of all, as well as Lord of the Church, requires the ultimate loyalty of his subjects and followers."[17] While Ellis has deliberately examined worship as a key expression of such core convictions,[18] exploring not simply what congregations believe, but how they act upon those kin-dom beliefs, Walter Wink has taught us to understand the opposing powers as a "Domination System." These pervasive and idolatrous forces seek to usurp Christ and twist the patterns of our lives to their own ends. These powers are not simply the people in control, but constitute "the institutions and structures that weave society into an intricate fabric of power and relationships,"[19] and "the spirituality at the core of those institutions and structures."[20] We may no longer call them Chronos, Moneta, Mercury, Cupid, or Mars, much less pay homage to the Babylonian deity Marduk,[21] but the fact that our world dismisses such powers as myth only enables the forces of time, money, speed, sex and violence to "strike from concealment and craze or cripple us without our having the slightest comprehension as to what has happened."[22] If, as G. K. Beale suggests, "what people revere, they resemble, either for

16. McClendon and Smith, *Convictions*, 97.

17. Ellis, "Duty and Delight," 342. This is echoed in the first part of the Declaration of Principle of the Baptist Union of Great Britain. For more specific comment on the political implications for Baptists and others see Haymes, "Baptism as a Political Act," 69–83.

18. Ellis has followed the trajectory of Alexander Schmemann, away from a "theology of worship" towards a more deliberate "liturgical theology." This approach is less interested in using theological systematics to analyze and define worship, but instead favors the study of worship precisely in order to uncover the theology embodied in our liturgical practices. In *Gathering* Ellis proposed a "fourth step" in this trajectory and extended Schmemann's thinking ecumenically and in particular to the worship of Baptist congregations. There he opened up the possibility of understanding worship as a key expression of the convictions of that community. See Ellis, *Gathering*, 223–24.

19. Wink, *Theology for a New Millennium*, 1.

20. Ibid., 4.

21. Wink explores Paul Ricoeur's commentary on the Babylonian myth of Marduk as a vital way of understanding the widespread myth of redemptive violence. See Wink, *Engaging the Powers*, 14–16, 24, 26.

22. Wink, *Unmasking the Powers*, 108.

ruin or restoration,"[23] then such powers remain the false gods which humanity, including the church, may come to resemble, either through unwitting or deliberate reverence, unless they are named, unmasked, engaged and redeemed.[24] The importance of resistance to the deliberate formation of Christian character is, for Wink, clear:

> Naming the powers identifies our experiences of these pervasive forces that dominate our lives. Unmasking the Powers takes away their invisibility and thus their capacity to coerce us unconsciously into doing their bidding. Engaging the Powers involves joining in God's endeavor to bend them back to their divine purposes.[25]

For the early church, such resistance was practiced within the catechumenate, an integrated approach to discipleship, mission, and worship that rehearsed pagans into the alternative values of the gospel. It was likened to the regular exercise regime undertaken by Greek athletes, only here the worshipping community trained to perform their kin-dom lives within the world and at "full stretch before God."[26] This *askesis* of worship formed converts into a new worldview, that Bob Ekblad sees as essential for the church again today, namely a cosmology that takes account of the "microforces that assault people in forms such as anger, jealousy, lust, and greed, labeled by the early church fathers as 'passions' or 'demons' and the larger macropowers such as legalism, nationalism, discrimination, and the like, labeled by social prophetic writers according to the biblical vocabulary surrounding 'principalities and powers.'"[27] To now fail to worship in this way is, by default, to offer devotion to the powers because, as James K. A. Smith suggests, we are,

> "liturgical animals," creatures who can't not worship and who are fundamentally formed by worship practices. The reason such liturgies are so formative is precisely because it is these liturgies, whether Christian or "secular," that shape what we *love*. And we are what we love.[28]

---

23. Beale, *We Become What We Worship*, 16.

24. Wink's trilogy of books are entitled, *Naming the Powers*; *Unmasking the Powers*; and *Engaging the Powers*. See also *When the Powers Fall*.

25. Walter Wink, *Theology for a New Millennium*, 34–35.

26. The evocative phrase is borrowed from Anderson, and Morrill, *Liturgy and the Moral Self*.

27. Eckblad, *A New Christian Manifesto*, 68.

28. Smith, *Imagining the Kingdom*, 3–4.

Smith's conclusion, "that we are what we love," takes us beyond the traditional maxim of "*lex orandi, lex credendi*" (our patterns of prayer, become what we believe),[29] and encourages worship that deliberately shapes how we behave.[30] The new maxim, becomes, "*lex orandi, lex credendi, lex vivendi*,"[31] i.e., worship shapes not only what we think, but how we engage the powers. Such worship, as Hauerwas notes, "requires that our bodies be formed by truthful habits of speech and gesture. To be so habituated is to acquire a character befitting lives capable of worshipping God."[32] Such habituation requires imagination.

IMAGINATION IN REHEARSAL AND PERFORMANCE

This habituation into the *lex vivendi* requires the people to imagine it being performed in a world transformed by Christ. Much as a musician in rehearsal might imagine the audience and concert hall in which they will perform, worship becomes a font of imagination that hosts a new reality, one shaped by the eschatological promises of God, where the kin-dom, if not fully realized, is still continually present as an ethical alternative. In this exercise of "prophetic imagination"[33] worship is more akin to books and radio than television and film; it is evocative of how an alternative world might be, rather than fixing it in concrete description. Thus it offers space for the Christian to grapple with the choices between Christ or the powers, to rehearse an ethical "performance before the performance"[34] and "believe the future into being."[35]

---

29. Ellis has noted with approval Geoffrey Wainwright's comments that Protestants in general have been less persuaded by the notion of *lex orandi, lex credendi*, as "Protestantism characteristically emphasizes the primacy of doctrine over the liturgy," *Gathering*, 249. Yet even if in such a case the *lex credendi* shapes the *lex orandi*, there remains the question of how both inform how believers act.

30. Of course, when the balanced harmony is performed well, the two are not easily separated.

31. See Irwin, *Context and Text*, 55–56. Irwin is building on the work of Don Saliers, "Liturgy and Ethics: Some New Beginnings." Saliers refers to this third stage as *lex agendi*, the law of ethical action. It is worth noting how Lester Ruth argues that a market-conscious approach to emerging and contemporary forms of Christian worship results in a new liturgical pragmatism: "What must be done (lex agendi) establishes new rules for how the church should pray" (386–87). See Ruth, "Lex Agendi, Lex Orandi," 386–405.

32. Hauerwas, "Worship, Evangelism, Ethics," 158.

33. See Brueggemannm, *The Prophetic Imagination*.

34. Hauerwas, *Performing the Faith*, 98.

35. Wink, *Theology for A New Millennium*, 185.

We return to the fourfold pattern of worship present in Ellis's hymn, to explore in detail how each liturgical movement—Gathering, Word, Response, and Dismissal—offers opportunities to rehearse and perform the character of Christ.

REHEARSING AND PERFORMING: CHRIST IN THE GATHERING

There are broad parallels between the opening lines of Ellis's hymn and the liturgies of ancient and contemporary Christianity. Justin speaks of the people gathering in unity to read the "records of the apostles and the writings of the prophets."[36] Today, the WCC speaks of the assembly coming into "the grace, love and Koinonia of the triune God,"[37] followed by a time of reading and proclaiming Scripture.[38] Ellis suggests something similar as the congregation gather before the God who "finds us as we seek" and who "gives himself just as he gave his Word." Equally clear is the commitment that such worship will form character as the people learn Christ's will and "follow in his way." Within a period of Gathering, there are considerable opportunities to proclaim Christ as Lord through a variety of words, songs, and symbols, all of which might rehearse the people in engaging the powers. But with the flexibility of this Gathering movement, comes the responsibility to draw the congregation's deliberate attention to the formation being undertaken. Each activity ought to be named and explained as a performance of God's will and Christ's way. The opening prayer or "call to worship," might do so by inviting the congregation to share in words that declare Christ's Lordship over the powers. A good example of this from the Iona Community says:

> Leader: It is not true that violence and hatred have the last word, and that war and destruction have come to stay forever;
>
> All: This is true: for to us a child is born, to us a son is given, in whom authority will rest, and whose name will be Prince of Peace.
>
> Leader: It is not true that we are simply victims of the powers of evil that seek to rule the world;

---

36. Justin Martyr, *1 Apology*, chapter 67, in Lathrop, *Holy Things*, 31–32.

37. Best and Heller, *Eucharist Worship in Ecumenical Contexts*, 35.

38. Both Justin and the WCC invite prayers for others at the ends of this part of the journey, something Ellis reserves for verse 3 of his hymn.

All: This is true: to me is given authority in heaven and on earth, and lo, I am with you always, to the end of the world.[39]

Other prayers, such as those of confession and forgiveness might equally affirm the Lordship of Christ over the fallen powers, as might congregational litanies and a variety of symbolic rites. But given the role of singing within many streams of worship and especially within times of gathering, there is a growing responsibility to address the formation of character by those who select our hymnody. This is especially true for less liturgical denominations. Ellis cites with approval, Bernard L. Manning's comment:

> Hymns are for us Dissenters what the liturgy is for the Anglican. They are the framework, the setting, the conventional, the traditional part of divine service as we use it. They are, to adopt the language of the liturgiologists, the Dissenting Use.[40]

Manning's insight applies both to hymns and to the more contemporary songs often used in worship. Hymns have an internal structure that sees them move in a linear progression similar to more traditional liturgy. Modern songs serve a similar but distinctly different purpose. They tend to be more flexible toward repetition, allowing for a greater intensification of a truth or emotion.[41] The issue is not one of either hymns or songs but both/and, whichever best forms Christ-like character. If in worship we become like what we love, then rephrasing Jesus' interrogation of Peter as "Who do you sing that I am?"[42] offers a potentially rich critique of our hymnody. This presents challenges to those who compose and those who select music for worship. As well as proclaiming Christ as Lord the lyrics ought to deliberately form disciples of resistance. Worship leaders ought to ask how hymnody offers specific words of lament and protest against Mars, Mammon and Timorus, the false-gods of violence, greed and fear that rage against the weakest members of a global village or indeed against creation herself. The church's singing ought to stretch and rehearse how the rhythms of the kin-dom and the melodies of shalom might be performed by the church within a hurting world.[43]

39. *Iona Community Worship Book*, 72.

40. Manning, *The Hymns of Wesley and Watts*, 133, as cited by Ellis, "Duty and Delight," 340.

41. See Ellis, *Approaching God*, 87–92.

42. Adam Tice, "Who Do You Sing That I Am?" Senior Paper, Associated Mennonite Biblical Seminary 2007, noted in Kreider and Kreider, *Mission and Worship After Christendom*, 157.

43. There is also the challenge of not only what is sung, but how it is sung, particularly by the congregation. Sung worship should be as participative as possible. But

Of course the congregation's hymnody will usually be shared through each "movement" in of worship: there will be songs sung within the Word-Service, the Table-Service and the Dismissal. Some will lead the people into a deeper engagement with that aspect of the worship, others may take them from one part of the service to the next, but each opportunity to sing offers a rich potential to undergird how the people might participate in a fresh performance of Christ as their Lord. Every hymn or song ought to ask how it might enable worshippers to engage with Christ's redemption of the powers.

REHEARSING AND PERFORMING: CHRIST IN THE WORD

Ellis's hymn then takes us into the ministry of the Word, when in a variety of ways, the Scriptures are proclaimed. Here the gospel truth unmasks the ancient deceits of false gods like Mendacius and the contemporary powers of spin and falsehood. This revelation may occur through preaching or discussion, testimony or silence, perhaps in drama and other art forms.[44] In the reading of the Scriptures, "the corporate memories of the community are recalled and reinforced."[45] These are not just the memories of a particular congregation, but a retelling of the "upside down values"[46] of the gospel. Here it is important that preaching is not simply giving the congregation information about God and so shaping what they believe, (although that must be included) but about stretching them in rehearsals of transformation, that are then performed beyond the time and space of worship. It is "from the hearing of God's Word repeatedly read in public worship that a life of faith takes on something of its measured rhythms and cadences its distinctive orchestration, but also its peculiar vision."[47] As Charles Campbell notes in a book devoted to this approach, the preaching of the Word becomes "an

---

if it is led by musicians in a "performance style" of a concert, then there is the danger that congregations are lulled into an audience mentality which is disengaged from the formation of character. Of course this can happen equally within either hymns played on the organ or in more contemporary styles of sung worship.

44. Justin records how, when the Scriptures have been read, "the president in a discourse admonishes and invites us into the pattern of these good things." Justin Martyr, *1 Apology*, chapter 67, in Lathrop, *Holy Things*, 31–32.

45. James White, *Introduction to Christian Worship*, 141.

46. Kreider and Kreider, *Worship and Mission After Christendom*, 67–69. Kreiders' argument is that the gospel can be "overwhelmed by conventional stories if it is not told and retold." See also Meyers, *Missional Worship, Worshipful Mission*, 82.

47. Foder, "Reading the Scriptures: Rehearsing Identity, Practicing Character," 141.

act of nonviolent resistance to the powers" and central to "the formation of Christian communities of resistance."[48] It is among such communities that the "unsettling news" and "unwelcome threat"[49] of the gospel engages with the powers. It is here Christ unmasks their false depictions of reality and invites the believer to die to their allegiance. Encountering the Word like this, rightly read and heard, says Marva Dawn, "will kill us."[50] She explains that, "Everything we do in worship should kill us, but especially the parts of the service in which we hear the Word—the Scripture lessons and the sermon."[51] This death is of course the death of the false and fallen self, the self still enthralled by the multiple illusions spun by the powers. But the Word of God is a word of Life and so she adds, "Once worship kills us, we are born a new to worship God rightly"[52] and goes on to conclude:

> The ultimate test is whether sermons turn the hearers into theologians and activists. Do they grapple with texts and teach the people how to question? Do they wrestle with faith and invite the listeners to know that victory is assured? Do they struggle against the world's pain and challenge believers to create justice? Above all, do they bring us all into God's presence to hear his Word to us?[53]

Dawn summarizes how the rehearsed Word must then be performed by this community of "theologians and activists" with a vignette from Richard Caemmerer:

> "Pastor, that was a wonderful sermon," said the parishioner at the door after the service.
>
> "That remains to be seen," said the preacher.[54]

---

48. Campbell, *The Word Before the Powers*, 4.
49. Brueggemann, *Finally Comes the Poet*, 1.
50. Dawn, *Reaching out*, 206.
51. Ibid., 206.
52. Ibid.
53. Ibid., 238.
54. See Caemmerer, *Preaching for the Church*, 51, cited in Dawn, *Reaching Out*, 240.

REHEARSING AND PERFORMING: CHRIST IN COMMUNION

The second verse of Ellis's hymn takes us into the heart of the Eucharist. This is Ellis's affirmation that, as Eleanor Kreider has argued, "Communion shapes character."[55] Of course, much Protestant worship is not Eucharistic and Ellis has persuasively argued that it distorts our understanding, "if we forget that most Sunday assemblies do not gather around the Lord's table for the sharing of bread and wine."[56] While this may be true, by including the Eucharist in this hymn, Ellis points us toward the rich potential of Communion to shape the character of the people. This character might well be explored through a consideration of the sheer grace and giftedness of communion or how Christians learn there, how to serve others with humility. But Eucharist is also particularly important to the Christian disciplines of generosity and of peacemaking. If communion is often absent from some Protestant services then those responsible for planning such worship might consider what opportunities are thus lost to forming disciples with these particular Christ-like virtues.

The hymn suggests that the Lord is present as we share in Communion and that sharing, in and of itself, is counter-cultural to the dominant myths of society. Powers of avarice compel the human heart, not only to keep what we already have, but to appropriate the goods of others. This greed arises from a false-narrative of scarcity promulgated by the fallen powers. Brueggemann has helpfully named this as a cultural paradigm of scarcity, tracing it back to the biblical time of Joseph, Pharaoh and the seven years of famine.[57] Anticipating poor harvests, the Empire of Egypt stockpiled food reserves and took control of the means of distribution. Their demands for payment reduced the Israelites to poverty and eventual slavery. While this Empire narrative of scarcity insists that there is never enough Brueggemann suggests that in the biblical counter-narrative, God not only initiates abundance in creation, but goes on to liberate Israel from Pharaoh's manipulation of scarcity. Exodus is then a contest between the powers of scarcity and divine generosity—a contest that continues globally today, not only with regard to food, but to water, healthcare, shelter, and so forth.

It is in Jesus, (who brings life in all of its abundance) that we see the fullness of God's unending generosity. Brueggemann's examination of Mark chapter 8, where Jesus feeds the hungry crowd, sees the disciples rooted

---

55. See Kreider, *Communion Shapes Character*.
56. Ellis, *Gathering*, 43.
57. See Brueggemann, *Journey to the Common Good*, 1–35.

in a world of pragmatism, efficiency and above all scarcity. There is not enough. But Jesus who inhabits the transformative generosity of the Father, shares out of God's abundance. In feeding the people, Mark notes that Jesus took the bread, gave thanks, broke it, and gave it to the crowd. The pattern of words are echoes in the Eucharist. Christ's presence in Communion calls the church into such abundant generosity. If it does not exercise such munificence, perhaps it is because they have failed to be rehearsed in the limitless generosity of God, and failed to imagine how sharing with your neighbor recreates the world. As such the church's learning to share bread and wine becomes a rehearsal of how well physical resources, time and justice are shared within the worshipping community and by them in the world. If Communion speaks to the church of the unconditional grace of God then as Brueggemann suggests, too often, it has been understood as "solely a theological phenomenon instead of recognizing that it has to do with the reordering of the economy of the world."[58]

This is well illustrated by the story of the Food Pantry in San Francisco. Sara Miles was a new Christian who discovered that God is revealed not only in Eucharistic bread and wine, but whenever we share food with others—particularly with strangers. Over the objections of some of her fellow parishioners she began a food pantry in the center of the sanctuary, where they gave away tons of oranges and potatoes and cereal around the same altar where she had "first eaten the body of Christ."[59]

Such generosity extends to our willingness to be reconciled with those at enmity with us. If as Ellis suggests, in Communion we are called to live a new way of life, then reconciling peacemaking is at the heart of our redeemed character. It would be easy to slip over the lyrics that speak of life "in offered peace," but the Eucharist offers rich opportunities to rehearse the performance of shalom, resisting powers that demand obedience through violence or coercion. Traditionally Communion offers such a space through the "sharing the peace." While this has often been minimized, in even the most liturgical of congregations, it retains deep potential for people to seriously explore the realities of conflict resolution within a congregation.

More importantly, the bread and wine invite a congregation to remember Christ's death not as a simple "in memoriam," but eschatologically, in the proleptic light of the future shalom. The recollection ought to affirm that on the night he was betrayed Jesus faced death as he had lived, rejecting violence, praying for his enemies and commanding his disciples to do likewise. But communion might go on to create an imaginative space for

---

58. Brueggemann "Enough is Enough."

59. Miles, "Real Bread," 3.

people to engage with the promised kin-dom of peace and this expresses their resistance to the "myth of redemptive violence."

Wink argues that this "myth" is the all-pervading cultural narrative, spun by the powers. It argues that violent means can bring about peaceable ends. But if, as the hymn affirms, "the Lord is here," shaping the character of our worship then, in Communion, Christ will compel us to show love to our enemies. Such a suggestion runs contrary to the normative liturgies of violence embedded in contemporary culture. As Wink says, "No other religious system has ever remotely rivaled the myth of redemptive violence in its ability to catechize its young so totally."[60] These people grow up to be leaders, policy makers and voters and are largely unable to resist the myth because they have heard no alternative voice. But resistance to the powers is not only far from futile, it is the secret of the Christian's joy.[61] It is around the Communion table that Christians are reminded that while Christ has died and is risen, so too he will come again, bringing with him a kin-dom that is already breaking in amongst us. The fullness of shalom may be "not yet," but in bread and wine the church is called to inhabit it within the "now," bringing peace into a violent world. They leave the Table consciously an "echo of their future selves."[62] As N. T. Wright suggests through a similar metaphor, Christians may know how the play will end, but until the *eschaton*, they are called to offer an "improvisatory performance of the final act as it leads up to and anticipates the intended conclusion."[63] We may not know the full nature of such a performance, but we do know that in each part we allow "peaceableness to shape our lives"[64] and so become an echo of what we shall one day be, participating in the reconciling work of Christ.

REHEARSING AND PERFORMING: CHRIST IN SYMBOLIC ACTION

The third verse of Ellis's hymn hints at the invitation to mission that is addressed again in the final verse, but it also focuses on how the church might respond to God through symbolic action and prayer. Tellingly this verse affirms that Christ waits for the church to join him in the world beyond their worship, and does so both needing their help and offering his assistance.

---

60. Wink, *The Powers That Be*, 54.

61. "Resistance is the Secret of Joy," is the title of a PhD dissertation by Lieve Troch, noted by Grey in *The Outrageous Pursuit of Hope*, 20.

62. Wright, *New Heavens, New Earth*, 12.

63. Wright, *The New Testament and the People of God*, 141–43.

64. Cunningham, *These Three are One*, 268.

Most worshippers are familiar with seeking the intervention of an omnipotent deity on their behalf or that of others. But here there is a clear direction to the suffering God who Bonhoeffer famously asserts is the only God who can save humanity. It cannot be developed here as deeply as might be hoped but Bonhoeffer's theology is clear: it is not by his omnipotence that Christ helps us, but by his weakness.[65]

Such a theology is a striking alternative not only to the cultural assumptions of "power and might" that pervade the world through myths propagated by the powers, but much of the triumphalist theology and hymnody that is present in the church. Such triumphalism seeks only to rehearse the congregation into the successful pain-free Christ of Easter Sunday and avoid the human being who dies in weakness and in shame upon the cross. As such it does little to equip the church to engage with the seeming paradox that their Lord is one who favors weakness over might, nor does it help form the character of people who should be resisting the cultural narratives of strength and victory adopted by the powers.

The lyrics also remind us of the need to join together deeds and prayers, again evocative of Bonhoeffer's advice to his young godson about the church of the future which he claimed would be limited to two things, prayer and action for justice.[66] Bonhoeffer himself was only imagining a practice that drew on his own theological affirmations that,

> In Christ we are invited to participate in the reality of God and the reality of the world at the same time, the one not without the other. The reality of God is disclosed only as it places me completely into the reality of the world. But I find the reality of the world always already borne, accepted and reconciled in the reality of God.[67]

If the congregation is to discover and perform the truths of Christ as Lord within the reality of the world then there might need to be the opportunity for such deeds and actions to be imagined and rehearsed within the worship. However, other than the established liturgical rites such as communion and baptism, actions, (whether imagined, symbolic or practical), have often been neglected by the church. The rich potential of the imagination in itself to envision alternative realities has already been noted. So to invite a congregation to "see themselves" within an imagined situation can be helpful. It may be, for instance, to envision that they, like the friends who

---

65. See Bonhoeffer, *Letters and Papers From Prison*, 473–82.
66. Ibid., 389.
67. Bonhoeffer, *Ethics*, 55.

once lowered their sick companion through a roof, can "see" their loved ones or some situation, lowered in prayer before the Lord.

But there is too, a rich potential in marrying the imagination with a reinforcing physical action that is symbolic of further deeds of character to be performed within the world. Congregations rarely move or act in worship. However the rise of what became known as "alternative worship" saw fresh creativity in how participative actions might enable people to rehearse and perform the alternative realities of life lived in the kin-dom of Jesus. These could be rites of comfort, designed to bring assurance in times of communal disorientation[68] or they might be rituals designed to deliberately disturb the people beyond the lulling comfort offered by the powers.

One brief example may illustrate the point. In a service held immediately after the events of 11th September 2001 the congregation were shocked and needed both to express their grief over those who had died and their solidarity with those working in the on-going emergency relief operation. At the front of the church were placed newspaper pictures of the disaster and a large pile of unwashed stones. As a lament was sung, people were invited to come (or imagine doing so) and move the stones, in solidarity with the rescuers who were still at that time removing rubble from Ground Zero. As they did so, they were further invited to build the stones into a cairn of remembrance for those who had died and to then commit themselves to personally seek out paths of peace. After this, prayers of assurance and commitment were offered. This was both a comfort to a disturbed people and an opportunity for them to move beyond disorientation. Of course, the polyvalence of a symbolic action may suggest many meanings to the congregation, allowing different members to respond, each according to their own personal context. In this way the same action may be comforting to one and disturbing to another.

If worship is, at least in part, about rehearsal of the kin-don of Christ in defiance of the powers, then the opportunity to engage in participative rituals such as these may be important in helping congregations imagine new ways of behavior. For if, as Hauerwas suggests, "the Christian faith is 'primarily an account of divine action' and 'only secondarily an account of the believing subject,'" then "God is a performing God who has invited us to join in the performance that is God's life."[69] Here in imagination and symbolic action, the people glimpse how they might "double the parts" of what Christ is already performing in the world. Indeed it may be through imaginative prayer and creative action that the congregation discovers that

---

68. The terminology is taken from Brueggemann, *The Message of the Psalms*, 19.

69. Hauerwas, *Performing the Faith*, 77.

they themselves might be the answer to their prayers, for often "prayer is not so much about convincing God to do what we want God to do as it is about convincing ourselves to do what God wants us to do."[70]

REHEARSING AND PERFORMING: CHRIST IN INTERCESSIONS

In the traditional shape of Christian worship established by Justin and adapted in more contemporary patterns, prayers of intercession are often found within the ministry of the Word. To place it later, as suggested in the Ellis hymn, need not be problematic. What is important is the shape of the liturgy should intentionally lead the people through their encounter with God, rehearsing them in the moral character to be performed as they depart the sanctuary. While Ellis asserts that the Spirit moves through deeds as well as prayer, clearly prayers, and particularly prayers of intercession remain necessary. While such prayers ought, in some way, to involve the whole congregation, the point is not to ask about what style the church adopts for its intercessory prayer. The issue is not about whether it involves prayers that are read in full, open times of spontaneity, or bidding prayers that encourage imagined but silent congregational responses. All of these approaches (and more) will be valid in any particular context. The concern is that in addressing God, those who pray might imagine just what is possible and purposed by heaven. So Wink argues in a series of key passages that,

> The act of praying is itself one of the indispensable means by which we engage the Powers. It is, in fact that engagement at its most fundamental level, where their secret spell over us is broken and we are re-established in a bit more of the freedom that is our birthright and potential.... Intercessory prayer is spiritual defiance of what is in the way of what God has promised. Intercession visualizes an alternative future to the one apparently fated by the momentum of current forces. Prayer infuses the air of a time yet to be into the suffocating atmosphere of the present. History belongs to the intercessors who believe the future into being.... Intercession, far from being an escape from action, is a means of focusing our action and of creating action. By means of our intercessions we veritably cast fire upon the earth and trumpet the future into being.[71]

---

70. Claiborne and Wilson-Hartgrove, *Becoming the Answer to Our Prayers*, 11.
71. Wink, *The Powers that Be*, 80

Such prayers for the wider world lead the congregation to the point where they are ready to leave the confines of the sanctuary and be sent back into the world. Such a sending changes how the people will next pray. With this understanding of vision of intercession comes a "moral intentionality"[72] that takes people beyond well-meaning sentiment and into a Christ-centered solidarity with those oppressed by the powers. In this way, as Byron Anderson notes, "for each thing we ask of God, the intent is our action in the world in God's name and power."[73]

REHEARSING AND PERFORMING: CHRIST IN DISMISSAL

Action in the world in God's name is the focus of the final verse of Ellis' hymn and the final movement of the liturgy through the dismissal of the congregation. This is the charge for the rehearsed community to go forth in mission to perform the gospel of Christ as Lord, resisting, contradicting and participating in God's redemption of the powers in the world around them.[74] This dismissal must not be prematurely truncated into a moment when, in effect, the people simply say "we are finished for today." This is the final pattern to shape the community's Christ-like character, and how they are sent out may well determine the missional virtues (or lack) in their living beyond the confines of the sanctuary. Gregory Augustine Pierce reminds us that in Roman Catholic liturgy, "when we are sent forth from the Mass, we are sent forth to go out and try again to help transform the world along the lines that God intended and Jesus preached."[75] He goes on to add that the word "mass" comes from the Latin dismissal, *Ite missa est,* meaning, "Go, we are sent forth," and tellingly concludes, "Sometime in church history, some people thought this was an important enough part of the liturgy to name the entire thing after it."[76] This "sending out" demands that those who plan worship consider how a congregation is formed in missional character through the final actions of its worship.

---

72. Saliers, *Worship as Theology*, 134.

73. Anderson, "Linking Liturgy and Life," 68.

74. Of course, all elements of worship should reflect this missional imperative, not just the "sending out." For a practical guide for how this may be done, see Lomax, *Creating Missional Worship*.

75. Pierce, *The Mass is Never Ended*, 38–39 cited in Meyers, *Missional Worship, Worshipful Mission*, 182.

76. Ibid., 182.

One practical aspect to the dismissal is that the people are sent out with an offering. In Justin's early description of the worship service, the final actions of the congregation engage people seeking out the common good of the Christian community and finding any and all of the wider community who may be in need. An offering is collected and dispersed to offer succor to the "orphans and widows and those who, through sickness or any other cause, are in want, and those who are in bonds and the strangers sojourning among us, and in a word takes care of all who are in need."[77] There is something of great virtue in sending such a rehearsed people to perform acts of compassion and justice in the world. But even before such deeds are performed the act of making an offering speaks out against the dominant powers of the Market that so dominate the global society. Some churches have recently stopped bringing an offering within worship, arguing that most members give through their bank and that the "collection" sends an unwelcome message to visitors, i.e., "the church just wants your money." This is understandable, but it is worth asking, where else might anyone witness and participate in an alternative to the pervasive "secular liturgies" of Mammon? James K. A. Smith notes that "kingdom economics" mean that:

> The liturgical practice of the offering indicates that Christian worship—which is a foretaste of the new creation—embodies a new economy, an alternative economy.... The Sunday offering in gathered worship is not disconnected from other systems of commerce, distribution, and exchange.[78]

He concludes that Christian worship ought to be "marked by cruciform practices that counter the liturgies of consumption, hoarding, and greed that characterize so much of our late modern culture."[79] Of course, the church is not unique in offering alternative liturgies of generosity in this way, many of other or no faith do so too, but if congregations offer no *askesis* of resistance to its members, surely they will have fallen short of their vocation to participate and perform God's mission of justice, peace and reconciliation?

But together with being sent to seek those in need of help, there is also within the Ellis hymn the intimation that the worshippers are to seek and find God too. This interpretation of the words reminds people that it is not the church of Christ that has a mission, but the mission of Christ that has a church. They are sent to discover that God is already near them in the world. The world beyond the sanctuary is neither God-forsaken nor unholy.

---

77. Justin, *I Apology*, ch. 67, as cited in Webber, *Common Roots*, 106.
78. Smith, *Desiring the Kingdom*, 204–5.
79. Ibid., 205.

For all the domination of the powers, Christ remains Lord of all. There is no convenient sacred and secular divide, but God can be found inhabiting and blessing all times and all places. In seeking and sharing the rhythms of God they have rehearsed in worship, the church is then more attuned to discern where the kin-dom is being established and add their lives in participation of what heaven is already performing. In adding themselves to what Christ already does, it is hoped that all creation and indeed the powers may rediscover their true and given vocation. In this way the church fulfills its vocation to be a part of humanity where Christ has really taken form. If so, as Aidan Kavanagh suggests, then it will be able to show the world what it is for the world "to actively co-operat[e] with God in its own rehabilitation"[80] and so "the world may say—'The Lord is here.'"

This final movement of worship then turns the people "inside out," orientating them towards the existing work of God in mission and sending them out to participate in the kin-dom and the redemption of the powers in the world. As Meyers reminds us, "Although these are the final actions of a worship service, going forth is not an ending but a beginning."[81] This final act of sending is "the primary element of preparation for a demanding aspect of worship (action) that lasts typically from one Sunday morning to the next. During the week the faithful are engaged in outward worship, the work of God's people which might be called 'the living liturgy of discipleship.'"[82]

CONCLUSIONS

Ellis's hymn and these reflections on it have taken us on a journey through the character-forming potential of those who, in worship, would regularly declare the "Lord is here" and week by week be explicitly attentive to Christ's presence in a particular time and place and people. It has sought to integrate how the *lex orandi and lex credendi,* might rehearse the congregation in the rhythms of a *lex vivendi* whose performance in the world engages and participates in the redemption of the fallen powers. The hope is that this brief exploration might encourage those who plan, preside over and participate in worship to ask how its structure and content enables the people not only to become free from the powers but to free the powers themselves, to discern how they can together rehearse and participate in the performance of Lordship of Christ. Then the church, with all of liberated creation, can

---

80. Kavanagh, *On Liturgical Theology,* 168.
81. Meyers, *Missional Worship, Worshipful Mission,* 182.
82. Ibid., 182.

join with the Psalmist's worship and declare, "O Lord, our sovereign, how majestic is your name in all the earth."[83]

---

83. Ps 8:1.

The Best Way of All

At the heart of all things
There is love, as Christ has shown
God of love we praise you:
Healing, binding, making one.

Pulsing through creation,
Life of God and life for all:
Love is invitation,
Human future, God's own call.

Love is kind and patient,
Never boastful, never rude;
Love can cope with all things,
Overcoming selfish mood.

Trusting, hoping, loving:
Jesus shows us how to care;
Love is still the best way,
Sign of life for all to share.

3

"God of Love We Praise You"
Baptist Worship and Congregational Song

Shona Shaw

BAPTISTS LOVE TO SING, and when we sing it is from our hearts as much as with our voices.[1] Chris Ellis, writing on worship has drawn our attention to this phenomenon in two publications: *Gathering: Theology and Spirituality in Worship in Free Church Tradition* and *Approaching God: A Guide for Worship Leaders and Worshippers*. Whilst music in worship has continued to be a controversial subject, Ellis has been at the forefront of writing that seeks to engage worship leaders and worshippers in deeper reflection on our song writing and singing. Although much has been written on the history of hymnody and the Baptist tradition, it is Ellis in *Gathering* that invites a critical engagement with liturgical theology. Influenced by the Schmemann-Kavanagh school of liturgical theology, Ellis asks us to consider the place and practice of our worship as the source of our theology and identity. To take the example of congregational song, Ellis argues that our experience of singing together in worship not only rehearses the stories of our faith but directly forms and shapes them. We are literally rehearsing *and* performing our theology as we sing together. In this sense our hymnbooks have been our sung liturgy. Much of Ellis's own hymn writing took place during his ministry in an LEP in Swindon (1981–90). His collection of hymns

---

1. See Ellis, *Gathering*, chapter 8 "With Heart and Voice: The Spirituality of Congregational Song," 153–57.

illustrates the need for sung theology to shape a congregation's worship during Lent, Easter, Pentecost, Advent, and Christmas. There are also hymns for rites of passage such as baptisms and infant dedications. A later composition entitled "Hymn for councils and committees" was written for the Baptist Union's Denominational Consultation in 1996. It seems fitting therefore to turn to Ellis's hymns in exploring the particular ways congregational singing enables Baptists to rehearse and perform our theology. In particular we will consider the theological themes of encounter, inclusion, sacrifice, and embodiment that recur in Ellis's hymns.

After hymn singing was accepted as befitting Baptist worship by the mid eighteenth century, hymns became for almost the next two hundred years, the main liturgical building block of our denominational worship. We were not distinctive in this practice, sharing with most of the Free Church tradition a strong affinity with the hymn-prayer pattern of worship. Nonetheless hymns carried our story, declared what we believed and subsequently shaped our identity. However, whilst preaching and the exposition of the word have largely been credited for constituting our worship as Baptists, the place of congregational song, although a constant presence is often ignored. Brian Haymes in his essay, "Still Blessing the Tie that Binds" makes reference to the hymn of the title, noting it was for many years regarded as the unofficial national and international "anthem" of Baptists.[2] But by the 1990s, when travelling around UK Baptist churches, Haymes discovered it had fallen out of favor, and been replaced by "Bind us together Lord, with cords that cannot be broken." Haymes questions whether this change, although small, may have theological significance:

> I have often reflected on this small particular change in our common life as British Baptists. Does it indicate anything significant? Did one generation know something that we have almost forgotten? There is a difference. One affirms a great conviction, celebrating the tie that binds as the gift of God. The other, for all its doctrinal verses, sounds more like a prayer. Are they two sides of one coin, affirming what God has done and then expressing our hope that God might do what we cannot do and give us what we find so hard to achieve?[3]

Haymes's personal observation of change is supported by a national survey of Baptist worship undertaken by Ellis in 1996, which uncovered the shift more generally from hymns to choruses. By 1996 less than half of Baptist Churches in the UK were using a hymn prayer pattern in their

---

2. Haymes, "Still Blessing the Tie that Binds," 100–101.
3. Ibid., 101.

worship, choosing instead to incorporate a sequence of worship songs. Some churches had dispensed with hymns entirely.[4] This trend was reflected in the poor reception of the last Baptist hymnbook to be published, *Baptist Praise and Worship* (1991), which went out of print soon after. Instead the likes of *Mission Praise* and *Songs of Fellowship* had become the favored hymnbooks for worship.[5] Ellis' survey of worshipping congregations provided for the first time a unique record of Baptists' current practice. In doing so, his research marked the significant shift that was taking place as regards the place of hymns, but also underlined the ongoing formative influence of congregational song on our worship and theology.

Whilst it is difficult to prove the reasons for the change, both Ellis and Haymes observe the impression these changes have made upon our sung theology. Ellis notes the move from the linear narrative of our sung theology in hymns to the cyclical and experiential nature of choruses (I would also add Taize chants to this category). Haymes suggests the corporate theological memory loss in the demise of the Baptist "anthem." If research were to be carried out today in our UK churches, what practices in our congregational singing would it uncover? Perhaps an even greater diversity in our song preferences, maybe, but certainly a continuing adherence to theology in song.

LOVING ENCOUNTER

Worship expresses what the church is and what she will be as we are transformed in encountering a loving God. This theme opens "The Best Way of All" in verse one: "At the heart of all things / There is love, as Christ has shown / God of love we praise you: / Healing, binding, making one." Ellis returns to the theme of encountering God's love again and again in his hymn writing, from the playful "Here and There Praise": "He came in Jesus to show his love, / He is below as well as above, / God is here and God is there: / Always around us offering care." And in the recurring couplet in each verse of the more expansive "Living God": "Here is love and here is glory, / life of God for all to share."

---

4. Ellis conducted this survey for the Baptist Union and the report was published as *Baptist Worship Today*, 14–18.

5. Some have suggested the rise of the charismatic movement and the song writing it inspired, together with the increased access to recorded worship on tapes and CDs contributed to the poor reception of *Baptist Praise and Worship*. See Neville Clark's reflections on being part of the editorial committee of *BPW* in Clark, "Baptist, Praise and Worship."

For "Living God" Ellis suggests two tunes: *Hyfrydol* or *Ode to Joy*. Whilst the tunes are quite different, both reach a musical climax on this recurring couplet. The music draws the attention of the singer to this point in the song, underlining the declarative, "Here is love and here is glory" and elicits an emotional response of elation. The result is a deeper sense of arrival, but also a feeling of moving beyond the familiar. Music encapsulates this ambiguity of encounter in that we experience a sense of now and not yet. Ellis's choice of hymn tunes for "Living God" make use of this quality to great effect.

Early General Baptists were cautious about allowing hymns into their worship for the cultural influence hymns might exercise in a way they could not control. For a denomination that puts so much emphasis on discerning the "mind of Christ" as its guiding principle and practice, we prize above all other modes, a faith that can be discerned *intellectually*. Whilst songs appeal to the intellect in their lyrics, they are embedded in a non-verbal mode of communication: music. Music like other art forms communicates with the intellect but it also reaches beyond the mind to the body. In this sense, hymns were a risk, liturgically and theologically, to worship that sought to be validated by cerebral means alone. To be scripturally authentic, meant remaining loyal to a form of congregational song that kept the biblical text as its focus and music firmly subordinate: this ensured purity of thought and the body in check. But what the early Baptists did not fully appreciate was the capacity for even plain, monotonous music to defy subordination and communicate on its own terms.

Such a simplistic perception of music is present in worship throughout our Christian history. As Jeremy Begbie observes, music's capacity to be formative of our worship has gone undetected and unchecked.[6] In particular we have been largely ignorant, Begbie argues, of music's workings and its "heightened sensitivity to currents of social and cultural thought and practice, and to their theological dimensions."[7]

We might observe then in congregational singing that a combination of music and text communicate through multiple senses increasing the response or "heightened sensitivity" of heart and mind. The interplay between sociocultural currents and theology that Begbie identifies can be seen at work not only in the song making of an individual but during a congregation's singing.

It is interesting to note Ellis utilizes the tune for "Bind us together Lord," (the song Haymes observed had replaced the older "Blest be the tie

6. See Begbie, *Theology, Music and Time*.
7. Ibid., 274.

that binds,") for a setting of "A Prayer for Justice." For his hymn on the "I Am" sayings, he turns to another contemporary tune, Graham Kendrick's "The Price is Paid." In using well-known tunes from more contemporary writers, Ellis utilizes the current musical memory of the gathered church and arguably gains from the sociocultural references of the music, identified by Begbie. This is not a new practice, for hymn writers have not always set their words to particular tunes and the standardized meter of hymns allowed a flexibility and variety in their settings that contemporary worship songs often lack. Singing the same words over time can be formative but it can also become rather boring. The interchangeability of hymn tunes allows words to be brought alive once again by a new key or melody. Ellis often has this in mind with suggestions of alternative tunes for his hymns. A good example is "Open this Book" where two tunes are suggested: Woodlands (Tell out my soul) with its fanfare beginning of perfect fourths compared with the more reflective and lesser known: Toulon, with its gentle undulating tune.

This corporate experience of singing will be explored further in the next section but to summarize we might say congregational singing is our sung liturgy for it is the work of the people expressing their encounter with a God of love. Whilst spoken liturgy maybe formative for other denominations, the liturgy of congregational song has been formative over the years for Baptists as we have sung our faith. In particular we recognize the equal part that music has played alongside the words in the formation of our sung theology.

INCLUSIVE PERFORMANCE

The line from verse one of "Living God": "Life of God for all to share" expresses song as an active performance of our shared faith. Baptists emphasize the shared "priesthood" rather than an individual's license to preside over acts of worship. Mindful of Begbie's point on music's sociocultural and theological meanings, we recognize that music is not merely contained in text but is a performed event. Music in corporate worship is made and performed by a group of people. Ellis calls this "a company of love" in his final line of "Faith and Future." Again in "The Communion of Saints" he refers to Christ's "loving company": "Come and look at one another—/ In each other Jesus see. / Come and let his Spirit bind us / As his loving company."

Pursuing the theme of performance in congregational singing, "a loving company" or "company of love" suggests a company of artists, players or actors. As with any artistic endeavor there is a shared responsibility for the creative process and performance. By including the congregation's singing, in addition to the musical text, instrumentalists or worship leaders, we acknowledge that each member of the congregation is a musical performer and integral to the performance.[8] Every voice is required to lift the song of the church and express the encounter with their distinct voice, as James K. A. Smith describes:

> [S]inging is a full bodied action that activates the whole person. . . . Singing requires us to call on parts of the body that might otherwise be rather dormant-stomach muscles and vocal cords, lungs and tongues. . . . Thus in song there is a performative affirmation of our embodiment, a marshalling of it for expression-whether beautiful songs of praise or mournful dirges of lament. The delights of harmony also attest to an aesthetic expression of interdependence and intersubjectivity. And the riggers and pleasures of musical creation attest to our vocation as subcreators. In short, music and song seem to stand as packed microcosms of what it means to be human. How appropriate then, for song to be such a primary means for reordering our desires in the context of Christian worship.[9]

Singing connects us, both physically and spiritually, with one another and with God. This is the "performative affirmation" to which Smith refers. Musical performance in worship is often viewed negatively for its implied vanity, but in this sense it describes the experience of performing faith together. It is both rehearsal for what is to come and performance of our experience now.

The presence of the gathered members enables and gives meaning to our worship rather than ecclesial license. There is a helpful provisionality in our congregational singing when reflecting upon the imperfections of our worship. It is good to be reminded of opportunities to learn together and practice, rather than expecting faultless performance. It is unrealistic to expect everyone to sing like professional musicians, but this should not devalue or exclude our contribution. What the congregation believes they are doing when they sing together is more important than the quality of their performance but this is often lost from our liturgical discernment. We may sing together in harmony even if we are unable to agree on everything, this is another mark of the provisionality of our discernment.[10] For some Christian traditions the importance of preserving historical accuracy may

---

8. Porter, "The Developing Field of Christian Congregational Music Studies," 151.

9. Smith *Desiring the Kingdom*, 170.

10. Rebecca Slough observes this phenomenon in her research. See Slough, "Let Every Tongue," 175–208.

have resulted in the marginalization of the congregation's performance in worship. However, even in more clergy led worship, as Schillebeeckx notes, this perspective is being challenged:

> Nowadays we are no longer looking for the prehistoric origin(s) of ancient rituals. The focus has shifted to the immediate "roots" or living matrix of rituals. And these origins are not in some distant past . . . but in the here and now of what is known as live performance.[11]

Sadly, the performance of our congregational singing can be drowned out by the volume of the instrumentalists or amplified singers. If we are to encourage a truly inclusive performance in our song, it may be time to review the balance of players in our "loving company" each week. This may require more than shifting the music group to a less prominent space. In more traditional buildings the acoustics lent themselves to amplify the sound of voices naturally and often allowed congregations not only hear one another but see one another. In this way the performance was rooted within the congregation, rather than being led by a minority of "specialists" at the front. This not only encouraged a multiplicity of voices in song but rehearsed the sense of inclusive discernment in our congregational government.

Before we move onto consider congregational singing and ritual we recognize the formative influence that congregational song continues to bring to our Baptist experience of inclusive performance and discernment. The inclusive performance that we bring is at once transformative but also fleeting. Ellis captures this contradictory experience of resting and striving in the "Song of Creation": "You are the wind that rushes through the heavens, / The breath that gently feeds us from our birth: / We rest in you, our source and goal of living, / We strive for you as stewards of your earth."

SACRIFICE AND SILENCE

We next turn to the concept of sacrifice in congregational song. In worship we experience sacrifice most explicitly through the Lord's Supper, remembering Christ's body and blood poured out. The ritual of sharing the bread and wine has been without music for many Baptists. We may sing a song of preparation before communion or response and thanksgiving following it, but a respectful silence traditionally marked sharing the elements within the congregation. In some churches, the point at which bread and wine begin to be shared with the congregation is the cue for the musicians to strike

---

11. Schillebeeckx, "Towards a Rediscovery of the Christian Sacraments," 12–13.

up again, providing appropriate music to ease the transition and provide a focus for our ears.

There is nothing wrong with this practice, however, it may be worth considering the value of silence at this moment of worship. We may not consider silence as part of our congregational singing, but silence is a part of the shared performance. As musical performers know the moments of silence within a piece of music are not passive, they mark time and require the performer's attention to return to play when the moment arrives. Unlike musical rests the silence during worship may not be controlled or quantified but requires our attention and cooperation all the same. Silence is kept, it does not happen by default. In falling silent during the sharing of the elements we are reminded that this is not our part but Christ's, for it is Christ's love and glory "for a needy world outpoured" (Ellis, "Living God").

Total silence can be uncomfortable or difficult to sustain, particularly with children present, but this should not worry us or preclude members of our congregation. As we were reminded earlier this is not a faultless performance with *perfect* silence. Silence may intensify unwanted feelings of unrest or emptiness within us, but maybe these responses are fitting as we encounter the mystery of Christ's sacrifice.[12]

As singing returns to mark the end of the Lord's Supper, the temptation is to relax the tension and return our minds to less troubling thoughts. But congregational song can maintain a response to communion that is turned outwards to God's mission.[13] Ellis's hymns for preparation and conclusion of the Lord's Supper keep this relationship between Christ's sacrifice and the need for response. In "A Sign of Unity" the verses provide a narrative for not only preparation, but also thanksgiving and sending out. It would work just as well as a shared spoken liturgy as a sung response at the end of the meal. John Bell insists singing should never be substitute for action, but should respond to and embody action.[14] In "Exodus Hymn" he weaves together the wilderness journey with the Lord's Supper, emphasizing its provisionality, of

---

12. The concept of sacrifice is explored by Michael Shaw in his *Baptist Times* article "True worship, hurts," where he argues that our need for familiarity and comfort in worship have meant we no longer engage in worship as sacrifice. See: http://www.baptist.org.uk/Articles/439677/How_true_worship.aspx

13. During his presidency of the Baptist Union, Ellis invited local congregations to reflect more broadly upon their gathered worship, aided by the resource *Let's talk about worship*. The eight sessions are structured around a conversation with Ellis and supporting scriptural texts. The focus is devotional, but deals with identity, the relationship between worship and mission, and the benefits of being open to learn and experience new ways of worship. See *Lets Talk about Worship* at http://www.baptist.org.uk/Publisher/File.aspx?ID=131866&view=browser

14 Bell, *The Singing Thing*, 84.

sustenance for us on the journey "until he comes": "You gave the travellers food in the wilderness, / Strengthen us now with the bread that we share; / Bread for the struggle and wine for rejoicing, / In Christ you free us and teach us to care."

As Baptists we may rehearse and perform our response to the Lord's Supper through shared silence and congregational song that marks and shapes our response to Christ's sacrifice. We will next consider how participation in God's mission might be rehearsed and performed through our singing.

IMPROVISING FROM THE HEART

In congregational singing the living liturgy of the people is affirmed for its inclusive and performative nature. Singing in this multi-sensory understanding becomes less the "work of the people" than the response of the body to loving encounter. Ellis puts it like this in his hymn "Ends and Means" on the struggles of discerning right actions: "The way of love will see us through / When questions challenge, 'Why?' and 'How?' / Come, let us struggle, seeking right, / Living the life of Jesus now!"

Congregational song is therefore a part of its body language that facilitates our loving response to God. It is more intimate and instinctive than we have acknowledged in the past, for to sing together is to *be as one* in a way that joins people's hearts and minds. It is also experiential in a way that does not compete with the intellect but empowers it to improvise a fresh response.

Ritual theory supports liturgical theology in its assertion that much of our theological knowing is perceived through our senses before it is recognized and known by our intellect. In his article "On Ritual Knowledge" Theodore Jennings expounds this theory: the first "moment" of knowing he proposes as a mode of enquiry and discovery, or "ritual as coming to know."[15] Ritual's capacity to generate knowledge gives ritual forms an autonomy and this has two implications. Firstly, ritual action is not sheer repetition: the same hymn sung by the same congregation on three different occasions. According to Jennings' argument this would demonstrate differences in detail that would have a bearing on the meaning of the ritual action. Secondly, the exploratory character of ritual action "seeks to discover the right action or sequence of actions" and is "constitutive of, not accidental to the ritual process." However, Jennings argues this is not a cerebral response, intellectually articulated and subsequently acted upon, but is critically recognized as

---

15. Jennings, "On Ritual Knowledge," 111.

embodied response. As Jennings, commenting on the relationship between worship and ethics in Romans 12, observes:

> It is not so much that the mind "embodies" itself in ritual action, but rather that the body "minds" itself or attends itself through ritual action. . . . I do not think through the appropriate action and then "perform" it. Rather it is more like this: My hand "discovers" the fitting gesture which I may then "cerebrally" recognize as appropriate or right.[16]

The process that Jennings outlines is reminiscent of musical improvisation when musicians experienced in performing together are able to go "off script" without disturbing the musical flow. The concept of flow is well known in the behavioral sciences and refers to a state in which "thinking, feeling and acting are unified, generating an experience that feels fluent and coherent."[17]

A freedom to improvise action in God's mission may arise when congregation's become experienced in performing their heart response in song. From these embodied actions flow God's love and glory.

SIGNS OF LIFE

"Love is still the best way, / Sign of life for all to share."

The living liturgy of congregational song is extremely resonant for Baptist discernment: we affirm and recognize according to Scripture the life of Christ amongst us. The image of the living body has been formative in the theological imagination since the church in Corinth received its letter concerning community life. The body can be understood as an individual physical body or corporate spiritual body of Christ, present amongst the worshipping church. But the image is of a *living* body, breathing and moving in God's love the hymn "The Best Way of All" reflects. God's love is described in verse two as: "Pulsing through creation, / Life of God and life for all:"

What sometimes happens in our worship, is the extent to which we have allowed the intellect to subordinate all other noetic functions of the body in worship. This has led to a rather detached and static corporate body in worship. We notice this more acutely in our worship as it is the primary arena for the body to be gathered together and *to be* itself. We sense when

---

16. Jennings, "On Ritual Knowledge," 115.

17. Joanna Collicutt making reference to Mihaly Csikszentmihalyi's work in her *The Psychology of Christian Character Formation*, 149.

our worship fails to bring the corporate gathering alive, when we are estranged from one another or our sung theology does not match our actions. Nathan D. Mitchell in his *Meeting Mystery: Liturgy, Worship, Sacraments* extends the metaphor:

> Liturgy needs to retrieve its "body" language rather than mind over matter of Cartesian Christianity, "our bodies make our prayers"—through gestures, postures, and shared exertions of singing, responding, processing, lifting, moving, touching, tasting, saying, seeing, hearing.[18]

Mitchell's range of "shared exertions" alongside singing, challenge the static nature of our gathered worship as Baptists. Our worship can lack the multi-sensory experience to which Mitchell refers, and there can also be a disconnect between our sung intentions and what happens in practice. It is interesting to notice that throughout Ellis's hymn writing he never makes reference to liturgical actions such as singing, shouting, lifting hands or bowing down. This maybe coincidental or indicative of the liturgical context within which he was writing, or the place of his own spirituality at that time. It is a reminder that there is a provisionality about our song making, which may have an impact upon how congregation's develop their song making and performing. More regular reflection on what our current choice of hymns is, maybe required to register whether there is a disconnect between our singing and our theology. Thus, hymns written during Ellis' Swindon ministry may not reflect his liturgical position today or indeed the current position of the congregation. This should not exclude from our current selection the hymns and songs from our shared past, but we would do well to be mindful of their cultural, social and theological content as indeed we are for the "new" or "latest" songs. Do both new and old songs invite a greater exploration of our shared "body language"? Does singing about kneeling, raising hands or bowing actually encourage a congregation to perform these "shared exertions" anyway? If we reflected more on the content of our songs maybe, this would be the case. At the very least our congregational song that is sung from the heart with full voice is a declaration to the world that Christ's body is indeed alive and invites others to join the throng.

Whilst we have affirmed the ongoing centrality of congregational song in Baptist worship today, we may consider Mitchell's call as an invitation to explore further what it means for us to follow "Love as the best way" and the "sign of life." Rather than viewing these actions as alien and thus undermining to Baptist worship, improvised for our own context, they may

---

18. Mitchell, *Meeting Mystery*, 219.

reawaken a conviction in our shared theology and confidence in its shared performance.

CONCLUSION

Taking Ellis's hymns as inspiration we have explored the liturgical themes of loving encounter, inclusive performance, sacrifice and silence, improvisation from the heart and embodiment. The tension of rehearsal and performance in singing our faith is ultimately characteristic of Ellis's song writing at a particular time in his Baptist ministry. Ellis's vision for worship is that we might deepen our loving encounter with God and with one another. Throughout his own writing and practice of congregational song, Ellis is keen to emphasize the element of the unknown, a sense that we are yet to arrive. This keeps a humility in his insights, an openness to learn from what is unfamiliar and an appetite to worship.[19] In so doing, he has encouraged others to assume the same attitude in their singing and their song making as we continue to praise the "God of Love."

---

19. Ellis picks up on the richness of ecumenism in sharing worship together in *Lets Talk About Worship*.

A Living Sacrifice

Come, Israel, hear, the Lord your God is one;
He is the Lord and worthy of our praise.
Love him with all your strength and heart and mind,
Bring all you are and serve him all your days.
Your neighbour love as you would love yourself:
Discover here the Kingdom's hidden wealth.
My gracious God, I answer now your call:
A living sacrifice, I give my all.

Do not conform to this world and its ways,
But be transformed, renewed in heart and mind.
Our loving God has offered on the cross
A sacrifice of love for humankind.
Sisters and brothers, by his mercy come
And in obedient living find your home.
My gracious God, I answer now your call:
A living sacrifice, I give my all.

O depth of all the wisdom of our God!
This mystery we cannot understand:
How we are rich in mercy and in grace,
For he is all and in his love we stand.
Receive the Father's love through his own Son
And by the Spirit let your heart be won.
My gracious God, I answer now your call:
A living sacrifice, I give my all.

4

"In Obedient Living Find Your Home"
Reflections on Baptists and Discipleship

Paul Goodliff

Chris Ellis has served Christ and his church as pastor, theologian, college principal, liturgist, hymn writer, ecumenist, and spiritual guide. He is also an enthusiastic painter. It is my privilege to know him as friend. Few can have had such a varied ministry as he, and in this paper I want in a small way to reflect that variety: academic reflection upon discipleship, but also upon art and the spiritual life, and in a very inadequate way, perhaps, to reflect the man in whose honor this Festschrift is published.

Upon first reading through this hymn by Chris, the line that struck me was found in the second verse, "And in obedient living find your home." Obedience is not amongst the most widely observed characteristic of the life of discipleship today. It smacks of a blind following of another's will, of a rather infantile "doing what you're told" mentality that is out of step with the prevailing *zeitgeist* which stresses freedom, liberty and individual choice. We might occasionally sing the old hymn, "Trust and obey, for there's no other way to be happy in Jesus, but to trust and obey," but we do not really believe this is so. Instead we rather hope that being happy in Jesus amounts to some religious observance coupled with a spirituality that allows us plenty of choice.

However, the life of discipleship demands obedience in ways that are quite counter-cultural. If our Baptist forefathers Thomas Helwys and

Leonard Busher founded the principles that we recognize today as universal human rights by their plea for religious liberty for all,[1] they did not do so because they thought that obedience was redundant in the life of faith. It may have been that a few years after those pleas were first heard the ensuing sense of liberty of conscience was much more widespread, but accompanying it was also a recognition that, as in Paul's day,[2] liberty could be put all too easily to the pursuit of a libertarian or antinomian conception of the Christian life. In the church where I now have the privilege to be minister, Abingdon in Oxfordshire, one of the earliest causes for the church to seek wider advice in the mid-seventeenth century, in this case from the London churches that represented leadership amongst the Particular Baptists, was the abuse of that freedom in a life of sin disguised as liberty of conscience. The leaders of the churches in London offered the wonderfully entitled "Heartbleedings for professors' abominations" in 1650, denouncing those who thought "sin is only sin to him that thinks it so," and who counted all their actions good "being acted by their own spirits which (as they think) are God."[3] In the heady mix of radicalism in the mid-seventeenth century, there was plenty of scope for "using your freedom as an opportunity for self-indulgence" (Gal 5:13).

ANXIETY ABOUT REPRESSIVE SHEPHERDING

If one reason for the unpopularity of obedience as a virtue in the Christian life is the wider cultural disdain for conformity and its resulting libertarianism, another is the suspicion of recent attempts to re-invigorate it by the so-called "shepherding movement." A dimension of the broader Restoration movement, this influential expression of North American charismatic renewal taught that every believer must submit to a "shepherd" who had spiritual oversight of them. Arising from difficulties at the Holy Spirit Teaching Mission in Fort Lauderdale, Florida, four regular contributors to its New Wine magazine: Don Basham (Disciples of Christ), Bob Mumford (Assemblies of God), Derek Prince (an English Pentecostal), and Charles Simpson (former Southern Baptist) joined together for mutual accountability in 1970. Joined by Ern Baxter (a Canadian Pentecostal) in 1974, by the following year the "Fort Lauderdale Five," as they became known, attracted

---

1. Helwys, *A Short Declaration of the Mystery of Iniquity*; Busher, *Religious Peace; or, a Plea for Liberty of Conscience.*

2. Rom 6:1–4; Gal 5:15.

3. Cited in White, *The English Baptists of the Seventeenth Century*, 78–79.

4,700 charismatics to their conference in Kansas City.[4] It soon courted controversy, being denounced by Pat Robertson in 1975, and others similarly soon decried its excesses. By 1980 many of those leaders who had previously submitted to "the Five," and accordingly structured their own pastoral care in similar hierarchical ways, were leaving the movement in the United States, and internal tensions between the five strong personalities led to Derek Prince leaving the movement in 1983, and the whole leadership of the remaining four dissolved in 1986. Charles Simpson remained the principal advocate of the theology of shepherding, and in 1987 established the Fellowship of Covenant Ministers and Churches. Its impact upon the British charismatic scene came through the invitation to Ern Baxter to speak at the Capel Bible Week in 1974, and Bryn Jones's invitation to Bob Mumford to address the Dales Bible Week in 1978. Baxter and Mumford spoke at the Anglia Bible Week every year from 1982 to 1985. The early freedoms of the charismatic renewal soon took on a more structured shape as submission to those whose leadership was recognized by the wider Restoration movement became obligatory, and any who questioned its legitimacy found themselves marginalized.

At its heart was a desire to take discipleship and obedience seriously. "Every believer needed to become a disciple and every disciple needed a shepherd/teacher. Independent charismatic groups were to be gathered up together under shepherds, and shepherds themselves were to submit to translocal ministries, particularly to apostles."[5] But it proved susceptible to abuse, as any human structure has the potential to be, and allegations of unreasonable and abusive requirements of submission carried with them the taint of a sect or cult. Is there another way of developing obedience as a virtue, without the excesses of shepherding? And does our Baptist heritage of mutual submission offer a more hopeful course by which to pursue the virtue of obedience?

MONASTICISM OLD AND NEW

It is obvious that an emphasis upon submission and obedience to Christ within discipleship courts greater controversy when that submission is incarnated within the church. The development of a "spiritual elite" in the form of the medieval monastic movement, with all of its expectations that the religious would carry the spiritual expectations of the greater mass of the community—which is reduced to spectating the spiritual life—required

---

4. Moore, "Shepherding Movement," 1060–62; cf. Kay, *Apostolic Networks*.
5. Kay, *Apostolic Networks*, 31.

obedience in shaping the monastic life. St. Benedict's Rule says little about the life of contemplative prayer, except to refer Benedict's monks to John Cassian and Basil the Great, but it is most concerned with life in the community. The Abbot is the teacher of the brothers, and crystallizes the monastic teaching into three monastic virtues: obedience, silence, and humility. These virtues are won through "the abandonment of self-will so as to learn the will of God through the monastic superior."[6] While, compared with its predecessors, (such as the *Rule of the Master*), Benedict's Rule is marked by its compassion and humanity, with much greater sensitivity to human freedom and leeway offered to the abbot, the overall sense is still one of an austere and frightening God whose watchful eye pervades the monastery. The overall aim is loving identification with Christ, and in fighting the wayward human spirit, obedience is primary in shaping conformity to Christ, if at the cost of a vision of an overly judgmental God. Do Baptists have an alternative that draws upon a portrayal of God closer to the Jesus of the Gospels?

In writing about the challenges to Baptist spirituality, Nigel Wright argues that the congregation is the setting for the actualization of what Anabaptists called *Gelassenheit*, willing "yielded abandonment" to Christ. "We are 'under' the 'rule' of Christ. In an age which values, perhaps more than anything else, both personal autonomy and self-actualization, and which reads the language of lordship as dominion and oppression, the concept of heteronomy—that I am called to find myself through submission to the rule of another—is both alien and offensive."[7] However,

> there is a demand which God-in-Christ makes upon us that can only be expressed by use of the language of authority, obedience, submission and duty. Any spirituality which does not contain these elements is deceiving itself. . . . Learning to live under authority, the authority of Christ over individuals and congregations mediated by the Spirit through the Scriptures is a fundamental configuring of any form of Christian, let alone Baptist, spirituality.[8]

This notion of a mutually submissive fellowship is given expression for Baptists in the gathered community of the church, with the local gathered *ecclesia* a form of laicized monasticism at its most visionary. Where monasticism in its classic form places the rule in the hands of the abbot, the Baptist vision is that this rule, with the same goal of conforming men and women to Christ's pattern, is placed in the hands of the whole gathered community.

6. Kardong O.S.B., "Benedict of Nursia," 180.
7. Wright, "Spirituality as Discipleship: The Anabaptist Heritage," 90–91.
8. Ibid., 91.

We "walk together and watch over one another in love." Perhaps some ministers of Baptist churches find themselves *de facto* those who administer that rule of Christ, and certainly the early Baptists thought of their pastor as exercising a form of rulership, but, at its heart, this is but a delegated authority from the church meeting—rarely exercised, and often subverted, but pregnant with potential for deepening the life of obedient following of Christ in a world at every turn animal to such a pattern.

In an attempt, in a small way, to adapt such a regime to the contemporary context of Baptist ministers who live dispersed from one another (i.e., not in community) and without the familiar vows of celibacy, poverty, and obedience to an abbot, The Order of Baptist Ministry offers a way of remaining faithful to baptismal and ordination vows through shared prayer, accountability and vision.[9] This form of value-laden obedience, rather than rule-driven legalism to vows, is one already explored by those fully committed to the historic religious life (the writings of Diarmuid O'Murchu, for instance[10]). Members of the Order meet regularly in a small group (maximum five people) termed a cell. An aspect of this that involves submission, and corresponding obedience, is in the commitment to the use of the Order's Daily Office. Members are expected to use this, as an expression of fellowship and shared journey, but, with permission, a member's cell may grant freedom to use some other form of prayer. This may seem a small step, but it expresses a deeper desire to be accountable for the life of discipleship. In the *examen* that is a major component of the regular meeting of the cells which give form to mutual accountability, openness to the insights of the cell's members, and, by implication, occasionally submission to them (voluntarily and out of love of Christ) is enacted. Thereby, something of the corrosive influence of the individualism of the age, together with its privatization of the life of the spirit so prevalent within British Christianity, is withstood. Fear of cultish intensity no doubt prevails over the desire for a deeper and more extensive accountability and obedience, but it is symbolic of that desire to "walk together as pilgrims and companions."

Might such a pattern be adapted to the life of a Baptist church? Certainly the familiar structures of mid-week House Groups have given small groups a familiarity born now of many decades of use. That they often singularly avoid the kind of honest reflection upon personal discipleship in favor of a less threatening format of singing, shared Bible study, and mutually supportive prayer, does not mean that with a will, they might not be co-opted to serve the purposes of mutual accountability.

---

9. http://www.orderforbaptistministry.co.uk.

10. O'Murchu, *Poverty, Celibacy and Obedience*.

OBEDIENCE AND THE GROWTH IN VIRTUE

The distinctive way in which Baptists might rediscover the central place of obedience in the Christian life of discipleship is by a renewed focus upon those practices of the life of Christian discipleship whereby the virtues are developed. In the context of ministerial formation, (understanding ministers to be, amongst other things, "exemplary disciples,") I have written more extensively elsewhere about how the practices inherent in ministry are the means by which the virtues of the life in Christ (or the character and spirituality of the minister) are formed.[11] The accusation may be made that to concentrate upon those charged with the leadership, oversight and care of the church of Jesus Christ smacks of elitism (a charge I would defend) but certainly what is true of the minister's character and spirituality must also be true of those whom they pastor. In this area, at least, there should be little to distinguish the minister from any other mature believer. Attention to the practices of worship, prayer, witness, hospitality, sabbath-keeping, silence, and godly fellowship (to name but some) in the life of every disciple inevitably forms the virtues of courage, integrity, generosity, humility, kindness, and compassionate love, but only if there is an element of submission in their transmission: submission to Christ by the Spirit, through obedience to Scripture's demands and engagement with its story, and at times a willing submission to the guidance and mutual concern of fellow believers. If I do not pray, or practise hospitality, and am willing to be honest and transparent about my struggles to engage with those practices, then submission to those who have a concern for my growth in grace (or, indeed, avoidance of making shipwreck of my faith) may be the essential element in enabling me to live out those practices, and grow in their attendant virtues. The avoidance of such honesty combined with willing submission may be the most significant element in my remaining weak in faith, vulnerable to the predations of the spirit of this age and defective in my discipleship.

How might discipleship, viewed through a lens of the practices that form the virtuous life, refresh the age-old challenge of "forming Christ" in us? It may be freighting one phrase too heavily with significance, but for Ellis, baptism, as a response of obedience to the gracious saving work of God, is where we begin:

> Baptism was therefore seen as a sign of that which was already accomplished in the person's life, an act of obedience and the conferring of blessing through a closer fellowship with Christ,

---

11. Goodliff, *Shaped for Service: Ministerial Formation and Virtue Ethics*, Eugene OR; Pickwick 2017

made possible by that very obedience and by an identification with Christ in his death, burial and resurrection. Again we can see the interaction of personal faith and a willingness to be obedient.[12]

The charge often leveled against the baptism of believers is that it reflects an expression of "faith as works," but, argues Ellis, that is to ignore the role that the doctrine of election and the work of the Holy Spirit play. "What we may say is that the baptism of believers has functioned as a part of the church's proclamation of the gospel of Christ and has been a liturgical focus of the invitation to personal discipleship and a life of fellowship 'in Christ.'"[13] The nature of discipleship as expressed through baptism is one of obedience, "As a divinely ordained means of human response to the saving work and call of Christ, baptism by immersion shows the character of that response to be one of whole-hearted consecration. Obedience and devotion belong together."[14]

The foundational act of obedience for Ellis is, therefore, baptism, and all ensuing obedience to Christ is a fulfilling of that commitment to follow Christ. To live in disobedience to Christ and his commands is, therefore, a contradiction of the baptismal vow to repent and follow Christ. Without resorting to the avoidance of post-baptismal sin through baptism at the point of death, any attempt to take more seriously that commitment, and ensuing obedience to Christ is to be welcomed. The "cheap grace" of baptism without the demands of the disciplined life that follows may be all too familiar, but it does not sanctify it through ubiquity.

CHRISTIAN FORMATION AND DISCIPLESHIP

Medi Ann Volpe asks in *Rethinking Christian Identity: Doctrine and Discipleship*,[15] "how do we think about Christian identity so that it is meaningful and specific without tying identity to a set of propositions or behaviors that remain precisely the same from one local and historical context to another?"[16] She answers that question by interaction with Kathryn Tanner, Rowan Williams, and John Milbank, as contemporaries, together with

---

12. Ellis, *Gathering*, 217.
13. Ibid., 221.
14. Ellis, *Gathering*, 221.
15. Volpe, *Rethinking Christian Identity*.
16. Ibid., 4.

Gregory of Nyssa. Her concern is with Christian formation in continuity with the tradition.

Volpe identifies five themes that can be identified in all three theological accounts: *fluidity* (faithful Christian practice varies from place to place and time to time), *continuity* with Christian tradition, the way in which identity is constructed is a function of the *imagination* (the neophyte begins to imagine herself as part of the Christian community, as distinct from the world), the recognition of considerable *ambiguity* in the theological accounts, Christianity is not conferred upon us but lived by us, which is *performance*. For Tanner, continuity depends upon our continuing participation in becoming disciples, for Williams it is faithfulness to the sources of the tradition (Scripture, creeds, and their interpretation through the ages), while for Milbank it is much more explicitly the Holy Spirit that ensures continuity.

For Tanner and for Williams Christian practice is a form of improvisational performance, and for Tanner, faithful practice "does not include all the same beliefs and practices from one generation to the next, and there are no means by which we might ascertain which of those beliefs and/or practices ought to remain the same."[17] Not that every belief will change, but that a new arrangement of practices and beliefs are negotiated in community with each new generation. Thus, the individual disciple, in Tanner's account, listens respectively to the accounts given around the table, where the voices from present and past are heard, then comes to her own conclusion. What is lacking is any notion of a magisterium, a teaching office that carries authority, and while this is inimical to Tanner's approach, Volpe argues that it is necessary, and turns to MacIntyre to show how an account of tradition helps. Discipleship is not a matter of choosing from a range of practices and beliefs and individually creating something that somehow coheres, but locating oneself in a tradition. It involves not simply discrimination, but also obedience.

Where Tanner sees Christian tradition as something that arises from cultural materials, and free from the authority of the community of practice, MacIntyre conceives of tradition as an inheritance that is passed on as its practitioners participate in the practices of that tradition. It is as they share in those practices that desire is formed, expressed in the virtues. Volpe argues that Tanner's failure to give an account of Christian formation fatally injures her account of what it is to live as a Christian.

> It is not merely a matter of learning the story, but learning how to live in the light of that story, coming to understand its

17. Ibid., 31.

significance for us and for the world. . . . Making the kinds of judgments Tanner sees as indispensable for Christian faith depends on knowing one's place in the story and being able to discern the meaning of the narrative for our thinking and action.[18]

In other words, obedience is crucial to enacting our role in the story. Turning to Williams, Volpe shows how he presents a more effective description of what it is to be formed as a Christian, and central to that vision is the notion of taking time, and that we understand who we are as Christians (our identity) only provisionally: our identity is always under construction as we attempt to "make sense" of who or what we are. This making sense is offered in a community of common interest, and is about learning to direct oneself towards God. The results are transformed social relationships, and a love that does not seek its own good but the well-being of others. This is precisely and most fully seen in Christ, and thus one follows Christ as one is drawn into God's love.

For Williams, the performance of Christian identity is, first, narration of the story that finds its richest description in the Eucharist.[19] Here we understand that God's grace is gift, and so we seek to transform the world into a community of gift and sharing. The identities both of individual Christians and the community they inhabit come together here. It is, secondly, a response to God's initiative, through human participation in God. It is as we take time and make sense that we grow in Christian discipleship, and grow into the image of Christ. The process of growth in likeness to Christ that Williams identifies, and of which Volpe approves, is traced by Williams in *The Wound of Knowledge*.[20] This is the conversion of desire, a process that is also shaped by the reality of sin.

Desiring God involves an opening up to the Other, of taking a risk, of being receptive to the object of desire. This is the character of discipleship for any who seek to follow Jesus.

> The conversion of desire from the inclination to control to the attitude of receptivity that characterizes transformed desire involves the development of the same habits of attention that make conversation fruitful: the willingness to take time and to forego explanation. To talk about the transformation of desire is thus to talk about the transformation of habits that give shape

---

18. Ibid., 51.

19. For Williams, the Christian seems more like Michel de Certeau's *raconteur* than Tanner's builder, the *bricoleur* of Pierre Bourdieu. See de Certeau, *The Practice of Everyday Life*, 80–82.

20. Williams, *The Wound of Knowledge*.

to everyday life. . . . [T]ransforming desire involves cultivating a vision of the world that orientates desire towards its proper object: God.[21]

The relationship of desire and obedience is significant in pursuing the way in which conformity to Christ is established. Far from obedience to Christ being the eradication of desire, its relationship is one of acting upon the ability to discriminate between desires, choosing those between the many desires and the deepest and most Christ-like, where "discernment is the way of sifting through a confusion of desires in order that our lives may be shaped by the best of them."[22] Desires will change through life, with context and through external influences, so this process of obedience in choosing the deepest desires, rather than simply feeding the most imminent or beguiling, is one that is never achieved, never complete. It is truly, to quote Eugene Peterson's Nietzchean phrase, "a long obedience in the same direction." And lest this process be understood as one of sheer human willing, Ignatius of Loyola reminds us that while we locate ourselves in the place where God will work by disposing ourselves towards him, or centering ourselves upon him, it is God alone who orders our desires aright. Rightly ordered desires bring consolation, "every increase of faith, hope and love, and all interior joy that invites and attracts to what is heavenly and to the salvation of one's soul by filling it with peace and quiet in its Creator and Lord."[23] Ignatius sees the Exercises as ways of ridding ourselves of "disordered affections," and both attending to, and being obedient to the Spirit's quickening of, the deepest longings of the soul.

THE OBEDIENCE OF MARY: FRA ANGELICA DEPICTING THE ANNUNCIATION

The archetypal instance of such discernment and obedience is, perhaps, the Annunciation. As portrayed in Fra Angelica's series of paintings of that Gospel story, Angel and Virgin mimic one another in humble greeting in the first depiction, originally an altarpiece in San Domenico do Fissile, near Florence and painted ca. 1425–27 (it is now in the Museo del Prado, Madrid), reminding us that obedience's prior disposition is humility.[24] In

---

21. Volpe, *Rethinking Christian Identity*, 70.
22. Sheldrake, *Befriending our Desires*, 80.
23. Ignatius of Loyola, *Spiritual Exercises*, 316.
24. Reproductions of these paintings are readily available on line using the more familiar search engines.

the second, ca. 1432, now in the Museo Diocesano, Cortona, while Mary remains bowed, the angel is all energy and speech as he declares "The Holy Spirit shall come upon thee, and the power of the Highest shall overshadow thee,"[25] with Mary's obedient response written upside down, "Here I am, the Servant of the Lord." "The urgency of the archangel's mission is emphasized by his forceful gesture, the thrust of his head and his tensely poised wings as he kneels before Mary."[26] In 1436 Pope Eugenius IV ceded the church and monastery of San Marco in the heart of Florence to San Domenico in Fiesole, Fra Angelico's monastery. Fra Angelico set about painting frescos in the renovated convent, and amongst them is the third great annunciation, found in the North Corridor. The fresco stands at the point of demarcation between the more public space for the lay brothers and those using the library, and the private dormitory of the friars. This marked "the threshold to the liminal, private space."[27] From here the friars journeyed through the Passion and Resurrection, and the joys and sorrows of the Virgin in murals on the walls of this private space. Everywhere Dominican saints meditate in these frescos, reminding the friars that contemplation was a surer way to God than scholarship.

This version excludes the expulsion of Adam and Eve from Eden (a feature of the two previous works) and is altogether simpler. The arms are once again crossed by both participants in the exchange, Mary's above her womb, the angel's in reciprocity; the setting is a loggia within a garden enclosed by a fence; and the angel's multi-colored wings depicting the polychromaticism of Paradise. Angelico understands something profound here about the relationship of desire and obedience: the capacity to be obedient is forged on the threshold of the public and private spaces, the liminal hinterland. It is public, insofar as the habits of obedience have concrete expression in the life of discipleship, but it is also private, for the discernment and struggles of will that enable the life of obedient following of Christ are located in that inner sphere of the human soul, like Mary, in the place of quiet contemplation.

Cell 3 of San Marco depicts the simplest annunciation. The angel is simply clad in a red robe, while Mary is in pink, devoid of her familiar blue cloak. She kneels on a prayer stool, while the angel stands, the pair within a simple arched room, while a Dominican friar, St. Peter Martyr, looks on in prayerfulness. There is no dove, nor words. The setting reflects the architecture of the convent itself, "heightening the sense of the Virgin's

---

25. Expressed through the words SPS S SUP..VEIET I TE VIRT ALTISI OBUBRABIT TIBI.

26. Ahl, *Fra Angelico*, 104.

27. Ibid., 137.

actual presence within the convent itself."[28] Here everything is stripped to the basic elements, allowing the friars to contemplate the incarnation with the minimum of disturbance, and respond to Christ, as she does, with "Let it be to me according to thy will." It is if, over a life-time of contemplating that scene, and expressing that contemplation through tempera and paint, Fra Angelico, has come to see that obedience does not become somehow easier, but merely starker, stripped bare of the extraneous, more transparent.

The obverse of this process is captured by psychotherapist Adam Philips when he writes "in flight from confusion and uncertainty about our desires and what we really want . . . we even hide from ourselves the fact that we are escaping. It is as though, if we can keep ourselves sufficiently busy escaping, we can forget that that is what we are doing."[29] Lack of attentiveness, failure to discriminate, inability to recognize our deepest longing and their resolution in obedience to Christ, contemporary culture finds obedience so hard because it lacks discernment of desire, to which many Christians are by no means immune.

In Ellis' hymn from which this chapter springs, this disposition of readied obedience is expressed as "My gracious God, I answer now your call: / A living sacrifice, I give my all." I can almost hear the Virgin singing it! "Do not conform to this world and its ways, / But be transformed, renewed in heart and mind," he writes, echoing Romans 12:1–2. This transformation unfolds as the disciple engages in obedience with the practices of the life of discipleship: attentiveness to God and his word, love of neighbor, and discernment of what is best. Paul has in mind a corporate process for the community of disciples, and the Baptist conviction that this transformation takes place within the covenant community of the gathered church, where we submit to one another (rather than to some elevated spiritual expert or "shepherd"), takes up this essentially communal practice. It is in this community of the obedient that we find our home.

The renewal of the mind that enables correct discernment ("be transformed by the renewing of your minds, so that you may discern what is the will of God—what is good and acceptable and perfect," Rom 12.2) evokes the restoration of the twisted mind that worships the creature rather than the Creator in Romans 1. In writing of renewal, ἀνακαίνωσις (*anakainōsis*), Paul uses the word for the first time in Greek literature, and is a word that is used later for baptismal regeneration, ἀνακαινίζω (*anakainizō*), "to make new." We return to the fundamental act of obedience, baptism, in renewing the person who is transformed by that renewing power by conversion and

---

28. Ibid., 140.
29. Phillips, *Houdini's Box*, 51.

obedience.[30] "The transformation Paul has in view here is shaped by the recovery of a realistic appraisal of ethical choices in the light of the converted community's experience of the "new creation" brought by Christ."[31] The basic sense of δοκιμάζειν (*dokimazein*) is "to test," or "to try" in a public arena,[32] and "Paul . . . implies that the discernment of the will of God will be followed by obedient acceptance of it."[33] Cranfield captures the importance of this for every disciple in obedient following of the discernment of the will of God,

> . . . it indicates the dignity of the individual Christian called as he is to exercise a responsible freedom, and is the decisive refutation of every impudent sacerdotalism that would reduce the Christian layman to a kind of second class citizenship in the Church. To know that it is God's intention that the ordinary Christian man should be so transformed by the renewing of his mind as to be able himself responsibly, in the light of the gospel and within the fellowship of the faithful, δοκιμάζειν . . . τί τὸ θέλημα τοῦ θεοῦ, τὸ ἀγαθὸν καὶ εὐάρεστον καὶ τέλειον is to know that one dare not patronize one's fellow-Christians.[34]

In such a way, renewal of discipleship through attention to the practices, formed out of the particular Christian tradition (Baptist, even) shaped by Scripture and historical contingencies, focuses attention upon this discipline of obedience. To follow Christ is to obey him, to desire him, to love him. "All who obey his commandments abide in him, and he in them," writes John in his first letter (1 John 3:24), "By this we know that we love the children of God, when we love God and obeys commandments. For the love of God is this, that we obey his commandments" (1 John 5:2–3), echoing Jesus's discourse in the Gospel of John, "This is my commandment, that you love one another as I have loved you" (John 15:12). Here is the broad horizon for that characteristically Baptist discipline of "walking with one another and watching over one another in love" in which we discover what it means to belong, to indwell the gospel command to love. Or as Chris Ellis puts it, "Sisters and brothers, by his mercy come / And in obedient living find your home."

---

30. Cf. Behm, "ἀνακαλίζο," 451–52.

31. Jewett, *Romans*, 733. Käsemann argues that this discernment cannot be restricted to the field of morals, Käsemann. *Commentary on Romans*, 330.

32. Grundmann, "δόκιμος," 256.

33. Cranfield, *Romans*, 609.

34. Ibid., 609–10.

A Hymn for Council and Committees

God of hope, you hold before us
Visions of your kingdom day.
Though we struggle in our grasping,
Help us find your servant way.
In our planning,
In our sharing,
May your will be always one.

God of joy, you hold before us
News that love is on the throne.
In our goals and in our methods
Help us choose what you will own!
In our dealing,
In our sharing,
May your will be always done.

God of peace, in Christ you show us
How forgiveness alters all.
Breathe into our human frailties
Loving kindness, lest we fall.
In our living,
In our sharing,
May your will be always done.

5

"Your Will Be Always Done"
Congregational Discernment as Contextual Discipleship

Stuart Blythe

THE PETITION OF THIS hymn is that those who gather may "grasp" the will of God so that it can be followed. In expressing this desire the words invoke some major Christian themes: hope, joy, peace, and love. The process as well as the outcome is clearly important. The concerns are those of the "kingdom" and not just the church. Such is the grandeur of the themes that the hymn may be considered to border on pious sentimentality. On the other hand, the theologically poetic weight given to this activity of gathering to know the will of God may indicate its central significance for the practice of contextual discipleship. That at least is the direction I will follow in this article.

CONTEXT

On the 18th of September 2014 the people of Scotland voted in a referendum which asked the question: "Should Scotland be an Independent Country?" This referendum was no surprise. The commitment to hold a referendum had been part of the Scottish Nationalist Party's election manifestos in both 2007 and 2011 when they contested the elections for the

Scottish Parliament. The SNP's outright victory in the 2011 elections meant that fulfilling this commitment became a possibility. On the 23rd March 2013 the First Minister Alex Salmond announced the referendum would be held the following September. One critique of this announcement was that it had taken the First Minister "some 700 days since he won a landslide in the Scottish elections to confirm the date."[1] In turn, the announcement meant both sides of the campaign had another 545 days to make their case.

In addition to being a well-publicized event the Scottish referendum was recognized as an event of considerable sociopolitical significance. At stake was a political union which had existed from 1707 and the attendant social and economic connections such entailed. This historic dimension was given additional piquancy in that it involved the expansion of the franchise to include sixteen and seventeen year olds for the first time.

The significance of the referendum was represented in the debate, discussion, and division which it generated at all levels of Scottish society. On the 12th September 2014 the BBC News reported:

> The debate is visible everywhere. Walk down any street in Glasgow or even wandering in tiny hilltop villages in the Borders, you are likely to see stickers on lampposts, billboards erected in fields, and posters in windows noisily urging "Yes" or "No."[2]

The level of public engagement around the issue is further illustrated by the turnout of voters on referendum day. "At 84.6%, turnout at the referendum was the highest recorded at any Scotland-wide poll since the advent of universal suffrage."[3] Reflecting on this turnout the Electoral Commission stated:

> This referendum showed that for young people, indeed for all voters, when they perceive an issue to be important and are inspired by it, they will both participate in the debate and show up on polling day.[4]

For a large number of people in Scotland, therefore, the referendum mattered.

To be sure other "contexts" could be highlighted rather than this one. The nature of contexts is that they are often particular and so varied. By the time this article is published the United Kingdom will have held a

1. Carrell, "Alex Salmond Announces Scottish Independence Referendum Date."
2. Webber, "Scottish Independence."
3. Electoral Commission, "Scottish Independence Referendum," 1.
4. Ibid., 1.

referendum concerning its membership of the European Union. Again, the nature of contexts is that they are changing. I choose this particular context, however, to highlight an event of sociopolitical importance through which I lived, and which fully engaged large numbers of people beyond the church.

SCOTTISH INDEPENDENCE AND CONGREGATIONAL DISCERNMENT

I consider myself fortunate that I was encouraged early to reflect theologically on issues of Scottish independence by my friend Doug Gay. In 2007 he delivered a talk at which I was present at the Greenbelt Festival entitled "Breaking Up Britain: How to Be a Christian Nationalist." This talk would develop into his book, *Honey from a Lion: Christianity and the Ethics of Nationalism*.[5] Doug stands in the tradition of Church of Scotland ministers concerned with public theology as it relates to church and nation.[6] It was he however, who encouraged me to try and reflect intentionally on the issue from a Scottish Baptist perspective. This immediately begged the question of whether there is such a thing as a Baptist perspective and if so what aspect of it could bring something distinctive to the conversation? For me the referendum was as much about governance as it was about national identity.[7] Church governance from a congregational perspective is also a distinctive feature of Baptist identity.[8] Reflecting, therefore, on a referendum about governance from the perspective of Baptist ecclesiology appeared an appropriate trajectory to follow.[9]

Where my reflections on Baptist ecclesiology led with respect to the issue of the Scottish referendum and independence is not the subject of this essay. Rather, my focus is on the practice of congregational discernment through church meeting as a specific expression of congregational governance. In this respect my theological reflections on congregational governance and the governance of Scotland made one thing clear. Few if any congregations were discussing this issue as a matter of communal discernment in their

---

5. Gay, *Honey From the Lion*.

6. We both for a time had William Storrar, author of *Scottish Identity: A Christian Vision*, as our PhD supervisor at New College in Edinburgh.

7. This is not the place to make this argument suffice to say that the eligibility to vote in this referendum was not based upon ethnicity but residence.

8. Holmes, *Baptist Theology*, 96.

9. Again this is not the place to make the case suffice to say that I was following and extending the argument that the "politics" of the church should albeit in a limited way be able to bear witness to the politics of the state concerning what the rule of God looks like in practice, Yoder, *Body Politics*.

congregational church meetings. Here, therefore, was an issue of considerable historic significance to Scotland and the United Kingdom as a whole. It was a topic which clearly mattered to the people of Scotland. It was being discussed and debated in a wide range of formal and informal communities. Yet, it was also a matter which was not being discussed by congregations in their designated place of meeting to discern the mind of Christ.[10] There was at least irony in my attempts to reflect on Scottish governance from the perspective of congregational governance when and where congregations appeared unable or unwilling to engage this specific matter in this way.

There are a number of possible reasons that can and were given for the omission of this subject from church meeting agendas over the many months and years when it was clear that the referendum was coming. These include: it was a divisive issue; it was a political not a spiritual issue; it was not a matter which affected local congregational life; it was not an issue on which a corporate decision had to be made; it distracted from the mission of the church. Perhaps these answers will satisfy some. On the other hand, it can be argued that these responses raise other questions as to what the inability or unwillingness of congregations to discuss this or similar issues demonstrates about our understanding of the church, mission, and indeed the Lordship of Jesus Christ. The Baptist ethicist, the late Glen Stassen, in his book *A Thicker Jesus* discusses the features of those who when tested in the "laboratory of history" have borne faithful witness to Jesus Christ.[11] Early in the book he writes this:

> Some churches seek to avoid offending any members, and so steer clear of controversial issues and confrontations. This is "Enlightenment lite": it reduces the gospel to private matters or general principles that do not clash with interests and ideologies. These churches fail to confront members in ways that provide the guidance we need in our lives, and they avoid addressing injustices and problems that threaten us. They offer something far removed from the Jesus in the gospels who challenges the religious and social complacency of his generation. Sociological studies show us that church members feel they need more specific instruction, even confrontation that calls us to grow in discipleship. Lacking this, "Enlightenment lite" churches lack

---

10. The language frequently used by Baptists to describe what they are doing in their church meetings when they gather for discernment is the language of knowing, seeking, or discerning, "the mind of Christ." Holmes, *Baptist Theology*, 100.

11. Stassen, *Thicker Jesus*, 8–10.

the depth of commitment and the vigor they need to avoid the decline and decay that constitute a growing crisis.[12]

From this perspective the failure of congregations to discuss and discern on matters of sociopolitical significance such as this referendum represent a crisis of decline and decay in congregational polity. It represents a failure of discipleship.

In response to the above I want to argue that church meetings should deal with "matters that matter," including those of a sociopolitical nature. To do this I will identify and expand upon a number of themes drawn from a statement by Ellis about congregational discussion and discernment in the church meeting. I am not claiming that he would support my explanation or expansion of his ideas. I am, however, claiming that what he writes in the hymn at the beginning of this chapter and then more specifically in the quotation I will cite provides a starting point for a reimagining of congregational discernment in church meeting with respect to the nature, content, and processes of the practice.

CONGREGATIONAL DISCERNMENT ON MATTERS THAT MATTER

Chris Ellis, in his book *Gathering: A Theology and Spirituality of Worship in Free Church Tradition,* writes:

> Lordship implies obedience, following and discipleship. Baptist and Free Church disciples gather as *ekklesia* for worship, and they gather as *ekklesia* for mutual discernment and governance in church meeting. Here is communal discipleship in prayer and decision-making. In both these spheres the Church looks forward to the Kingdom of God. In prayer it prays for God to act, and in church meeting it seeks to align itself to the divine will. This is an eschatological community, a group of people bound together in Jesus Christ, attempting to be disciples. This is the Church and it cannot be understood apart from these perspectives. Its common life is the contemporary life of the disciple band following Jesus, and the contemporary life of the apostles sent out in mission with the promise of Jesus Christ to be with them always.[13]

---

12. Ibid., 6.
13. Ellis, *Gathering*, 237.

Here, Ellis clearly identifies congregational gathering for discernment not simply as an aspect of Baptist governance but as an essential dynamic of their gathered life as "the church." From this I want to highlight a number of themes pertinent to a reimagining of congregational discernment and discussion as dealing with matters that matter, including those of a sociopolitical nature. In doing this I will use the language of congregational discernment as shorthand to describe the practice of discernment, discussion, and decision which takes place when a congregation gathers in meeting for this purpose. These various aspects and their relationship to one another will be discussed as the essay progresses.

THE LORDSHIP OF JESUS CHRIST

In the above quotation Ellis predicates the practice of congregational discernment upon the Lordship of Jesus Christ. This Lordship of Jesus Christ which he claims "moves inexorably towards a Trinitarian doctrine of God" is the "presiding conviction" that undergirds what it means to talk about the church as a "community of disciples."[14] The confession "Jesus is Lord," is more than "simply a theological statement." It has ethical "consequences for authority, behaviour, communal identity, and ways of viewing the world."[15] While the nature of the church may indeed be a Baptist distinctive, starting with the nature of the God who gathers that community is theologically valid in Baptist thinking.[16] On this Pat Took is cited as stating:

> Our Baptist tradition is not in the first place about government of any kind except the Lordship of Christ. Any Christian community which makes a form of government its central tenet is in danger of losing its soul.[17]

Of course Baptists do not have an exclusive claim on the Lordship of Jesus Christ or the ethical consequences of such confession. Yet, they have a particular way of understanding how that Lordship is to be experienced. This includes the direct rule of Jesus Christ over local congregations and their liberty to make decisions about their own life and ministries.[18] In practice,

---

14. Ibid., 229–32.
15. Ibid., 230.
16. Haymes et al., *On Being the Church*, 3–4.
17. Took, "It shall not be so among you," 14, cited in Rollinson, "The Attentive Community," 3.
18. Fiddes, *Tracks and Traces*, 6.

as Ellis indicates, this involves Baptist congregations meeting to discuss and discern the divine will and what it means to align themselves with it.[19]

I would argue, however, that despite the emphasis described above congregations need to go beyond a limited and static way of understanding what it means to discern the mind of Christ the Lord. A limited and static understanding of the rule of Christ will impact both the content considered relevant and the outcomes considered possible from such discernment activities.

A limited understanding of the Lordship of Jesus Christ is one which in practice confines its understanding of the Lordship of Jesus Christ to Lordship over the church. To be sure Jesus Christ is Lord over the church and it is an expression of faith that acknowledges this Lordship and submits to his rule (Col 1:18). On the one hand, this understanding should constantly press upon the church the task of asking: *"How must the church live to be the church?"*[20] On the other hand, the danger is that this approach can lead to matters that matter not being discussed because they are considered out of the proper realm of interest of the church. This is problematic because the Christian confession of the Lordship of Jesus Christ is actually a confession of his Lordship over all things whether this is presently acknowledged or not (Col 1:15–23). Ellis highlights the possible dimensions of this more expansive Lordship when he writes:

> We may speak *cosmically* of Christ being "Lord of all things," or *politically* of Christ being Lord over all earthly rulers, or *devotionally* of Jesus Christ as being the "personal Lord and Saviour" of an individual believer, or *ecclesiologically* of Christ being the Lord or Head of the Church.[21]

In this respect Stassen argues that it is precisely those individuals and communities who have recognized the "Lordship of Christ or sovereignty of God *throughout all of life and all of creation*" who have remained faithful in times of historical testing.[22] This more expansive rather than more limited understanding of the Lordship of Jesus Christ is arguably also implicit in what Ellis writes with respect to congregations discerning and deciding now in the light of a kingdom perspective and their eschatological hope.[23] When and where a more expansive understanding of the Lordship of Jesus Christ

---

19. Ellis, *Gathering*, 237.
20. McClendon, *Ethics*, 46, italics author.
21. Ellis, *Gathering*, 235, italics author.
22. Stassen, *Thicker*, 16, italics author.
23. Ellis, *Gathering*, 237.

is acknowledged then a wider range of matters that matter than those simply concerned with the immediate corporate life of a Christian congregation can be admitted to the table as issues requiring congregational discernment.

It is possible, however, not only to adopt a limited understanding of the Lordship of Jesus Christ but also a static understanding. This static understanding can limit the potential possible outcomes of discernment. The confession that Jesus is Lord is a resurrection claim. It is an affirmation that Jesus is alive. The community of disciples is "The Community of the Risen Lord."[24] To discern the mind of Christ, therefore, is certainly not less but is more than trying to understand together "the inescapable authority of Scripture."[25] It is to bring oneself with others into engagement with the living Jesus Christ. The great text for congregational governance Matthew 18:15–20 anticipates a living presence. This presence becomes a possibility through the resurrection. On this Nigel Wright argues:

> By the Spirit of God, . . . the risen Christ is in the midst of those communities of faith that look to him and keep his memory alive and believe that in so doing they share in the life of one who lives not just metaphorically or by force of human imagination, but truly and actually.[26]

Such thinking thickens our appreciation of the Baptist Union of Great Britain's Declaration of Principle when it states:

> That our Lord and Saviour Jesus Christ, God manifest in the flesh, is the sole and absolute authority in all matters pertaining to faith and practice, as revealed in the Holy Scriptures, and that each Church has liberty, under the guidance of the Holy Spirit, to interpret and administer His laws.[27]

In this understanding when a congregation gathers to discern the mind of Christ the Lord it gathers to encounter the promised presence of the living Christ.

To understand congregational discernment as an encounter with the living Lord creates a range of potential outcomes. What I mean by this is that rather than any *a priori* decision concerning what matters and what does not, and how it should be approached, and its relevance or not to a

---

24. Wright, *Vital Truth*, 9–23.
25. Wright, *Free Church*, 42.
26. Wright, *Vital Truth*, 11.

27. Baptist Union of Great Britain, Declaration of Principle. The Declaration of Principle for the Baptist Union of Scotland is very similar with respect to the point being made here about the Lordship of Jesus Christ.

congregation, these issues become themselves a matter for discussion and discernment. In turn, the possible outcomes of discerning on issues of "practical moral reasoning" can be either "loosing" or "binding" (Matt 18:15, 18).[28] More generally speaking, to seek the mind of the risen Lord exposes all of our traditions, interpretations, and institutions to the guidance and judgment of Jesus Christ. In this respect I resonate with the work of John D. Caputo who argues that Jesus Christ is the "deconstructive" inner "Truth" of Christianity.[29] To connect with this Jesus is, therefore, to invite change and transformation. Caputo writes:

> In a deconstruction, things are made to tremble by their own inner impulse, by a force that will give them no rest, that keeps forcing itself to the surface, forcing itself out, making the thing restless. Deconstruction is organized around the idea that things contain a kind of uncontainable truth, that they contain what they cannot contain. Nobody has to come along and "deconstruct" things. Things are auto-deconstructed by the tendencies of their own inner truth. In a deconstruction, the "other" is the one who tells the truth on the "same"; the other is the truth of the same, the truth that has been repressed and suppressed, omitted and marginalized, or sometimes just plain murdered, like Jesus himself, which is why Johannes Baptist Metz speaks of the "dangerous memory" of the suffering of Jesus and why I describe deconstruction as a hermeneutics of the kingdom of God.
>
> The "danger" Metz describes is the deconstructive force. As soon as the "other" tells the truth, as soon as the truth is out, then the beliefs or the practices, the texts, or institutions, that have been entrusted with the truth begin to tremble! Then they have to reconfigure, reorganize, regroup, reassemble in order to come to the grips with their inner tendencies—or repress them all the more mightily.[30]

To seek not simply the mind of Christ but the mind of the living Christ is to enter into a practice which has potential for the unexpected and the new in relation to a wide range of issues that matter. Given that the emphasis is on Jesus Christ the Lord present through the Spirit such encounter involves having Scripture readers that "are corporately engaged in placing Jesus Christ at the centre of Scripture in such a way that the prophetic vision

---

28. Yoder, "The Hermeneutics of Peoplehood," 40–67.

29. I have cited Caputo in other work I have written on congregational discernment, *What Would Jesus Deconstruct?* 29.

30. Ibid., 29.

becomes the present vision of the community."³¹ It also involves developing a *"thick, historically-embodied, realistic understanding of Jesus Christ* as revealing God's character thus providing norms for guiding our lives."³²

To approach congregational discernment from the perspective of the nature of the God who calls and gathers congregations is to affirm the Lordship of Jesus Christ. This Lordship in its expansive and living nature invites discernment on a range of issues beyond those which may narrowly be considered spiritual or pertaining to the church and creates a context in which the new and creative can happen. This activity, however, finds its focused attention in the practice of contextual discipleship.

CONTEXTUAL DISCIPLESHIP

I have argued above that in the quotation by Ellis he predicates what he writes about congregational discernment upon the Lordship of Jesus Christ. Interestingly as he continues in this quotation he does not collapse congregational discernment into worship. I do not think that this means that he would not agree with various writers that congregational discernment can be and should be located in a context of worship. Instead, however, he subsumes both "spheres" under the heading of "communal discipleship."³³ This approach sits very comfortably with the Baptist understanding of the nature of the church as a "believer's church" or "community of disciples."³⁴ The choice of the language of discipleship to describe the participants of congregational discernment, however, has wider significance for how we understand and practice congregational discernment. One of the things that the language of discipleship does when describing those who participate in congregational discernment is move us away from talk of a "members's" meeting where the qualification for attendance is formal membership. Instead, it locates the practice congregational discernment as an expression of people "attempting to be disciples."³⁵ This observation supports Wright's arguments that a reform of the practice of membership is required if we desire a reform in the practice of church meetings.³⁶ In this respect some alternative ways do need to be discovered for creating church communities

---

31. McClendon, *Doctrine*, 479.
32. Stassen, *Thicker*, 16.
33. Ellis, *Gathering*, 237.
34. Wright, *Free Church*, 49–67.
35. Ellis, *Gathering*, 237.
36. Wright, *Free Church*, 49–67 but also *Challenge to Change*, 110–14.

which are "open at the edges and committed at the core."[37] In this model the core will consist of those who voluntarily submit to the discipline of attempting to be disciples through the participation in certain practices including congregational discernment.

Describing those who participate in congregational discernment as disciples also emphasizes the communal nature of discipleship. These are people "bound together in Jesus Christ."[38] This in itself may be worth emphasizing as corrective when and where the private and individualistic aspects of discipleship are highlighted.[39] The communal nature of discipleship, however, has at least two dimensions that are not always distinguished and which have significance for the content and practice of congregational discernment. On the one hand, there is the individual life of a disciple shaped and guided by the community to which they belong. On the other hand, there is the shared life of discipleship as expressed by the community in its common life and activity together. To put that differently, discipleship is expressed in lives scattered and gathered. When a congregation gathers for discernment it can be concerned with individual and or corporate activity. The concern for individual activity is seen biblically and historically in what is known as church discipline. Studies indicate that such matters were often the content of Baptist congregational meetings in earlier centuries.[40] This certainly should not be romanticized as at times "in practice the concern was for the maintenance of a few, rather arbitrarily chosen moral markers."[41] In turn, how such discipline may actually be applied today requires careful consideration.[42] The point here, however, is that congregational discernment need not necessarily result in a congregation deciding that the same behavior is required of everyone. The outcome of the discernment may in fact be that on particular issues believers are actually free to follow their own conscience with or without any attending qualifying guidance from the congregation. One of the texts cited in support of congregational governance is Acts 15:1–35. The decision, however, that seemed "good to the Holy Spirit and to us" (Acts 15:28) did not require all to follow the same behavior. This being the case items need not be excluded from the processes of congregational discernment on the *a priori* grounds that not everyone

---

37. The original provenance of this term is a matter of some debate.
38. Ellis, *Gathering*, 237.
39. Pilli, "Discipleship," 44–56.
40. For some discussion and descriptions based on congregational minutes see for example, Egner, "Re-imagining the Covenant Community."
41. Holmes, "Knowing Together," 172–88, 178.
42. Wright, *Free Church*, 64–66.

will agree. Rather the outcome may well be one of freedom but informed by the perspective and the insights of the believing community. In this respect the outcome of discernment on the issue of the Scottish referendum may have been that Jesus Christ had no common expectation of his people as church. Yet by engaging in the process of seeking the mind of Christ individuals would have voted having at least heard the voices of their believing community.

Following on from the above, describing those who engage in congregational discernment as disciples also indicates the type of matters that should be the content of church meetings convened for this purpose. They should be matters that impact the faithful discipleship of believers gathered and scattered. Here it is worth returning directly to what Ellis writes on this subject for in his statement he identifies the "contemporary" nature of discipleship.[43] These believers who gather to discern are an eschatological community attempting to find out what it means in their context to be the "disciple band" and the "apostles sent out in mission."[44] To put this in terms of James W. McClendon's "Baptist vision," those who are engaging in discernment are those who together in the light of Scripture are seeking to embody contemporaneously the story of the people of God as found in the "that" of Scripture and the "then" yet to be of God's eschatological future.[45] From this perspective the content of church meetings for the purposes of discernment should be those matters that relate to faithful discipleship in context. This, as Stassen suggests, includes the current and the controversial.[46] This is important because along with an understanding of the Lordship of Jesus Christ over all things, and a realistic and embodied understanding of Jesus Christ, faithful discipleship requires a Holy Spirit context where the dominant and prevailing ideologies which can capture our allegiance need to be challenged and repented of.[47]

---

43. Ellis, *Gathering*, 237.

44. Ibid., 237.

45. McClendon, *Doctrine*, 44–46. Ellis shows in various places an explicit appreciation of McClendon's work. For a piece of writing which addresses in detail the subject of congregational discernment from McClendon's perspective see, Heidebrecht, "James Wm. McClendon Jr.'s Practice of Communal Discernment," 45–68.

46. Stassen, *Thicker*, 6.

47. Ibid., 16–17. Interestingly for this discussion Stassen includes nationalism among such ideologies. In this respect while I am favoring engagement with "culturally-pressing" issues I am quite prepared that this process will lead to them being exposed as "idolatries," Holmes "Knowing Together," 187.

PROCESS FOR DISCERNMENT

What Ellis does not offer in his description of congregational discernment is a process for engaging in the practice. As such this will not address the concerns of several writers who wish to reimagine the practice of congregational discernment through church meetings because of bad experience. This is a common theme in a number of the writers I have already cited. Some of the negative evaluations tend to be anecdotal and at times rather dated and repetitive rather than evidential.[48] This said, experience tends to suggest that there is indeed a "mismatch" between the experiences of such meetings and the theological weight which they carry.[49]

For those concerned with practice, therefore, what Ellis and indeed I have written, may simply add further theological freight to an activity which cannot bear the already existing theological weight given to it. In response I would want to say several things.

First, the nature of the practice of congregational discernment should be determined by its purpose. My argument is that the purpose of congregational discernment is to discern the mind of the living Christ. This discernment should be focused, therefore, on issues that pertain to allowing believers to be faithful disciples of Jesus Christ in their scattered and gathered contemporary missionary contexts. Such discernment will not necessarily require all people to be bound by a common decision or even a common decision to be agreed but should always be open to the new and unexpected through the presence of Jesus Christ. The specific issues considered in this way should be distinguished from other matters which congregations can deal with differently. These can be delegated or indeed decided in a democratic way.[50] The process of discussing and deciding what issues should be dealt with and in what ways can be seen as a matter for congregational discernment and such consideration could be a starting point for new practice.

---

48. Some of the cited negative references go back to the 1980s.

49. Holmes, "Knowing Together," 173.

50. Congregational discernment as is often stated is not about democracy. At times, however, in some of the writing there appears an almost negative understanding of democracy per se. I do not share this. In this respect with Holmes, "I want to celebrate" historic Baptist practices that extended participation in decision making processes to those who were otherwise culturally excluded, such as "working men" and "women," "Knowing Together," 182. While Wright is one of those who has rightly challenged the idea that discernment is about democracy he yet states "there are worse things than democracy," *Challenge to Change*, 101, and is indeed willing to describe discernment as "guided democracy," *Free Church*, 134.

Second, the practice of congregational discernment should be both expressive and formative of discipleship. That is, engaging in congregational discipleship should be regarded as an activity required of those at the core of a congregation attempting to be disciples. Simultaneously, the process should help them become disciples. In this way the process as a practice is not simply an end to an alternate means but is an end in itself.[51] This means indeed the practice of communal discernment should draw upon, model, and teach the spiritual discipline of attentiveness as an integral part of making disciples.[52] It also means, however, that participants have to have the opportunity to discuss and disagree on matters of contention. If this is not allowed or encouraged the matters that matter may remain off the agenda. Appropriate skills and practices which foster a context in which this can happen should be encouraged and utilized.[53] In recent literature there are a number of helpful suggestions concerning such skills and practices even though the authors may be approaching the subject from a different perspective than me.[54]

Third and following on from the above, I think that there are some particularly important practical issues that require mention. The reason, meaning, and value of the practice of congregational discernment in its various dimensions have to be constantly explained and taught. Since the practice is valuable and formative time can and should be given to matters that matter and the process of discernment. People should be constantly encouraged to be free to speak, free to listen, and free to change their minds. This includes the repeated reminder that no-one's statements will be treated as their last word on a topic but as part of a process in which the voice of Christ to this congregation at this time is being sought. The humility to acknowledge that one can be wrong even in sincere convictions should be recognized as a feature of "attempting to be disciples" and applicable to common decisions as well as to individual ones.[55] While discussion and discernment can take place in a variety of contexts there should yet be times as intentional as gathering for worship when a congregation gathers as congregation to discern.

Four, a goal of leadership should be to enable congregations to lean to discern in these ways. In some discussions of leadership and congregational discernment the primary focus appears to be on how the direction

51. Here I begin to push in the direction of a more technical understanding of "practice," McClendon, *Ethics*, 172–76.

52. Rollinson, "The Attentive Community" is helpful on this.

53. For an interesting discussion on the potential use of the "circle process" see Schelin, "Unbreaking the Circle," 19–32.

54. Jump, *Healthy Church Meetings*.

55. Ellis, *Gathering*, 237.

of leadership and the discernment of the congregation are to be related.⁵⁶ This is a valid discussion as various forms of leadership have a part to play in the process of discernment.⁵⁷ My point, however, is different. My point is that it should be regarded as a critical function of leadership to facilitate a congregation growing in maturity with respect to its ability to discern what the living Christ is saying to it. This is surely a way in which leaders act "for the body."⁵⁸

CONCLUSION

The items considered appropriate for discussion as part of congregational discernment are determined by our understanding of the nature and purpose of that practice. Developing from the work of Ellis I contend that congregational discernment is a practice of contextual discipleship to seek to know and to obey the mind of the Jesus Christ the living Lord. Given that discipleship is contemporaneous, and the Lordship of Jesus Christ expansive, this should draw into the practice of congregational discernment matters that matter pertaining to the life of the church scattered and gathered in the complexities of the societies and cultures in which we are seeking to bear faith witness in mission. Not only, however, should the processes of discernment be expressive and formative of discipleship but, given the nature of the living Christ, we should always be open to surprise, challenge, and change.

---

56. Pexton, "A Theological Reflection."

57. For some albeit limited discussion on leadership in the "fellowship of the Spirit" see McClendon, *Doctrine*, 477.

58. Shurden, "Baptists and the Priesthood of All Believers," 64–87, 66.

Open This Book

Open this book that we may see your Word
Embodied in the drama of our earth –
Stories of people that your Spirit stirred,
Glimpses of hope and visions of new birth.

Open this book that we may meet the one
Who came as word-made-flesh for all to see;
Show us his life, all that was said and done,
That we might see ourselves as we could be.

Open our ears that we may hear you still;
Teach us to live as well as speak your word.
Open our eyes that we might face your will –
The word-made-flesh in those who call you Lord.

6

"That We Might See Ourselves as We Could Be"

Baptist Interpretations of Scripture on the Complementarity of Male and Female

BETH ALLISON-GLENNY

IT WAS IN A conversation with Chris Ellis, as I was exploring a call to ministry, that I was first introduced to the Declaration of Principle of the Baptist Union of Great Britain. Before this point I had understood that as Baptists we had a common conviction on baptism and on local church governance, but it was only then that I discovered that the basis of our Union also contained a conviction about how we read Scripture together: "That our Lord and Saviour Jesus Christ, God manifest in the flesh, is the sole and absolute authority in all matters pertaining to faith and practice, as revealed in the Holy Scriptures, and that each Church has liberty, under the guidance of the Holy Spirit, to interpret and administer His laws." It was the first time I had appreciated not only that there was a Baptist hermeneutic, but that it was carefully nuanced. A Baptist hermeneutic contained within the Declaration of Principle emphasizes the role of the local church for the interpretation of Scripture. This means that Baptists emphasize the provisional nature of scriptural interpretation for each context and give significant space to the importance of dissent. This principle suggested that our interpretation of Scripture was much more provisional than anything I had encountered in a broader evangelical environment to that point, as we were to be intentional about that the limitations of our interpretations, interpreting always into local settings with live challenges, and measuring our interpretations against the person of Christ and the guidance of the Holy Spirit. It was a defining moment in my developing Baptist identity, as a theology undergraduate who had become bored and frustrated with the line often spouted in church settings that "the Bible *clearly* says . . . ."

There was one issue in particular that I found unclear: what it meant to be embodied as male and female. Was the drama of embodying God's word something performed differently by men and women? This was a conversation that repeatedly occurred in my emerging ministry, and which Chris patiently discussed with me: was there something different about being a woman in ministry? Was my embodiment (as some had argued in the closest Baptist church to my university) a bar to ordination and leadership? Or was it something that would be an asset—others informed me that women in ministry were great because they brought with them a pastoral care perspective and insight, or they brought collaborative styles of leadership. Connected to this conversation around embodiment was another key debate: the church's response to those who are LGBT+, or, as it is normally focused on the question whether same-sex marriage can be affirmed by the church. Both these conversations seemed to ask whether being embodied as one of two sexes mattered for people's behavior and more precisely, how it should matter.[1]

Women in ministry and same-sex marriage are also two recent issues on which British Baptists have sought to read Scripture, not simply at a local level, but as a Union. These two issues have been handled differently, but they have both been the subject of Council statements, which have emphasized a denominational position on what Scripture is understood to say. These two subjects are therefore connected by being questions upon which we have formed a denominational interpretation, but I also hold that the normative reading we have developed on women in ministry is linked to our normative reading on homosexual practice. Both of these positions start from what I will describe as a "soft complementarian" position on what it means to be embodied as women and men in the image of God, which controls how we view and understand the texts. In what follows I will show how this

---

1. There are also people who do not fit easily into the language of man or woman, or male or female. These people need to be listened to by the church—and theologically reflected with—as well, but such an important topic would require its own article. The emphasis of this chapter will therefore be same-sex marriage, as this is the debate currently within the Union, but I am aware that this is also something that challenges a binary view of complementarity.

soft complementarity has been developed by Baptists theologically to justify women in ministry, as a softening of harder, patriarchal complementarity held by a more conservative evangelicalism. However, I will also offer two cautions: firstly, that this complementarity is still limited to a binary view of male and female means it is ultimately unhelpful for the emancipation of women, and secondly, that complementarity has shaped our view of embodiment when we talk about same-sex marriage. If the Union is going to come to interpretive norms on women in ministry and homosexuality, then we need to ask whether this underlying belief of what it is to be male and female is an adequate theological articulation of our embodiment. As the Baptist Union's own working party on homosexuality asked:

> And while one might want to argue that issues of human sexuality are of a different order to issues of slavery and gender, this merely begs the question: whether these issues are similar or dissimilar is precisely the issue that necessitates careful, prayerful and reflective theological discussion.[2]

DEVELOPING INTERPRETATIVE NORMS: SIMILARITIES AND DISSIMILARITIES BETWEEN HOW SCRIPTURE IS READ AS A UNION ON WOMEN IN MINISTRY AND HOMOSEXUALITY

Even though the basis of Baptist Union is a Declaration of Principle that locates interpretation in the local church, on both of these issues Council has produced, to borrow its own terminology, an interpretive "norm." For women in ministry this "norm" is the acceptance of women in ministry, and whilst dissent from this is allowed, the emphasis is that to do so is to be at odds with the Union's "gospel conviction":

> Commitment to the full inclusion of women in leadership is our "norm." . . . Those who want to disagree and want to be part of the family have to reckon with that. There is a place for dissent . . . but dissent as a Baptist is to speak up for justice at great personal cost; it is not to perpetuate injustice at great cost to others. In other words, we should not allow dissent to be a cover for prejudice and discrimination that inflicts pain and hurt on the women among us.[3]

---

2. *Baptists Exploring Issues of Human Sexuality*, 14.

3. *The Story of Women in Ministry*, 72. *The Story of Women in Ministry* was originally "Women in Leadership among the churches of the Baptist Union of Great Britain"

Although local Baptist churches cannot be forced to call women in ministry, the Union structures that discern calling to ministry are committed to ordaining women and in the light of continued challenges faced on women being settled in churches, Council has advocated an interpretation of Scripture which commends women in ministry and has described the Union's position as one where this interpretation is generally accepted.

Similarly, both Baptist Steering Group and Baptist Union Council have emphasized a Baptist "norm" on marriage, affirming that it is between a man and a woman: "Council positively re-affirms and commends to our churches our Union's historic Biblical understanding of marriage as a union between one man and one woman, and calls them to live in the light of it."[4] This also has implications for ministry, since the rules for accredited ministers state, "Homosexual orientation (whether male or female) is not of itself a reason for exclusion from the Ministry, but homosexual genital practice is to be regarded as conduct unbecoming."[5] There has also been much discussion about whether ministers of churches who register for same-sex marriage can be allowed to perform these marriages without risking their accredited status. In 2014 Baptist Steering Group allowed ministers the freedom to follow their Church Meeting in conducting same-sex marriages, arguing, "As a union of churches in covenant together we will respect the differences on this issue which both enrich us and potentially could divide as we seek to live in fellowship under the direction of our Declaration of Principle."[6] Whereas by 2016 Baptist Union Council said, "recognizing the costs involved and after careful and prayerful reflection and listening, we humbly urge churches who are considering conducting same-sex marriages to refrain from doing so out of mutual respect."[7] Although this freedom of ministers to follow the will of their Church Meeting was technically not removed, great discussion was had about whether churches who registered for same-sex marriage should and could be expelled from the Union, resulting in a greater questioning of the local church's freedom to interpret the will of Christ than anything seen in the women in ministry discussion. Interestingly, the Declaration of Principle was cited in both statements on same-sex marriage: in the first as an argument for the freedom of the local

and was a report presented to the Baptist Union Council in March 2010.

4. Statement from the Council of the Baptist Union. March 2016. http://www.baptist.org.uk/Groups/273782/Same_Sex_Marriage.aspx

5. Baptist Union of Great Britain, *Ministerial Recognition Rules*, 20th March 2014, 13.

6. http://www.baptist.org.uk/Articles/463892/Responding_to_the.aspx accessed 24th April 2016.

7. Statement from the Council of the Baptist Union. March 2016.

church, and in the second as a way of arguing that churches of the Union were covenanted together and so should refrain from disrespecting other churches in the Union by conducting same-sex marriages. This suggests that the freedom of the local church to interpret Scripture and then act accordingly, even if it dissents from the normal reading of Scripture by the Union, is something that is not agreed upon by all members of the Union. It is also noteworthy that this "humble urging"[8] of churches has been a much bigger feature of the debate around homosexuality than the ordination of women. In both debates the Union through its structures has sought to come to an agreed interpretation of the texts. However, the agreed norms have different trajectories: the historic position on women in ministry is to be reversed, and the historic position on homosexuality is to be maintained. The ability of the local church to dissent from these positions is also different in both cases: nothing is done to force churches to accept women in ministry, other than to remind them they dissent from the Union; however the Council is asking local churches to refrain from registering their buildings for same-sex marriage and the ministerial recognition rules currently prevent those who are in same-sex marriages from being ordained.

AN UNDERPINNING THEOLOGY OF BINARY COMPLEMENTARITY

As well as women in ministry and homosexuality being comparable examples of how the Union has developed a denominationally advocated reading of Scripture, there is also a shared underlying theological question about embodiment. Language about the complementarity of male and female is found in both of the Baptist discussions of homosexuality and women in ministry, but with comparatively little theological reflection on homosexuality, compared with that present in the women in ministry debates. For example, in *Making Moral Choices* it states:

> the complementarity of men and women in marriage reflects a basic characteristic of the divine nature, since God made men and women in his own image and likeness. As Creator, God has given to humankind the task of continuing the human race through the gift of sexuality. Therefore to disparage sexuality is

---

8. This is the language used in the statement from the Council of the Baptist Union, March 2016. Precisely what this means and how strongly this censors churches and ministers has been the subject of a lot of discussion.

to repudiate something that lies at the very heart of the divine purpose.⁹

It is thus worth unpacking the theology of complementarity as it is found in the discussions around women in ministry, in order to understand better the Baptist starting point for a theology of human embodiment for sexuality. The complementarian answer developed by a multiplicity of Baptist authors in light of women in ministry helps to explain why the Union has advocated a change in how Baptists interpret the fact of women in ministry, but maintains a historically conservative position on human sexuality.

The nodal point to complementarianism is the idea that there are two biological sexes, a male sex and a female sex, which in some way "complement" each other. This position holds that there are differences between men and women because of their bodies, a position known as biological essentialism. Elaine Storkey summarizes this position about human biology, "Men and women are not only sexually different, they are different chromosomally, reproductively, anatomically, hormonally and in terms of weight, height and brain usage."¹⁰ Defining complementarianism in church life involves conversations about hierarchy, whether there is a created, "ontological" difference between men and women and, if so, how this continues into the roles they take on within society.¹¹ The vocabulary used in this chapter is trying to get to the heart of this conversation, and uses "complementarian" to mean the view that men and women are different to one another in a way that is essential of their biological sex, and these innate differences of man and woman are designed by God to complement the other sex and together reflect the *imago Dei*. This means that men, because they are created men, have certain innate tendencies and abilities, and women, because they are created women, have other innate tendencies and abilities.

Complementarianism is often used as a descriptor of a theology of gender propounded by conservative evangelicals, that men and women, whilst having equal worth before God, were created for different roles and functions. This position used to be called hierarchicalism, because it understood men were created to be the head of women in domestic, social and

9. *Making Moral Choices*, 22.

10. Storkey, *Created or Constructed? The Great Gender Debate*, 14.

11. Ontological difference refers to the idea that men and women are different in their very being in a way that goes beyond biological difference. Essential difference refers to the way men and women are different in a way that is essential to their biological sex, drawing from a platonic understanding of an eternal essence that manifests in particulars. These two terms are often used by different feminist theologians to denote the same things, as the idea that there is created essential sex difference implies something in God's ordering of the world. See Thatcher, *God, Sex and Gender*, 19.

church life, having the authority, preaching and teaching, whereas women were created to take on other roles, especially in the domestic sphere as wives and mothers. Such a view is typified by authors such as John Piper and Wayne Grudem, who argue, "He [God] designed our differences and they are profound. They are not mere physiological prerequisites for sexual union. They go to the root of our personhood."[12] This position, which will be termed "hard complementarity" in this discussion, continues to find expression within the more conservative evangelical tradition. For these churches, women cannot be ordained because it is ontologically impossible for them to lead men; women were created to be submissive. This position is predicated on ideas which reinforce male dominance and female submission and sees patriarchy as part of God's ordering of creation.

However, there is also a prevalence of language about the complementarity of men and women used by Baptists who would be fully in favor of the ministry of women. This egalitarian complementarity seems to have a similar understanding that men and women are created differently and need to work together for the mutual flourishing of both sexes, but the aim of this position is producing equality instead of hierarchy. This position of "soft complementarity" has been used as a core argument for the ordination of women amongst Baptist authors over the past thirty-five years: because women are created different to men, the church cannot be a full reflection of the *imago Dei* without the gifts and styles women bring, and so the male dominated church needs women to bring these different styles and gifts into a collaborative ministry with men in order to save the church from patriarchy.[13] The language used in soft complementarity holds to a binary paradigm of embodiment and gender, questioning the conclusion but not the original concept. This is an understandable move, because it challenges hard complementarians on their beliefs about women in ministry, without asking them to change their original doctrines around embodiment. However, whilst this reliance on the same understanding of embodiment produces a clever rebuttal to hard complementarians, questions must be asked about whether this works and produces the egalitarianism hoped for, and whether holding on to the binary paradigm without subjecting it to further scrutiny is desirable. The binary model of the complementarity of men and women could be itself a flawed and limited understanding of what it is to be created in the *imago Dei*.

---

12. Piper and Grudem, *Recovering Biblical Manhood*, 32.

13. Allison, "A Feminist Discussion of 'Complementarian' Arguments for Women in Ministry, with Particular Reference to the Baptist Union of Great Britain, MTh thesis, Oxon., 2015.

SCRIPTURAL INTERPRETATIONS OF COMPLEMENTARITY AS AN ARGUMENT FOR WOMEN IN MINISTRY

Baptist literature on women in ministry amongst those within the Baptist Union over the past thirty-five years constructs a dominant narrative that there are two complementary and divinely created genders essential to biological sex and that these are held as irrefutable norms. This brief overview will show that ontological gender is understood to be something that is revealed through Scripture, both in the creation narratives and in the New Testament understanding of gender within the church, especially Galatians 3:28 and 1 Corinthians 11. It will show how Baptists have drawn arguments from Scripture that women and men are created as complementary partners, that man and woman together reflect the *imago Dei*, and so we need to keep or reclaim these gender distinctions, especially femininity, in order to fully reflect the image of God.

The first interpretation of Scripture is that men and women were created to be complementary pairs. This is typified by Pat Took, who considers that man and woman were created to be different and live in mutuality, looking to the fall as the source of domination and misogyny. Women were created to be "the companions and colleagues of men. . . . Someone who was essentially the same but who was also interestingly different: bringing further resources, fresh intelligence, new ways of seeing something, a deeper companionship."[14] Her argument is that in their ontology women are there to exist alongside men, and this companionship included bringing "further," that is, different, resources, intelligence and ways of perceiving the world. She elaborates that man and woman were made for each other to image God together and with only one gender that image is lost. She goes on to examine the many ways gender affects our identity, from the relationships we have grown up in to the culture and history that we have, arguing that men have been unable to govern without women and women without men: "if either man or woman were to try this alone they would be radically disabled by the loss of their proper colleague in the enterprise."[15] This "original partnership" is essential for creating life and is likewise essential to "all aspects of human endeavor, including the church."[16] Took highlights the importance of mutual creativity and male and female "complementing one another."[17] She

---

14. Took, "In His Image," 3.
15. Ibid., 6.
16. Ibid., 6.
17. Ibid., 8.

concludes with the terms mutuality and complementarity to make the case to men that "you need us.... In the body of Christ you urgently need us."[18]

Took's argument that a complementary relationship based on gender persists in numerous texts about women in ministry. A brief snapshot of the continued use of the creation narrative justifies the view that complementarity was divinely intended. Adam Eakins, for example, maintains that people are not made gender neutral. God created us with gender so it is "important that men are men and women are women."[19] Elsewhere, in an earlier text, George Beasley-Murray considers Jesus's examination of creation passages and concludes, "the partnership between man and woman exists apart from marriage."[20] For Anne Phillips, complementarity becomes a solution to patriarchal oppression; she develops her argument that creation is intentionally diverse and that "men and women generally but not exclusively display different characteristics and abilities intended to be utilized in complementarity and equality."[21] Phillips's other writing suggests that she may now object to such a heteronormative interpretation of her complementarian language and so the cautious phrasing of "not exclusively" in this quotation should be emphasized.[22] However, it is hard to hear this as critical of the multiplicity of Baptist authors who do argue this viewpoint by using the same language, such as Derek and Dianne Tidball, who argue that the two genders were created to be different by God as no individual or one gender was created to be self-sufficient and "through relationship each can become a more complete person."[23] Looking at creation they argue that "Eve is going to be the counterpart, complement, companion and partner to Adam."[24] This persistent language of complementarity as designed by God is a recurrent theme in Baptist texts as the answer to patriarchy and hierarchism. The created differences of the two sexes are intended to be used in partnership together. The emphasis on men and women as created partners also blurs talking about marital relations and general partnership at work in the world. For the above Baptist authors, making a distinction between sexual partnership and wider working partnerships does not seem to be

---

18. Ibid., 10.
19. Eakins, "That Joke Isn't Funny Anymore," 2.
20. Beasley-Murray, *Man and Woman in the Church*, 3.
21. Phillips, "Who Is the Problem? Reflecting on Leadership and Gender in English Church and Society," 2.
22. See Philips, *The Faith of Girls*.
23. Tidball and Tidball, *The Message of Women*, 35.
24. Ibid., 37.

necessary: rather a general natural rule can be derived that men and women are complementary pairs.

The second interpretation, that men and women together reflect the image of God, is argued by multiple Baptist authors. They argue that distinctions between the genders do not need to be erased in order to claim equality, rather the opposite is true; soft complementary is seen as designed by God and so the recovery of femininity will see the undoing of patriarchy. Stephen Ibbotson, referring to the *imago Dei*, maintains the differences between male and female and argues that the existence of otherness and its embrace is not an obliteration of difference.[25] A binary understanding of male and female remains even if that difference must not be rendered in terms of authority and hierarchy. Instead the mutuality of otherness is described by Ibbotson as beneficial and fruitful.[26] Ibbotson's position is that gender is re-ordered from divisions that are hierarchical to egalitarian. Few, similarly, considering the legacy of Eve and the damage done to women, suggests instead male and female "in complementarity reflect the image of the deity."[27] This egalitarianism is connected with reclaiming the femininity that is present within God. The church will only have full ministry and representation of the *imago Dei* if there are both men and women in ministry.[28]

This soft binary complementarity is evidenced in the treatment of New Testament texts by Baptist authors. Although Galatians 3:28 might offer a less binary view of male and female, that in Christ there is "no longer male and female," the maintenance of an ontological male and female in complementary partnership continue in Baptists' treatment of the New Testament, and especially the aforementioned text. Authors again maintain the distinctions between male and female as part of equality. Beasley-Murray offers an ontological view of gender as he considers Jesus' treatment of men and women in the coming kingdom of God. He argues that man and woman will no longer maintain their physical relations but that does not mean that there will be no such thing as man and woman and, if this is an eschatological goal, then this should be what we strive for in our existence: "man and woman in genuine partnership in the service and love of Christ."[29] Referring to Galatians 3:28 he emphasizes that it is the divisions (not the distinctions) between male and female that disappear. In his treatment of the household codes in the epistles Beasley-Murray is keen to resist any understanding that

25. Ibbotson, "Following the Trajectory," 7.
26. Ibid., 7.
27. *The Story of Women in Ministry*, 36.
28. Ibid., 36.
29. Beasley-Murray, *Man and Woman in the Church*, 5.

these distinctions between male and female involve male dominance and female submission, but he concludes "the distinctions between them are no longer divisive but complementary. Their partnership in the kingdom of God is likewise an equality of service which is complementary."[30]

Similarly, Winter looks at Galatians, arguing that male and female is a deliberate allusion to the *imago Dei* in Genesis 1:27 and that Paul does not think that gender differences are erased through baptism, again stating "Christians are not androgynous."[31] Instead he argues that baptism obliterates the dominance of one gender over another. This theme continues with Ibbotson, who shows that baptism as a symbolic rite that is inclusive of women would have been remarkable in the Corinthian society where symbolic rites would have divided and differentiated the genders. Thus, baptism is a re-ordering of gender, but the re-ordering of divisions of hierarchy not the removal of binary norms.[32] The Tidballs also state that Paul was concerned that the distinctions between men and women, and the institution of marriage, were still respected.[33] Again, they conclude that "essential gender distinction inherent in the creation of male and female" should be respected and the distinction was that of difference not hierarchy.[34] They continue, "men should not seek to behave or dress like women and women have no need to imitate men to exercise their gifts in the church."[35] Although they argue for different behavior and dress for men and women, this gender distinction pertains to character and personality rather than role. They continue that the distinctiveness of each gender completes what is lacking in the other, "God's creation design was that men and women should complement each other as equals."[36] In texts on women in ministry, it is clear that Baptist interpretations of Scripture are keen to maintain essential binary differences between men and women which play out in relationship if not in church hierarchy. This sets up a normative interpretation on gender embodiment that has the potential to be used not simply for women in ministry but for human sexuality. The emphasis on maintaining gender distinction seems to be because women in ministry are seen to reflect the feminine present in God. Responding to the idea that a Father God necessitates male leadership *Women, Baptists and Ordination* offers, "the image of God is seen most

30. Ibid., 13.
31. Winter, "God's Inclusive Story," 7.
32. Ibid., 7.
33. Tidball and Tidball, *The Message of Women*, 216.
34. Ibid., 222.
35. Ibid.
36. Ibid., 281.

clearly in the complementary natures of female as well as male."[37] In its brief discussion of the *imago Dei*, it considers that Scripture gives us images of God "that many would acknowledge are more female than male."[38] It does not clarify what would make an image of God male or female, rather it assumes this is apparent and continues the theme that maleness and femaleness in God are split into the two sexes, which combine to make the image of God. Thus, the second interpretation develops into the third, that the difference and otherness of women is something to be lauded as God-given, and the argument begins to emerge that Baptists should ordain women *because* they embody their gender, as this will reclaim the intended image of God in the church.

This begs the question about what Baptist authors think Scripture says these gender differences are. For many authors maleness and femaleness is seen to be self-evident, but for a few other authors the distinctiveness is not always agreed upon, and the binary nature of the language is even challenged. Woodman draws the analogy between man and woman, Christ and humanity and God and Christ in 1 Corinthians 11, which he suggests shows us something of how man and woman should relate to each other. He argues, "the relationship is not one of subordination, but is rather a relationship of interdependence and unity."[39] The language of interdependence continues to advocate complementarity between male and female; however the difficulties of this argument later emerge as he comments, "Paul welcomes the freedom of women to minister in his churches except where it was exercised in such a way as to compromise the church's unity and witness."[40] Woodman's interpretation of the scriptural passages used to argue against women in ministry show that the challenge of arguing that men and women require each other too often leads to the argument that women can minister, but their ministry is still provisional on other social norms. Male ministry assumes neutrality, whereas women's ministry may only complement when appropriate. This would not be Woodman's intended argument, as Woodman cautions that as long as there is no equality of opportunity then social stereotypes will prevent the discovery of finding "the real distinctiveness between male and female that reflects the distinction in God."[41] He argues for a "distinctive" male and female that together reflect the *imago Dei*, but challenges that the social stereotypes of this are often inaccurate. Woodman

---

37. *Women, Baptists and Ordination*, 28.
38. Ibid., 28.
39. Woodman, "Presentation to Baptist Union Council on the Difficult Passages," 2.
40. Ibid., 5.
41. Woodman, "A Biblical Basis for Affirming Women in Ministry—Part 2," 13.

looks to Galatians and argues that it is not appropriate to "distinguish one person from another using divisions based on race, class or gender."[42] This subtle difference in argument is to be noted: there is still something about a binary complementarity of men and women in ministry, but it is impossible to know exactly what this is in advance of having women in ministry, and social stereotypes and norms should not be used to predict these.

Paul Fiddes takes this nuance one step further, again trying to develop a complementarity that is not based on binary stereotypes of men and women. Initially his argument echoes those heard above as he constructs a strong understanding of complementarity, where it is noteworthy that women are again listed in the binary pairs that include humanity and the church, rather than God. He argues that each partner has their own contribution to the relationship which cannot be confused with the other, "this suggests that in the male-female covenant, there is also a particular contribution made by each sex which cannot be replaced by the other."[43] He argues strongly that the question surrounding male-female relationship is one of hierarchy rather than difference, "the difference must not be obliterated in belief about fundamental equality in Christ; the 'otherness' of male to female . . . must be respected and allowed for as a factor that enriches the relationship." However, he then draws on Rosemary Radford-Ruether as he discusses the mutuality and interdependence of male and female in husbands and wives, emphasizing the need for both to be subject to the other. He suggests that a doctrine of *perichoresis*, the interpenetration of the different persons of the Trinity, combined with the gender mix in both a male and female genome suggest that there could be a blend of male-female characteristics in both men and women. However, he is quick to caution against any view of androgyny in the creation accounts, suggesting Paul may have been writing 1 Corinthians 11 to counter gnostic groups that were arguing for this asexualism.[44] The challenge for both Woodman and Fiddes as they seek to develop a complementarity that is not based on social stereotypes of men and women is that they continue a binary understanding of gender, if not a binary view of sexual embodiment. However, amongst Baptist authors this is an important nuance compared to a widely accepted and un-interrogated view of binary complementarity and could be the starting place for developing a more considered view of embodiment.

---

42. Woodman, "A Biblical Basis for Affirming Women in Ministry—Part 1," 8.
43. Fiddes, "Woman's Head is Man," 372.
44. Ibid., 372.

THEOLOGICAL CONCLUSIONS DRAWN ABOUT MALE AND FEMALE PARTNERSHIP FOR BAPTIST MINISTRY

The theological conclusion, having established that a soft binary complementarity is scriptural, is that ministry ought to embody this male and female binary partnership. This manifests in a number of different ways, but significantly for the discussion on human sexuality it emphasizes the partnership of men and women in co-ministries over sole pastorates of women. This idea that women's difference will bring something to ministry that will benefit men and undo a patriarchal society permeates many of the texts. For example, Shirley Dex argues that women have a mission to bring tenderness and other humanizing elements to men.[45] In the recent *Story of Women in Ministry* reader, Took is cited as arguing that men need women, because of the previous definition of ministry in terms of status and success instead of collaboration and mutuality. The discussion draws from Took that "in other words, ministry has been defined in male terms, something which not only inherently excludes women, but also diminishes those men who find themselves drawn into such unbalanced expressions of leadership."[46] Woodman argues that because male models of leadership dominate ministry we are unable to gain from the complementary richness that women bring because they will face the expectation that they have to become honorary men. Gender equality means "women would be called to ministry as women and free to minister as women."[47] This need for women to be women in ministry is essential to the undoing of patriarchy, as the church will only be fully able and staffed when every church has a male and female minister.[48] This also finds articulation by Rob White, who states that the church, by presenting a masculine God, has presented a lopsided one; he continues that women, who have the ability to look deeper than the surface and are very forgiving, have been hurt by male leadership which is "unthinking, unfeeling and boorish. The male ego can be a brutish thing—unbending and irrational when aroused."[49] Instead he argues that there is a need for women ministers in order to present a full picture of God, which they would do by bringing "intuition, nurturing nature, and ability to empathise."[50] Interestingly White moves from this to encourage married couples to minister together,

---

45. Dex, "The Church's Response to Feminism," 323.
46. *The Story of Women in Ministry*, 41.
47. Woodman, "A Biblical Basis for Affirming Women in Ministry—Part 2," 13–14.
48. Few, "Hats and WI(w)GS," 15–16.
49. White, "Mr. and Mrs," 5.
50. Ibid., 5.

suggesting men should encourage their wives into ministry, showing the extent to which this binary view of complementarity overlaps with a heteronormative view of marriage.[51] Stephen Rand offers a variation on this theme, arguing that the real discussion should not be about whether women can be in sole ministry in the same way as men, but how we develop shared leadership of men and women together. He argues that this complementary partnership in leading churches is the more significant issue. Here the alternative to sole male ministry where women are marginalized is not sole female ministry, but shared ministry.[52] Shared ministry is seen as a goal of many authors, for example, in *The Story of Women in Ministry*, co-ministries and co-principalships are held up as a model.[53] The argument for women in ministry is not simply that biological sex is not a bar to ordination, but that women should be ordained in order to minister in a man-woman partnership, married or otherwise. This aim might seem subtle, but it is a significant comment both on women's independent ministry and on the best partnership being between those of different sexes.

For the broader conversations about LGBT+ inclusion and acceptance, it is also important to note that the majority of Baptist authors are keen to maintain a binary view of gender norms. The church needs women to be ordained because of their femininity as a way of countering patriarchy and so those women, and the wider Union, must seek to reclaim femininity in their ministry. Examples of this include when the Baptist Colleges committed themselves "to encourage women . . . and actively to affirm the particular gifts and insights that they bring."[54] This was seen to be something structural as well, as they committed "to encourage the development of patterns of ministry in which the complementarity of gifts might be expressed."[55] Likewise the Baptist Union Regional Team Leaders agreed with the 2007 Blackley Declaration's concern at the lack of women in ministry, saying, "this represents a great loss of gifting and experience to the churches."[56] Recently the Women in Leadership Consultation also produced recommendations on ways "the leadership styles of women can be more fully understood and affirmed within the life and structures of church denominations and

---

51. Ibid., 5.
52. Rand, "Can Anyone Here Play the Piano Better Than My Wife?" 2.
53. *The Story of Women in Ministry*, 68.
54. Baptist Union Colleges, *Statement of Intent*, 2nd April 1990.
55. Ibid.
56. Baptist Union of Great Britain, *Statement by the Regional Team Leaders Regarding Women and Men in Leadership*, May 2008.

ecumenical institutions."[57] The gifts and styles of leadership offered by a minister are seen to be observable and connected to their sex, as the Tidballs comment, "there are obvious distinctions between men and women, not least biologically."[58] The Women in Leadership Consultation considered the symbolic difference of female biology, commenting "women's bodies, their experiences and their ways of knowing are different from men."[59] Kate Coleman, a former President of the Baptist Union, has written a course to help women in ministry and other leadership roles in which her premise is that "there is increasing recognition that men and women bring different gifts to leadership."[60] She claims there is no dispute that there are differences between men and women. Whereas men have been developing their leadership styles, women are only just beginning to discover what their unique issues and problems might be. A feminine style is seen as consensual, relational, caring, inclusive, multi-tasking, open, and transparent and she argues that whether this is femininity is derived from genes or society does not matter.[61] She goes as far as to state, "God calls us because we are women and because we have something distinctive and valuable to contribute."[62] This feminine style is echoed by Phillips, who describes men as naturally competitive and women as naturally collaborative.[63] Elsewhere she argues in line with Coleman about the gift of women's ministries "which bring welcome change and rich blessing."[64] Similarly the Baptist Union document *Women, Baptists and Ordination* argues, "Women tend to be more aware of their emotional strengths and weaknesses and may be more likely to seek the support they need. Women may be better at building a team approach to the work. Intellectually, women are just as able as men."[65] Elsewhere, the recent Baptist Union booklet *The Lydia Question* mentions in one story that "women very often preach differently from men, in completely fresh styles."[66]

---

57. *The Leading Question?* 2. The Women in Leadership Consultation involved Women's Justice Group of the Baptist Union and the Ecumenical Forum of European Christian Women.

58. Tidball and Tidball, *The Message of Women*, 35.

59. *The Leading Question?* 9.

60. Coleman, *7 Deadly Sins*, 23.

61. Ibid., 23.

62. Ibid., 65.

63. Phillips, "Who is the problem?" 2.

64. *The Story of Women in Ministry*, 71.

65. *Women, Baptists and Ordination*, 28.

66. *The Lydia Question: A Fresh Look at God's Calling*.

For many authors, the patriarchal structures mean the male style of ministry is flawed, and there is something about redeemed womanhood that needs to be discovered, but the solution will not be about "aggressive" sharing in masculinity.[67] Phillips comments that the pain of some women in ministry has led to "the uniform modelling of male leadership styles."[68] Instead the solution is to find a true womanhood that is not determined by men, which means being not degraded and objectified through popular culture, especially advertising.[69] Significantly this true womanhood, as Dex expresses it, "will be different from an approach where women seek to become (token) men."[70] There are therefore a number of negative comments about women who were perceived as trying to be masculine. Dianne Tidball's study shows the desire not only to reclaim femininity, but that this spills into a criticism of women who were seen to reject this femininity: "women trying hard to be men—to be noticed."[71] This is echoed by a later Baptist Union briefing paper:

> There is a need to deconstruct the traditional patriarchal styles of the delivery of learning. For example, the Women Tutors from the different colleges deliberately ran a recent Joint Colleges Conference in a more collaborative manner, breaking with years of unquestioned tradition.[72]

Similarly, a report to Baptist Union Council was written to address the problem that in the Baptist Union "male patterns of power and authority remain normative."[73] Written for Baptist Union Council, it is aware that "Even the 'debating chamber' forum of Baptist Union Council is one which inherently fosters competitive masculine discourse."[74] From the outset the paper assumes there is a male style of leadership, and the problems this creates for those who wish to see collaborative, relational discourse. It does not assume that this is only women, but leads from this to a later comment cited that "women think in terms of people not profits, creation not destruction."[75] In Baptist discussions there is a frowning upon women who

---

67. Dex, "The Church's Response to Feminism," 323.
68. *The Story of Women in Ministry*, 68.
69. Dex, "The Church's Response to Feminism," 323.
70. Ibid., 323.
71. Tidball, "Walking a Tightrope," 391.
72. Baptist Union of Great Britain, *Briefing Paper for the BUGB Faith and Unity Executive on the meeting on 31st July 2008*, 4.
73. *The Story of Women in Ministry*, 6–7.
74. Ibid., 7.
75. Ibid., 28. The comment was from Hedger, "Some Experiences of a Woman

behave like men in ministry, because part of their intended ministry is to be womanly. Thus, the discussions surrounding the reclaiming of femininity as a way of dismantling patriarchy and the fall not only embed a strong binary view of gender, but they connect this view of gender with redemption. The implications of the gender narrative found in the women in ministry discussions, reduced to *ad absurdum*, are that those who are LGBT+ who would not wish to fit in to gender roles, or are not able to, are thus colluding in the sinful structures of the world.

These views on complementary embodiment of men and women may have been developed for the conversation about women in ministry, but they have created an interpretative and theological norm for how we also consider human sexuality. Developing a theology where male and female partnerships are set up as exclusively the image of God leaves those who are not in those partnerships as less than God's image: similarly those who minister in sole pastorate or those who are single or in same-sex relations. Furthermore, it places extra expectation on women in ministry, that they must operate their ministry in a way which reclaims femininity in order to fix the patriarchy of the church. It seems that this places an undue emphasis on women, not to mention that there is too little caution that what is seen to be feminine in popular culture has been developed itself in a patriarchal world. Women risk becoming "other" to men, and by seeing their ministry as different in some fundamental way this provides credit to those who argue that for their next minister they really need a man. Such a theology is thus limited in its ability to emancipate women in ministry.

REDISCOVERING DISSENTING INTERPRETATIONS: BEYOND BINARY COMPLEMENTARITY

Baptists have argued for a complementarity of male and female embodiment, developing their theology of women in ministry on the belief that ordaining women reclaims a femininity that is understood to be part of the *imago Dei*, yet this view of femininity—and by extension, masculinity—as something that is binary and divinely ratified should not be accepted without interrogation.[76] From within the Baptist literature there have also been voices that have challenged such a limited understanding of complementarity. Although in the minority, these dissenting interpretations offer a wider

---

Minister," 252–53 cited in Briggs, "She-Preachers, Widows and Other Women," 347.

76. Elsewhere I have dealt extensively with the problems arising from binary gender norms, considering the critiques proposed by recent feminism, such as Judith Butler.

view of human complementarity. Fiddes offers the greatest nuance amongst the discussions of female styles and gender difference, reflecting on how this should be understood:

> Christian theology may expect to find some "gender differences" in human existence, or distinct characteristics of personality and approach to life that can be called "male" and "female," beyond the basic biological differences. Theologians ought, however, to be open and questioning in discovering *what* these qualities are, and *how* they are to be connected with the particular functions of men and women in personal and social spheres.[77]

Fiddes commits to this complex understanding of gender-difference and gender-sharing, utilizing Reuther's understanding of a feminine way, suggesting that the differences can be felt more easily than they can be defined:

> We might perhaps think of a range of characteristics in different proportions in men and women, and also a blend of different ways of integrating these elements. Distinctive male and female functions will lie somewhere, mysteriously, in the midst of these factors.[78]

Fiddes argues that this alerts us to the complexity of expressing what gender differences are, suggesting instead that there is a spectrum of gender available to both men and women: "the task of women's movements might then be to get men to recognize and employ their feminine aspects that have lain dormant."[79] Whilst this still has a binary view of gender, it is one that is disconnected from human embodiment. There is something male and female, but different people will embody them differently. In a Union which has a strongly developed theology of gender as biologically essential, this could be a starting point for a wider view of complementarity than the one currently utilized. It would also, interestingly, allow for the idea that complementary partners do not require different biological sexes.

Another author who critiques such a narrow view of complementarity is Ruth Gouldbourne, who addresses the concept of complementarity between male and female by offering some challenges in the use of this language. Her first challenge is to look at this in terms of our understanding of the church as the body of Christ: that complementarity goes beyond that of male and female, because, as the body of Christ, "we all need each other,

---

77. Fiddes "Woman's Head is Man," 379.
78. Ibid., 381.
79. Ibid., 380.

in all our variety, not simply in the differences between male and female."[80] She also suggests that complementarity is a problem when applied to Christ as this results in the scandal of particularity; if Christ has not taken on the fullness of humanity, then how can women be redeemed by him? Her next challenge is that language about this role of women perpetuates a cultural stereotype which is unhelpful for all who minister: "it carries two assumptions with it: that men cannot care and women can do nothing else."[81] Lastly, she looks at the research of Leslie Francis on Eyseneck personality analysis research on Anglican clergy, which discovered that compared to the general population the gender expectations were reversed, with female ordinands recording a more characteristically masculine profile and the male ordinands recording a characteristically feminine profile, which suggests, amongst other things, that male ministers are good at caring and that female ministers may be less good at this. Her ultimate conclusion however is to return to the idea that complementarity is for the whole church in all its variety: "of one thing I am sure: when God calls us to the service of the church in ministry it is as individuals, uniquely gifted and with the weaknesses that are ours as well. We are not called in categories, nor can we serve in such."[82] Gouldbourne's view would also allow for a fuller view of human complementarity that is not based on a binary pairing of male and female partners, but allows for a variety of people responding to God in different ways. These two authors begin to develop a different Baptist narrative of gender, and possibly sexuality, that challenges the consensus view within the Union that sees male and female embodiment as so fundamental to what we bring to the church and to our partnerships with others.

CONCLUSION

The Baptist Union has decided to interpret Scripture at a denominational level on two issues: women in ministry and homosexuality. Both debates thus contain procedural similarities, and they contain the same underlying question about embodiment; however on the former it has offered significant and sustained theological reflection, on the latter it has offered less, yet it has used some of the same language of "complementarity." Looking at how Scripture has been interpreted and what has been meant by complementarity in the debate on women in ministry thus gives an insight into the theological presuppositions that are now shaping the debate on same-sex marriage.

80. Gouldbourne, "Do Women Complement Men in Ministry?" 7.
81. Ibid., 7.
82. Ibid., 10.

It is clear that the Baptist Union has sought to respond to questions about the ordination of women by reinterpreting a conservative doctrine of complementarity to reach an egalitarian conclusion. However, Baptist authors do this not by challenging the binary paradigm of gender and biological sex upon which it is founded, but by questioning the conclusions of hard complementarity: twisting the arguments so that the difference between men and women are precisely the reason Baptists should ordain women. In turn this binary theology of embodiment, that men and women are created to be different but complementary halves of the *imago Dei*, has shaped the interpretative landscape for our conversations around human sexuality, because it sets up a view of partnership that must necessarily be between men and women, as the ideal reflection of God's image. It is important as Baptists to be aware that this is what we are doing as we seek to interpret and live out God's word in these two discussions. There are questions emerging around how appropriate soft complementarian theology is as a basis for arguing for women in ministry, and so this invites us to listen again to the dissenting Baptist thought which offers a wider view of complementarity than that of two genders. After all, if there is to be a Union "norm" on what Scripture says about embodment and how we should act that out, then we must form that norm conscious that it is also part of our Union's shared theology of Scripture both to listen to the differing interpretation and to appreciate our constant need to revisit what more Scripture has to reveal to us. So let us do what Chris urges and open the book again, that when we consider our human embodiment, "we might see ourselves as we could be."

Baptismal Hymn

Here at the water we confess
The word of God has been made flesh,
For when he in the waters bathed
He shared the fate of those he'd save.

As Jesus to the Jordan came
So we have come to do the same:
Then let us all from evil turn
And ways of love from Jesus learn.

The water buries like a tomb
Yet there new life springs from the womb.
We stand and sing what we believe—
That all in Christ new life receive.

We share one life and own one name:
"Jesus is Lord" we all proclaim;
Called to be one, his body we,
A sign of hope for all to see.

We set our feet upon the Way,
To speak for Christ in all we say;
Through Spirit's power in fire and dove,
To do his work and live his love.

7

"The Water Buries Like a Tomb"
Baptists and Baptism

SALLY NELSON

"I AM THINKING OF being baptized."

Dropped casually into the conversation after church coffee; whispered fearfully under a repressive regime; breathed out quietly in the face of death: this is the statement that reminds us that God will be God, and that God's call to the human heart comes always miraculously, sometimes irresistibly, and often in spite of our best efforts at ministry. At this point our hearts will miss a beat because *something has happened* in a life near us.

Like others, I have had the privilege of witnessing, and sometimes being part of, some unusual and varied baptisms—in my case often because of time spent in chaplaincy, working with the dying and those *in extremis*, as well as (in my domestic life) those with disabilities. Some of these encounters have been in ecumenical settings, in which I have had to think hard about what I believe as a Baptist—what *must* be retained? what *could* be relinquished?—without loss of integrity, because primarily we try to follow Jesus, who prioritized compassion over law.

An essay like this one is truly a luxury, argued on paper and not in the pressure of the pastoral moment! In it, I would like to explore (in a Baptist context) one of the key scriptural metaphors associated with baptism—that of dying and rising with Christ, referenced in verse 3 of Chris Ellis's thoughtful baptismal hymn. I am not engaging with the key divisive debate centering on "who does what" in baptism,[1] but I would like to think about the character of the *community of the baptized*: those who live in the familiar world with its joy and brokenness, but have explicitly identified their hope in a different kind of creation through this mysterious act of baptism.[2] They are both dead and risen. Karl Barth suggests that "The baptized man differs from the unbaptized in all circumstances as one who has been placed under the sign of the death and resurrection of Jesus Christ, under the sign of His hope, His destiny, His advent, . . . whether he reflects upon it or not, whether he takes notice of it or not, whether he does it honor or not."[3] In thinking about the community of the baptized, which has this explicit dual existence, we can also think about the significance of the act of baptism through which people enter it, with particular reference to the dying and rising metaphor.[4]

THE TREASURES OF A HELPFUL METAPHOR

Dying and rising is not the only baptismal metaphor. Paul Fiddes identifies in his essay, "Baptism and creation," a series of dramatic motifs connected with baptism, all of which are grounded in the biblical narrative. These motifs are birth, cleansing, conflict, refreshment and journey.[5] Each is instantly recognizable to us as revelatory of an aspect of the power and role of baptism in a Christian's life. Other scriptural metaphors associated with baptism include circumcision (e.g., Col 2:11–12), new clothing (e.g., Gal 3:27–28), and, perhaps more tenuously, exodus (e.g., 1 Cor 10:1–2).

---

1. The extremes being that baptism is a work of grace and more or less God's doing; or that baptism is a response to grace and more or less our doing. It is dangerous to identify these too closely with denominational positions since in reality Christians often have a nuanced view. See Ellis's helpful comments in "Baptism and the Sacramental Freedom of God," 25–26; John Colwell's discussion of God's freedom within sacraments in the chapter on baptism in *Promise and Presence*; Brian Haymes's comments on believers' baptism as affirmation of the saving grace of God in *A Question of Identity*, 9–10.

2. Ellis writes "Baptism gains its shape from the story of Jesus and its promise and challenge from the union with Christ of the believer who continues to live in the world that crucified Jesus," Ellis, "Baptism and the Sacramental Freedom of God," 27.

3. Barth, *The Teaching of the Church Regarding Baptism*, 59.

4. There is a different dynamic within paedobaptist circles. For the purposes of this argument I will work with Karl Barth's idea that while infant baptism cannot be "ineffective," it is less than the ideal of "free and responsible" baptism (see ibid., 52). This view of baptism does, however, leave a question about how those with learning difficulties or speech and language problems, for example, may articulate a free and responsible decision for faith. I offer some comment on these matters later in the essay.

5. Fiddes, "Baptism and Creation."

This multiplicity is surprising: yet we need all these metaphors to provide anything like an adequate picture of what baptism is, means, or does; just as any discussion of the atonement which relies on a single metaphorical picture (victory, penal substitution, sacrifice, love, etc.) will be insufficient and distort our understanding of the work of Christ.[6]

This abundance of metaphorical descriptions persuades me that metaphors are a very useful way of revealing, without defining or limiting, the actions of a transcendent yet immanent God. Each metaphor helps a bit; none is adequate alone. We gain sufficient insight through a good metaphor to be able to grasp something of the work of God in us, and the love of God for us, yet the metaphor does not allow us to appropriate that insight in such a manner that we usurp the power, the majesty, the sheer limitlessness of God's being. Thus, the range of metaphors used "keeps us 'umble,'" since we cannot pin a single one down and make it a matter of litigation against our sisters and brothers in Christ (though over the centuries we have certainly tried to do so). Jesus, in his teaching, presumably avoided prescriptive explanations for this very reason: a countercultural tactic then as now, since boundaries and rules do so warm the human heart and make us feel that we know where righteousness is to be found!

The whole Bible is rich both in metaphor and story (not least in its use of parables, both in the OT and in the teaching of Jesus). There is plenty of scholarship that explores the enduring fascination of humanity with narrative and metaphorical form, and of course narrative is also very much in vogue in popular cultural thought. For example, if you listen to BBC Radio 4's *Open the Book*[7] it will not be long before there is a discussion of narrative; and, in a completely different discipline, "narrative medicine" has been advocated as a better way for physicians to engage with patients since the mid-1980s.[8] The books on this subject have a deeply pastoral and moral dimension that resonates happily with Christian theology.

The philosopher Paul Ricoeur was one of those brave enough in the mid-late twentieth century to challenge the modernist juggernaut of fragmentation and reductionism. His method of "phenomenological hermeneutics" took human experience seriously as a legitimate starting point for reflection. As Christians and pastors (and here I do not just mean ordained ministers, but the calling to compassionate living that belongs to us all), this is a helpful and refreshing place to begin—it's a bit like the Bible, in which all human life is exposed! Ricoeur argued that the properties of language

---

6. Stephen Holmes discusses the various metaphors in *The Wondrous Cross*.

7. A radio broadcast about contemporary literature.

8. See, for example, Charon, *Narrative Medicine* and Frank, *The Wounded Storyteller*.

that we call metaphor and narrative were fundamental qualities of reality. In other words, metaphor and narrative help us to make sense of the world because the world is actually constructed after the form of these linguistic building blocks in some way.[9]

In his classic text *The Rule of Metaphor*,[10] Ricoeur established that words have an inner and vital characteristic, known as "polysemy" or the possession by a word of multiple referents.[11] In life we experience this in the ambiguities and misunderstandings of everyday conversations ("I thought you meant . . ."), as well as in the problems of translation from one language or dialect to another. There is no simple one-to-one correspondence between a word and its referent: a word is always used contextually and grammatically.

We might initially think that this is a disaster with echoes of Babel—and sometimes it is! However, Ricoeur explains how polysemy is also indicative of a healthy language,[12] since it allows the language to develop intuitively and be understood by others without simply adding more and more new words, thus making a language impossibly large. The shared appreciation of parameters of meaning is one aspect of shared culture. As social beings, we need to find descriptions of our world that are collectively understood. Since we cannot live inside one another's heads, and experience exactly what everyone else experiences, we are able to make use of polysemy to grasp a sense of the inner world of another. For disciples, followers of The Way, this intentional process is the minute-by-minute, Spirit-filled, ongoing Pentecost project of trying to understand the feelings, experiences, and emotions of "the other," and to live with compassion on the earth, reversing the divisions and aggressions of Babel. It is the first step towards our discipline of loving one's neighbor.

There is another fascinating aspect of polysemy in addition to these benefits of social cohesion. There are indeed intuitive boundaries to possible meanings: while a word may not always mean the same thing forever, it does not mean just anything at all. Ricoeur argues that the inner flexibility of words gives rise to the *creative and dynamic* potential of metaphor

---

9. Christians will readily make the connection that God "spoke" or "called" the world into being.

10. Ricoeur, *The Rule of Metaphor*.

11. See ibid., 134.

12. Ricoeur says: "A language without polysemy would violate the principle of economy, for it would extend its vocabulary indefinitely. Furthermore, it would violate the rule of communication, because it would multiply its designations as often as, in principle, the diversity of human experience and the plurality of subjects of experience demanded," ibid., 134.

to expand language and understanding. Metaphor establishes similarities, but is never a matter of simply substituting one word for another: a true metaphor will always expand understanding and bring new things to light. A metaphor famously has "is and is not" properties that take us into new territory[13]—a metaphor suggests that an entity "is" something else but also "is not" that something else. When there is a new discovery, something that has never been seen, heard or experienced before, we have to create a new set of words for it. If these words have no connection to the familiar, then the new thing remains effectively undiscovered.[14]

A metaphor, with its creativity, can thus surprise and even shock us! "For this is the function of metaphor, to instruct by suddenly combining elements that have not been put together before. . . . It is from metaphor that we can best get hold of something fresh"[15] (possible because metaphors can depict abstract ideas in concrete terms). A metaphor is only a metaphor for as long as it teaches us new things; once we no longer feel that surprise (which Ricoeur describes as its "impertinent attribution"), it is "dead"; it is no longer creative and dynamic, and it can be put into a dictionary (thus the "leg" of a table was metaphorical once, but is now a dead metaphor since we do not even think of other "legs" when we use it).

Because the metaphor introduces this "semantic impertinence," as Ricoeur terms it, the original referent of the word becomes less obvious and new meaning breaks in. The suggested metaphor is either successfully understood and adopted into language, or it is discarded. So, the "eye of the storm" is helpful, but the "arms of the rain" does not really convey anything meaningful in our current worldview (though perhaps it will in some future era). The reader has to consider what a storm and an eye, or rain and arms, have in common; then decide whether our understanding of the event is expanded or not. Both are metaphors, but one is valuable and the other is not.

BAPTISM AS DYING AND RISING

We can now move on to consider the specific metaphor of baptism as dying and rising with Christ. Romans 6:3-6 gives us the image:

13. See Teselle, *Speaking in Parables* and McFague, *Metaphorical Theology*. Ricoeur refers to the paradox of metaphorical process as correlating sameness and difference ("Creativity in Language," 108), and discusses it extensively in Ricoeur, *Rule*: ". . . the wonderful 'It was and it was not,' which contains *in nuce* all that can be said about metaphorical truth," 265.

14. An example might be the difficulty of the non-computer generations to grasp newer technologies: the language is alien and the concepts remain hidden.

15. Ricoeur, *Rule*, 24-38.

> Do you not know that all of us who have been baptized into Christ Jesus were baptized into his death? Therefore we have been buried with him by baptism into death, so that, just as Christ was raised from the dead by the glory of the Father, so we too might walk in newness of life. For if we have been united with him in a death like his, we will certainly be united with him in a resurrection like his. We know that our old self was crucified with him so that the body of sin might be destroyed, and we might no longer be enslaved to sin.

One of the apostle Paul's recurring themes, indicated in this passage, is our new being "in Christ" (see Morna Hooker's discussion of our solidarity with Christ—sometimes termed the "interchange" theory).[16] This calling to believers to dwell intimately in the story of Jesus ("in Christ") is not just indicated in the various epistles as christological reflection on the cross and resurrection, but is present throughout the New Testament, including the gospels. For example, from Jesus's lips we hear the conceptual linking of baptism and death in his challenge to James and John: can they undergo the baptism he will undergo, or drink the cup that he will drink (Mark 10:35–44)? The good news of salvation requires us to indwell the entire story of Jesus, not a selection of highlights, and it is for this reason that I want to work with the dying and rising metaphor—it forces us into places we might prefer to avoid.

That was then; but this is now:[17] we are his followers today, and the question is therefore also posed to us in our own present. What does baptism as death and resurrection indicate for our modern journey of discipleship? I will offer here some thoughts with reference to the normal Baptist practice of immersion, although I recognize that there are good pastoral and practical reasons why candidates might sometimes not be immersed.[18] I will identify three features that I believe can be a countercultural witness to the power of transformation in Christ.

---

16. Hooker, "Interchange and Atonement," 26–41.

17. James McClendon's "Baptist vision" indicates that we take "the plain sense of Scripture as its dominant sense and recognize [our] continuity with the story it tells . . . [and] see past and present and future linked by a 'this is that' and 'then is now' vision," McClendon *Doctrine*, 45. See also Colwell's discussion of Jesus's story becoming our story, *Promise and Presence*, 121.

18. Barth suggests "One can hardly deny that baptism carried out as immersion . . . showed what was represented in far more expressive fashion than did the affusion which later became customary," *The Teaching of the Church*, 10.

1. BAPTISM IS A MULTISENSORY EXPERIENCE

Western culture is in thrall to sensation and experience. Extreme sports, gang behavior, heavy drinking/drug use and voyeuristic violence have all been identified as indicative of a fragmented society that lacks healthy mechanisms to deal with the deep human need for the transcendent.[19] This need in traditional societies is often met at key points of transition by appropriate ritual and liminal experiences, which for the West are in short supply now that most people do not practise any formal religion. Baptism responds to this liminal craving, the fascinating numinous hinterland between the transcendent and the material worlds. It is almost impossible, as a candidate or as a member of the congregation, not to be moved by a (credo-)baptismal service. For everyone present there are sounds and sights that speak of a special event; and, for the candidates, the feeling of being in deep water is powerful. Some people are truly afraid of water and of being "pushed" under, however well prepared they have been, and however gently it is done; and most people will experience a degree of anxiety as they wait for their turn. Indeed, as I write, the north of England and Scotland have experienced unprecedented levels of flooding (Christmas 2015), and the destruction reminds us that uncontrolled water is a serious threat—yet water is also life-giving, and in the baptismal pool, a sign of grace. Death and life are separated by a hair's breadth.

Haymes has written elsewhere about the significance of this fear—and how appropriate it is to experience it, if indeed baptism is a symbolic dying and rising again. Simply entering the water may often be a physical shock for the candidate. "Generally, for pastoral reasons, ministers work hard to set the candidates' fears aside. . . . We surround them with care and tell them that the water is warm and that everything will be all right. Might something be restored to baptism by keeping the water running, cold, such as takes breath away," he suggests.[20]

The New Testament is short on precise instructions for baptisms (hence the plurality of interpretations today). The *Didache*, on the other hand, does offer us some specific guidance: "But if you have no running water, baptize in other water; and if you cannot do so in cold water, then in warm" (*Didache* 7.2). In the twenty-first-century West, we inhabit a culture of safe domestication that, with all its regulation, somehow kills us with

---

19. For example, Rohr, *Everything Belongs*, 53. Turner in *The Ritual Process*, 193, discusses the important concept of "*communitas*"—the "at-one-ness" of a group, such as that found in the liminal phase of initiation. See also the discussion in Nelson, *Confronting Meaningless Suffering*, 141.

20. Haymes, "Baptism as a Political Act," 72.

inanity. Baptism has the possibility of reminding us that we *should* be rightly in awe of death; we *should* be glad to rise out of it, for it required nothing less than that the Son of God be tortured and crucified, to give his everything, to defeat this enemy of humanity. These reminders of dark power stir something deep within us that we often prefer to suppress with activity and consumables—but it needs to be stirred, for it is part of our human experience that we should die; and it is a healthy part of our human experience if sometimes we think of it and prepare for it.

There is also, of course, the death of self in another sense, for many approach baptism with some vestige of embarrassment, or at least self-consciousness—at the time of immersion, we have to make ourselves vulnerable in front of our brothers and sisters in Christ, and after the event we have to make ourselves vulnerable in sharing our witness in the world. "What did you do at the weekend?" "Well, I was baptized by total immersion." And so it begins. Our loyalties have changed and the old ones sink to the bottom of the pool, another necessary death. From this point we are irreversibly called to witness to our membership of the community of the baptized, whether or not we give it honor, as Barth would say.[21]

2. BAPTISM OFFERS US SIGNIFICANCE

Human beings always seek a coherent story in which to locate their own lives. Adriana Cavarero[22] discusses our driving "desire" for our own story, noting that at certain points of our own stories we are utterly dependent upon others for the narrative material (for example, the points of birth and death, which we cannot narrate for ourselves—and I would identify an added significance here for those with learning difficulties, since none of us is truly autonomous). McClendon understands theology as the work of the narrative community (i.e., the community with a significant story).[23] H. Richard Niebuhr considers the human need for a coherent narrative with a beginning and an ending;[24] while Ricoeur identifies our human sense of inner searching with our awareness of the conflict between what he terms human (lived) and cosmic (universal) time:[25] we become aware, as we develop, that after our own deaths there will be a continuing story (the cosmic story) in which we may personally be forgotten. A good story, one that en-

21. Barth, *The Teaching of the Church*, 59.
22. Cavarero, *Relating Narratives*, 1–4.
23. McClendon, *Doctrine*, 41.
24. See Niebuhr, "The Story of Our Life."
25. Ricoeur, *Time and Narrative*, chapter 4.

gages and enfolds us, and affirms our personal value, will always be a winner because we are made that way.

Ricoeur's analysis of metaphor led him to consider the nature of narrative, culminating in the 1980s in his three-volume opus, *Time and Narrative*. He identifies a function of narrative that is similar to metaphor—its ability to bring in the new—which narrative achieves by finding a "plot": "By means of the plot, goals, causes and chance are brought together within the temporal unity of a whole and complete action. It is this synthesis of the heterogeneous that brings narrative close to metaphor. In both cases, the new thing—the as yet unsaid, the unwritten—springs up in language."[26] The metaphor of dying and rising in baptism is part of the bigger narrative that invites us in and shows us something new.

Ellis discusses baptism as a sacramental act that reveals, among other things, something of "continuing incarnation." We live as enfleshed, embodied disciples in the world. The church and her rites embody an eschatological hope for all. Things can be better—things can be healed, redeemed—because our lives are now somehow enfolded into the life of Jesus. The sacramental use of bread, wine and water (material objects) tell us the story of salvation both as past act and future hope, linking creation (in the material objects) to redemption in visual and sensory acts of worship and proclamation. Chris sees the whole redemptive process as ongoing, with baptism as a focus. Baptism "may only be part of the whole, [but] it should never be referred to as 'only a sign' since it provides a lens through which the Spirit's activity may be viewed in the world and in the ongoing life of the church. Our understanding of the freedom of God is clarified when His activity in baptism is seen as a pointer to His activity elsewhere, as well as an example of that wide-ranging saving activity."[27]

The Christian practice of baptism by immersion offers an invitation into a story replete with imagery. There is water; there is a watching crowd; there are words of grace spoken over us. Then is now. We, today, "are" beside the Jordan, watching Jesus being baptized by John and affirmed by the voice from heaven: "*As Jesus to the Jordan came / So we have come to do the same*" in Ellis's story-hymn. The New Testament, argues Haymes,[28] always presents the life and ministry of Jesus as a radically new departure. We can see in the context of the present discussion that baptism is radically new, yet has continuity with the past. The sense of the new is endorsed as the older purification rite for proselytes is re-presented in the terms of the new

---

26. Ricoeur, *Time and Narrative*, vol. 1, ix.
27. Ellis, "Baptism and the Sacramental Freedom of God," 36.
28. Haymes, "Baptism as a Political Act," 69.

covenant: the opening of heaven, the outpoured Spirit, the voice of God speaking to God's people again, after centuries of apparent silence. God is among us! God is "accessible" in a way we have never imagined: *The word of God has been made flesh / For when he in the waters bathed / He shared the fate of those he'd save.* And here we have a metaphorical *act*—the old referent being used to point to something new.

The process of contextualizing our personal life stories by understanding them as part of a bigger, transcendent story, is essential to religious faith or indeed to any sense of *telos*, or significance to our existence. However, it is also inevitably distressing, since the process reveals painfully to us what we really are. We see ourselves at last as part of the bigger picture: part of the body, in relationship with Christ and our fellows; and we may not be what we had previously imagined. When we ask for and undergo baptism, we voluntarily identify with the cosmic story, which is in fact Everyman's story (we are "in Christ"), but is crucially also the story that every man/woman may not necessarily wish to own as theirs. Moving willingly from observer to participant in this story could be described as a key point of *metanoia*.[29] It is a metaphorical movement: we are and are not the same as we were before. The baptized person occupies this metaphorical space: s/he is both recognizable as the "old man" (the apostle Paul's term), yet also recognizable as the "new man" (in Christ). This baptized person has a revelatory role in the community—we could call that person a "spiritual Janus," looking both back and forward.

The only reason to be baptized is to respond to the divine invitation to participate in The Greatest Story. Being in this story meets our inner consuming desire for eternal significance, but comes at a cost, as we have described above. Being baptized with the baptism of Jesus means drinking the cup that Jesus drinks—and this may be more than we really feel we can handle. This challenge takes us to the next aspect of the metaphor of dying and rising.

3. THE ACT OF BAPTISM IS ABOUT CHANGED PRIORITIES

Christian life is shaped around Jesus Christ—indeed, it is shaped *like* Jesus Christ—not "a bit like," which pleasingly accommodates our compulsive

---

29. Niebuhr argues in "The Story of Our Life" that one cannot be both observer and participant, which is in agreement with relativity theory: that the presence of the observer affects the outcome. This area is also explored with respect to suffering in Nelson, *Confronting "Meaningless" Suffering*, 108.

consumerism—but "exactly like."[30] Fortunately for us, the body of Christ is our *corporate* identity; this *may* mean that not all of us are individually called to all of his sacrifice and all of his ministry: but that is not our decision. We do not always choose the journey of our discipleship; we merely follow it. Corporately we *will* experience all that Jesus experienced; although just because we can expect to undergo his baptism and drink his cup, it does not lessen the unique act of salvation that was—and is—his and his alone. We simply live faithfully according to his image or shape.[31]

The active and ongoing process of being so shaped is what we have historically understood as *metanoia*. It may mean a radical and obvious walking away from a sinful lifestyle; it may mean that we are open to being challenged more subtly by God in the hidden depths of the sinful being. *Metanoia* means setting our compasses towards God and not away from God; it is about personal and corporate transformation; it is active, not passive; it is journey, not destination. James Alison argues that in baptism we accept the death of our damaged "I," so that it "can start to be restructured from within by the One who forgives, and is towards others as God is. . . . Baptism presupposes the possibility of a radical restructuring of the 'self,' from within such that we become what humans were always meant to be, but are locked into resisting: bearers in the flesh of life, freedom and vitality of God."[32]

A single act of baptism does not equate to the whole process of *metanoia*. Baptism is a sacrament of grace and not a magical act, so the act of baptism does not necessarily initiate *metanoia*, even though baptism is generally recognized as an initiation into the redeemed community of Christ; and baptism definitely does not constitute *metanoia*, which has to be worked out in the daily or even hourly recommitment to Christ in the context of the life of an individual and community. However, perhaps we could argue that *metanoia* may necessitate hunger for baptism. Someone who wants to follow The Way of Jesus should normally be baptized, because

---

30. Ellis uses this language of the shape of Jesus in "Baptism and the Sacramental Freedom of God," 27.

31. This communal aspect is the way in which we hold our brothers and sister who may struggle with the "free and responsible" baptism of Barth's vision—I am thinking particularly of those with learning difficulty or speech and language issues. When we baptize, we usually include a form of words such as "I baptize you, at your own request and before this gathered community of God's people, in the name of the Father, Son and Holy Spirit". There is always a corporate commitment to this process of entry into the community of the baptized. We always hold one another; we enter this community of mutual exploration of personhood. Being able to say some stylized words at the right point is not the issue, and has never been a baptistic principle.

32. Alison, *Broken Hearts*, 171–72.

that is the shape of Jesus's life.³³ However, as John Colwell emphasizes, God is not imprisoned by the sacraments.³⁴ Although God has promised to be present in certain "places," most obviously baptism and the Lord's Supper (McClendon would add prophetic preaching), God is not confined to these and is free to act as God wills.

The act of baptism, then, is indicative of something: it indicates a willingness to travel the Jesus journey, to be "shaped into the Jesus shape"³⁵— though without being concrete about the nature of this shape, since we retain our personal identities.³⁶ It is indeed an initiation: but into a process of formation and change, not into a state; and into a process that occurs in community, because we learn most about our personal unholiness from the way we connect with others.³⁷ As individuals we become part of a baptized witnessing community—indeed, we cannot logically retain an untempered individuality in Christ. We do not stop being ourselves, but become ourselves in communion with others. Haymes has engaged with the individual-corporate poles of our Baptist life, identifying our modern tendency to individualism as a cause of weakness in our denomination. He comments, "Of course, believers' baptism affirms the essential personal response we are invited to make to the call of God but the calling and baptism is into the covenanted community of love in Christ, into the church of which Christ is head and Lord."³⁸

---

33. There are exceptions such as members of the Salvation Army, the Friends and other non-sacramental Christian groups.

34. Colwell, *Promise and Presence*, 125.

35. It might be helpful here to reflect on David Augsburger's discussion of discipleship as "reflecting" Jesus rather than trying to "repeat" his life—it means believing what Jesus believed and working out what that means. See Augsburger, *Dissident Discipleship*, chapter 1.

36. I think this approach may answer the difficulty about those with impaired cognitive function and the credo-baptist position. My own daughter has severe and complex needs, but is actively (in the sense of regular attendance) a part of a community that wants to be "on The Way." I do not see the need for her to articulate an independent commitment in her life of faith when she is utterly dependent on others in every other area of her life. She is unavoidably committed to community for even the smallest details. When considering her baptism we decided that because she is unable to speak and affirm her conviction, we would, as a community, reaffirm our baptismal promises together at that point. Her faith story would be shared in the form of testimony by other members of our community, who had seen faith in her. It might also be appropriate for the whole church to proclaim: "*We* baptise you . . . ," rather than the ministerial "I."

37. See McFadyen, *The Call to Personhood* for a discussion of the way in which our personhood is located through dialogue with God and with others.

38 Haymes, "Still Blessing the Tie that Binds," 98.

To be people "on The Way" is what God asks of us. What we encounter "on The Way" constitutes the precise nature of our calling, but the overall direction is deeper into God. The map and directions are given in the life of Jesus of Nazareth[39]—and yet they are not just map and directions, which we are objectively free to take up and put down. We are also initiated into a subjective union with Jesus, a depth of relationship that explodes our meager mental capacities. We do not undergo his baptism and drink his cup *because we have chosen to do so*, but because we are *"in him."*

Rites and rituals—and the practical and social elements of baptism do constitute a visible and tangible rite and ritual—are, as previously mentioned, the tools used by human communities to contain dangerous transitions so that the harmony and order of the community can be maintained.[40] The people in transition from one state to another occupy what is known as a "liminal" state, and are perceived as dangerous because they do not fit the normal structures and strata of the social group. So they are marked by the requirement of a ritual that facilitates their transition, and often by the sequestering of the liminal group while the transition and ritual is completed. So, for example, many primitive societies remove adolescents from the village and set a series of tasks or challenges, the end of which is to undergo a ritual marking their emergence as adult members. As noted earlier, Western society is rather impoverished in terms of such rituals, but an obvious example of a liminal group would be those who are terminally ill (in transition between life and death), who are marked by isolation from the community because we do not wish to be reminded so clearly of our mortality.

Baptism qualifies as such a transition ritual. The pool is indeed both "tomb and womb," as Ellis's hymn testifies. Those undergoing baptism are in transition from the old life to the new, from death to life. "Thus the believer rises from the water to live the resurrection life in the 'inbetween time,' between the ascension of Christ and his final coming in glory. Baptism gains its shape from the story of Jesus and its promise and challenge from the union with Christ of the believer who continues to live in the world that crucified Jesus."[41]

---

39. See John 14:1–6.

40. This material is covered in the classic anthropological studies, e.g., by Turner, *The Ritual Process* and Douglas, *Purity and Danger*.

41. Ellis, "Baptism and the Sacramental Freedom of God," 27.

THE COMMUNITY OF THE BAPTIZED

The community of the baptized, then, lives in a state of tension commonly understood as the "now but not yet." The community of the baptized lives as a people "on The Way," growing into Christ, yet already "in him." It lives as those who are part of the world that slew Jesus, yet who are also those who would serve him to the end.[42] Truly, the community of the baptized has "one foot in the grave," and could perhaps be described as a liminal community. We know that our churches have an eschatological character. We are marked by waiting, but this waiting should not be passive—rather an active yearning for and working for fulfillment: "[T]he goal of baptism . . . is one which looks beyond itself. . . . Its *telos* is transcendent, not immanent. . . . What was preached was not the bringing or representing of this coming One, but conversion towards him. . . . Baptism with water is a promise [which] points forward."[43]

It is no wonder that the community of the baptized is often identified as hospitable to the marginalized: liminal groups are sequestered for the good of everyone, after all! In the West, we have the ruins of Christendom all around us, and until recently there has been a general vague societal understanding and toleration of our status "on The Way." We have not yet been truly marginalized because of this Christendom legacy, although this socially constructed shadow of Christianity has little to do with union with Christ, undergoing his baptism and drinking his cup. Its loss might actually clarify the nature of baptism (if not its mechanism), and baptism's radical call to arms. The community of the baptized has the potential to become a mechanism of revelation within a hostile society: truly ethical, truly political, truly missional. The church herself dies and rises as a sign of eternal hope within the world; not just the individuals within her.

At this ending point I want to return briefly to thoughts about metaphor. Metaphors have a transitional quality: the "is and is not" of linguistic creative potential. They refer to the known but project it into the unknown and thus create—or reveal—something new. Metaphors are the stuff of the eschatological community: they bring into the field of vision that which is not yet, but which we know drives our deepest longings.

A person who has been baptized acquires this metaphorical character: s/he is and is not the same as before. S/he is a person who is part of a creative, dynamic process, a person on The Way. To return to my opening paragraph, Something Has Happened, and that Something is about stepping

---

42. Ellis, "Baptism and the Sacramental Freedom of God," 27.
43. Barth, *Church Dogmatics* IV/4, 70–71.

into the Jesus story. A person who has been baptized is and is not dead, just as Jesus is and is not dead. Jesus is resurrected (not revived, resuscitated, or reversed); he is full of new life. There is nothing that can stand against this divine creativity that brings life from death.

McClendon speaks of baptism as a *remembering* sign. When I am dying, and entering that in-between land from which there is no return, I hope that I remember the day of my baptism. I hope that I remember that I am already dead in Christ and yet alive in him too; that his resurrection, into which I am also baptized, will carry me like a highroad through the valley of shadow. Then is now; this is that. *Something has happened* in human time that reaches into the cosmic dimension.

> *We stand and sing what we believe*
> *That all in Christ new life receive.*

A Sign of Unity

The grain once scattered on the hills
Is gathered here in bread;
So may divided people come
And with one loaf be fed.

The bread is broken to be shared,
The love of Christ we see;
So love must now accept the cost –
In giving we are free.

The grapes once grown upon the hills
Are crushed within the cup;
The fruit of earth, the sweat of brow –
Thanksgiving offered up.

The peace we share is to be lived,
This meal gives energy,
To strive with hope and give the world –
A sign of unity.

We thank you Lord that still you share
Your life with us today;
So may communion be our style
In following your way.

8

"A Sign of Unity"
The Changing Theology and Practice of Lord's Supper amongst British Baptists

MYRA BLYTH

INTRODUCTION

THE OPENING WORDS OF this Communion hymn echo the Eucharistic prayer found in the first-century church manual, the Didache. That manual is the earliest comprehensive description of the way of life adopted by early Christian communities and it was an appeal for unity and order within the body of the church. Likewise, Paul's letters to the churches he founded sought to provide similar practical advice and guidance, and the Acts of the Apostles offered descriptions regarding community life in Jerusalem and in the churches of the diaspora.

Down the centuries, church manuals have often been produced with a similar intent to equip faithful living and the right ordering of the life of the worshipping community. Historically, though, attempts to make manuals normative, as in the 1662 *Book of Common Prayer*, have caused dissenters to shy away from written texts. They argued that prescribed liturgies, like "empty ritual," worked against the movement of the Holy Spirit in the hearts of believers. That said, texts such as early Baptist confessions, composed in response to accusations of heresy, were produced to explain and clarify theology and practice; their effect was to harmonize belief and practice within and between congregations.[1] By the eighteenth century, hymn texts were also important written sources for use in Free Church worship. Confessions and hymn texts supported Christian instruction and formation. During the twentieth century, manuals for ministers and those leading worship were published at regular intervals. These all have a descriptive rather than prescriptive function and, while not used by all ministers and leaders of worship, they have served to strengthen and equip, and to encourage unity and good practice across the churches of the Baptist Union.

This chapter surveys Baptist manuals for worship and, in particular, the orders or patterns for celebrating the Lord's Supper which have appeared since 1960, in order to see how Baptist Communion theology and practice have evolved, what factors may have influenced these developments, and what impact these developments have had for worship and polity. As well as both primary and secondary texts, my sources have included a number of one-to-one interviews with key individuals involved in the editorial teams. No less than four manuals for church worship have been published by the Baptist Union of Great Britain between 1960 and the present day.[2] Each of these has emerged in response to a felt need within the Union for guidance on orders for worship and on texts to enrich congregational prayer life. Commissioned but not official, these books have been described as aids to prayer and worship. In total they include as many as nine different orders for the celebration of the Lord's Supper.

In what follows, I will argue that Baptist views and practices around the Lord's Supper have changed in two respects. First, the content and practice of the Lord's Supper has expanded from a backward-looking memorial meal to a present- and future-oriented kingdom feast. There has been an ebb and flow between these two poles, determined by prevailing theologies and culture, and the interaction of the two. Second, particularly in the latter years, there has been a fresh focus on covenant theology and on the Lord's Supper as a covenant-renewing meal. Within the covenant theme, a prominent emphasis has been on unity within the body of Christ. This accent on

---

1. "From 1644 onwards the Particular Baptists issued a series of Confessions of Faith which stressed the conviction that unity in doctrine, polity and action was an important factor in being Church.... By the end of the 17th Century both General and Particular Baptists organized national assemblies at which the touchstone of acceptability was the agreed Confession," Hayden, "Baptists, Covenants and Confessions" in *Bound to Love*, 25.

2. *Orders and Prayers for Church Worship* (1960); *Praise God*, (1980); *Patterns and Prayers for Worship* (1990); and *Gathering for Worship: Patterns and Prayers for a Community of Disciples* (2005).

unity is not "the argument of the besieged ark—that in a hostile world we all need to keep together"[3] but, rather, that unity as God's covenant community is realized through relationship: when we walk together and watch over each other we embody Christ in the world.

The hesitancy Baptists feel towards printed texts has its roots in a dissenting spirit, which prefers extemporary style prayers. Written texts are felt to be counter-intuitive to free style worship. This concern is addressed in the introduction to each of the manuals. In different ways they all seek to reconcile the practices of extemporary and written prayers, and actively encourage extemporary prayer alongside the use of written texts. Respecting Baptist autonomy and freedom in worship, they offer written texts as an aid to preparation and a complement to extemporary prayer:

> In this book we have provided a large number of prayers both for the normal and for the special occasions of personal and church life. We do not envisage a Baptist minister reading all these prayers out of the book! There are indeed some occasions when it is fitting and helpful to read a prayer, but in general the prayers are intended to help the minister in (his/her) own preparation for free prayer. To study the ideal content of a prayer for a given occasion, can be of help in preparing both the sequence and the content of one's own free prayer.[4]

Notwithstanding the dissenting reservations about the use of written texts in worship, the publication of manuals gained momentum throughout the twentieth century, because those in leadership were convinced that texts enrich worship and help build unity within the body. Ironically, the case for written texts has not been won by theological argument but pragmatically, through the influence of popular culture and technology. In congregations today, for instance, songs, readings and prayers are often projected on to screens, along with visual images, and it seems that modern technology, creatively combining words with pictures, has won over the hearts and minds of Baptists where texts alone did not.

---

3. Fiddes, *Tracks and Traces*, 215.
4. Payne and Winward, *Orders and Prayers*, xv–xvi.

KEY DEVELOPMENTS IN BAPTIST COMMUNION TEXTS

Worship in Context

The worship manuals may be seen as a mirror on the story of Baptists within the twentieth century. Four phases unfold. The first reflects the confident ecumenical approach of church leaders in the post-war period, when they engaged pro-actively in unity talks and enthusiastically embraced the ideas for the renewal of worship inspired by the liturgical movement. The second reflects the impact of the 1960's spirit of revolution and change, when a growing number of ministers and churches became disillusioned with ecumenism and looked to leaders in the charismatic and church growth movements to help renew worship and mission. The third phase, a deeply contentious time, required the pastoral and peace-making spirit of Bernard Green (General Secretary of the Baptist Union, 1982–91) to hold the Union together. He skillfully united very diverse and fractious opinions. *Patterns and Prayers for Christian Worship* (1991), the manual published at the end of his term in office, embodies this consensual approach, seeking through worship texts to nurture unity in diversity. The fourth phase saw "worship wars" and theological divisions recede, and in their wake a new spirit of optimism and adventure emerged. Worship was enriched by both ancient and contemporary sources, which were playfully adopted and adapted to inspire missionary, incarnational and sacramental approaches. Baptists still "sit light" to written texts but the current texts are used and appreciated more widely than ever before.

Phase One:
Ordering Worship—Baptists and Liturgical Renewal

Orders and Prayers for Church Worship, edited by Ernest Payne and Stephen Winward, is a classic resource of high Baptist liturgy, entirely representative of Free Church worship in its time. The introduction is a beautifully crafted historical description of Baptist worship rooted in the Free Church tradition. It carefully elaborates the principles, which guided Baptist thought and practice from its beginnings. Ecumenical in spirit, it encourages ministers to treasure reformation principles and Baptist convictions, and also to embrace an emerging consensus within Western and Eastern Christianity on the shape and content of Christian worship. To that end, it draws inspiration from ancient sources and extensively borrows from the prayers of the church through the ages to inspire and deepen the prayer life of local

Baptists. It also breaks new ground by encouraging a new order for Sunday worship and commending the use of the lectionary for morning and evening prayers. Both of these proposals posed a strong challenge to operant practice in 1960 but they were defended by the compilers as consistent with Reformation principles and Baptist convictions.

In the section entitled, "Ordinances of the Church" (in the first edition), twenty outline orders of service are listed, two of which include the Lord's Supper. In the third edition, published in 1965, the presentation was revised and a new section entitled "Orders for Public Worship" was brought to the top of the contents list to give special place to the orders for the Lord's Supper, and for morning and evening prayers. Interestingly, there is no separate order for a Service of the Word, rather an Ordinance for the Lord's Supper is offered which combines the two. There is provision in the text for those not wishing to receive Communion to leave but the assumption that the word preached and the bread broken should be held together is beginning to be seen as the norm for Sunday worship. While this is discreetly implied rather than boldly stated in the ordinance text, the rationale for such an approach is clearly set out in the introduction:

> It is the combination of these two—synagogue and upper room, Scripture and sacrament, spoken word and visible word—which gives the complete pattern of Christian worship. It was this full diet that the great reformers endeavored to restore, a worship in which the "liturgy of the word" was consummated in the "Liturgy of the upper room." It is a departure from apostolic worship to celebrate the Lord's Supper infrequently or to regard it as a brief appendage following another complete service.[5]

For Baptists, the norm for celebrating the Lord's Supper has always been to turn to the words of the institution narrative as recounted in the Gospels or more often in 1 Corinthians 11. Payne and Winward maintain that tradition but a number of extra elements are added, such as offertory prayer, the *Sursum Corda*, the *Sanctus* and the *Benedictus*, plus a prayer of preparation followed by the prayer of thanksgiving. All of these additions significantly developed the shape and ethos of the Lord's Supper as practiced by Baptists.

Two sample thanksgiving prayer texts are offered, drawing on texts from the early church. The purpose behind this was not to discourage extemporary prayer but to encourage prayers—written and extemporary—modeled on prayer texts, which celebrate the story of redemption and recount the event of the cross from a past, present, and future perspective.

---

5. Payne and Winward, *Orders and Prayers*, xii.

They were seeking to correct a tendency in which the supper was reduced to a mere memorial of the event of Christ's death and lacked reference to the story of salvation, from creation to redemption, as well as a sense of joy in the presence of the Risen Christ and in the hopeful anticipation of feasting in the coming kingdom. At the heart of the thanksgiving prayer, words of remembrance (*anamnesis*) and words of invocation (*epiclesis*) are very intentionally used. There is a richness of the theology, as well as poetry and prose in these texts, which can easily be missed if put off by archaic language.

Mindful of the difficulties this thanksgiving prayer may present, the editors urge the reader to see the text not as a proposal to return to inflexible and fixed liturgy—from which the Reformation freed us—but as a challenge to "avoid that 'squalid sluttery' and uninspired disorder which comes from disregarding the traditional pattern and forms of Christian worship":

> Wherefore, O Father, commemorating the passion and death of thy son Jesus Christ, rejoicing in his resurrection and awaiting his advent, we thy servants do set forth this memorial according to his holy institution and commandment, giving thanks to thee for the perfect redemption which thou has wrought for us in him. | And we beseech thee to send down thy Holy Spirit, the Lord and giver of life, to sanctify us and these thy gifts of bread and wine, that the bread which we break may be the communion of the body of Christ and the cup which we bless the communion of the blood of Christ. Grant that we receiving these thy gifts in faith and love may receive Christ our Saviour anew into our hearts, and all together grow up in all things into him who is the Head . . . .[6]

Further, the provision of a two-year lectionary cycle for morning and evening prayers was a novel and controversial proposal because, as with written prayers, it challenged notions of freedom. Surely, argued the critics, a text should come to the minister inspired by the Spirit in the course of prayerful reading and preparation? The proposal is defended by the authors, however, by appealing to Baptist convictions and particularly to a high view of Scripture. They argue that God's Word needs to be studied with seriousness, and when freedom becomes license to read only what appeals to us then freedom is a curse rather than a blessing.[7]

It is often said by Baptists that this manual was written almost entirely by Winward and that Payne's contribution was moral and institutional,

---

6. Payne and Winward, *Orders and Prayers*, 150.
7. Ibid., xx–xxi.

encouraging Winward along in the task and giving the support of his name and office to the publication. Whether or not this is true, separate publications by both individuals, writing on the subject of the Lord's Supper show, that they shared many common concerns which are reflected in the manual.

In 1944, Payne wrote: "The Lord's Supper long had in the life of the local church a central position corresponding to that which the table itself occupied in the older meeting houses. The minute books of the seventeenth and eighteenth centuries contain many cases which show how exercised were the church members when one of their number failed to 'fill up his place at the Lord's table'"[8] Payne also had views on the specialness of the meal. His stance, as the following comment shows, was shaped by ecumenical discussions:

> Baptists no less than Christians of other traditions have regarded this as a specially sacred place and occasion. Baptists were not represented officially at the conference on Faith and Order at Lausanne in 1927. Had they been, it is likely that their spokesmen would have accepted the declaration that "the sacrament of the Lord's supper is the church's most sacred act of worship in which the Lord's atoning death is commemorated and proclaimed and that it is a sacrifice of praise and thanksgiving and an act of solemn self oblation," though they might have hesitated a little at accepting the word sacrament for some of their number have always been shy of the term.[9]

How, I wonder, should we interpret the current non-place of the Communion table in many Baptist churches today? I recall visiting a church recently where there was no Communion table, so the elements were perched precariously on top of hi-fi sound speaker. When the moment for Communion came, there was momentary confusion as to where the elements had been put, then, neatly spotted by a member from near the back row, the minister was able to reach up and retrieve them from their lofty position, everyone laughed and on we went! And what, precisely, exercises the minds of members today concerning participation in the meal? The issue is not—as in the eighteenth century—who is absent, but rather who is excluded. Those favoring the participation of children in Communion argue that we are all on a journey and table fellowship is there to nourish the seeker and the found. Those who take the opposite view lament that turning it into a "free for all" is losing the specialness of the meal!

---

8. Payne, *The Fellowship of Believers*, 58–59.
9. Ibid., 59.

I suspect that, given Payne's ecumenical stance and allowing for the direction of bilateral discussion today in which initiation is understood in terms of process rather than a single event, he would have had an open mind on the question of participation in the Lord's Supper. However, the absence of the centrality of the table (symbolically and actually) and a residual resistance to the term sacrament would be for him a much greater cause for concern. On the matter of sacrament, Payne wearied of those, such as Alexander McClaren, advocating aggressive forms of Zwinglianism.[10] From the pulpit, McLaren announced: "all our theories about the meaning and value of the communion service must be found with the four corners of that word . . . a memorial rite, and as far as I know, nothing more, nothing whatsoever."[11] Contra McLaren, Payne drew on the words of the eighteenth-century Baptist, Benjamin Beddome, appealing to his reader:

> . . . are not the words of Benjamin Beddome still true: "What are the outward means whereby Christ communicated to us the benefits of redemption? The outward and ordinary means whereby Christ communicated to us the benefits of redemption are his ordinances, especially the Word, Sacraments and Prayer, all of which are made effectual to the elect for Salvation." So (concludes Payne) "is not the Lord's Supper still rightly described as one of the 'effectual means of salvation'?"[12]

Payne argues as an historian and so draws heavily from Baptist history as well as the ecumenical movement for precedent. Winward, by contrast, was a local minister, passionate about worship. He wrote as a practitioner, and one for whom worship was honed Sunday by Sunday in his congregation. In *The Reformation of Worship*, published three years after the manual, Winward identifies with the sacramental language of the high reformers in which actions and the words together might be said to effect what they signify.[13] Thus he writes: "in the Eucharist there are four actions: taking, thanking, breaking and giving (Mark 14:22, 23). Together with the appropriate words it is by the performance of these fourfold actions that we, the church, 'do the Eucharist.'"[14] He explicitly speaks of the sacrament of the Lord's Supper and argues for a theology of sacrifice as central to the meal. The meal is more than a memorial; it is an act of consecration. He suggests that there are

10. Ibid., 68.

11. Ibid., 69 citing McLaren, *A Year's Ministry,* First Series (1884), 101.

12. Ibid., 70, citing Benjamin Beddome, *Scriptural Exposition of the Baptist Catechism* (1752), Quest XCIII.

13. Winward, *The Reformation of our Worship*.

14. Ibid., 70.

two senses in which sacrificial language ought to be used at the table of the Lord: "It is a sacrifice of praise and thanksgiving, . . . especially in the prayer of thanksgiving offered over the bread and the loaf, and . . . in response to the mercies of God in Christ, the worshippers offer themselves to God."[15]

The prayer which is suggested in the manual for use as a prayer of preparation and approach immediately before the prayer of thanksgiving is a particularly good example of Winward's emphasis upon consecratory and sacrificial theology. The prayer originates from the Eucharistic liturgy of the Church of South India.[16] Its function in that liturgy is to conclude the offertory actions, i.e., the collection, together with the bread and wine, are brought forward to the table, where an offertory or consecratory prayer is then said. The first part is read by the minister:

> Holy Father, who through the blood of thy dear Son hast consecrated for us a new and living way to thy throne of grace, we come to thee through him, unworthy as we are, and we humbly beseech thee to accept and use us and these our gifts for thy glory. All that is in heaven and earth is thine, and of thine own do we give to thee. Amen.

After these words, the congregation then pray:

> Be present, be present, O Jesus, thou good High Priest, as thou wast in the midst of thy disciples, and make thyself known to us in the breaking of the bread, who livest and reignest with the Father and the Holy Spirit, one God, world without end. Amen.[17]

Curiously, Winward only uses the congregational half of the prayer, but still he places it in the moment of the offertory, presumably with the intention to make this prayer of approach a consecratory act. The invocation, "Be present, be present, Jesus," stresses the notion that the meal is not mere memorialism and the address to Jesus as "thou good high priest" highlights Christ's priestly role and the sacrificial character of the meal. The subsequent plea to "make thyself known to us in the breaking of bread" further accentuates the sacramental and the mystical dimension to the meal. This prayer, in adapted form, can be found in the current Anglican service book, *Common Worship*, in the section entitled prayers for the preparation of the table.[18] It did not however make its way into *Praise God* (1980) nor any subsequent Baptist manual.

15. Winward, *The Reformation of our Worship*, 71.
16. Church of South India, *The Service of the Lord's Supper*.
17. Ibid., 11. For more on this prayer See Porter, "Be Present, Be Present," 158–59.
18. *Common Worship*, 292.

In summary, then, it is very apparent when comparing their separate writings on the Lord's Supper that Winward and Payne complemented one another. While Payne's contribution to the manual may practically have been little more than personal encouragement and institutional support, it is clear that this book was conceived through their common reflection and common convictions about worship, and the result was a book which is more sacramental and liturgically "high Baptist" than any manual that has followed.

Phase Two: Contemporizing Worship—Struggles within the Union

In 1980, twenty years on from the first edition of *Orders and Prayers for Church Worship*, a new publication entitled *Praise God* was produced, jointly prepared by Alec Gilmore, Michael Walker, and Edward Smalley. The work was divided up between the editors and, as Alec Gilmore recalls: "we basically respected each other's views so that while we would offer comments on each other's work it was left to the one who wrote the text to adapt and amend as they saw fit."[19] In the division of labor, Michael Walker was assigned to select and organize the prayers while Alec Gilmore complied the liturgies for communion, marriage, and infant presentation.

Massive changes within church and society, in the twenty years following the publication of *Orders and Prayers*, caused the compilers of *Praise God* to resist the idea of simply producing a further re-vision of the text, even though Winward had granted them permission to change it as they saw necessary. In the introduction, Gilmore notes that to emphasize ordinance or orders at this point would have been out of keeping with the zeitgeist. A new approach was needed. People did not want one book; they wanted choice, variety, and flexibility. The hunger for new Bible translations, as well as vibrant experimentation and innovation in music and the arts, was changing worship beyond recognition, not just in Baptist congregations, but also across the churches. The clear commitment of the editors of *Praise God* to support and encourage innovation was demonstrated by designing the book as a prayer resource, more minimalist in the range of service orders to be included, more inclusive and contemporary in its use of language, and more eclectic in its use of Bible translations.

There was significant continuity, however, on the liturgical level. Consistent with Payne and Winward, the book builds on two key achievements of the liturgical renewal movement: first, the affirmation of the service of

19. Myra Blyth, "Interview with Alec Gilmore" (March 2016).

word and sacrament as normative for Sunday worship and, second, the place of the church calendar in shaping worship on a daily, weekly and seasonal basis. Both of these developments were, in the minds of the editors, completely compatible with a more open, participatory and experimental approach to worship so popular at the time.

The outline for the celebration of the Lord's Supper in *Praise God* was a much simpler structure in comparison to Payne and Winward. For example, the words of the *Sursum Corda* remained but the *Benedictus* and the *Sanctus* are removed; as is also the offertory prayer from the church of South India. This minimalist approach was driven by Gilmore's strong conviction about the need to use plain and accessible language: "only when you put something into today's language can you understand what something is. Our language must be down to earth and thereby understandable." On this point, Gilmore has been utterly consistent. There was a second, less articulated, motivation for plain language which might also explain the absence of more sacramental prayers like the offertory prayer previously noted in Payne and Winward. There can be little doubt that the offertory prayer was intended by Payne and Winward to support a more sacramental and sacrificial understanding of the meal, or that *Praise God* left it out, not just in the interests of contemporizing the text but to reflect the theological turn within the Union away from sacramental theology in the second half of the twentieth century. What appears instead in *Praise God* and in subsequent manuals are Prayers of Preparation which focus on human unworthiness, and on the need to hear words of forgiveness followed by God's gracious invitation.

Back in 1963 (contemporaneous with Winward's publication *The Reformation of Our Worship*), Gilmore authored a chapter in a publication, entitled "Baptist Churches Today and Tomorrow," in which he outlined the essential features of the service of word and sacrament. Significantly, concerning the offertory, Gilmore writes:

> The offertory needs special attention because what we are pleased to call the offertory has degenerated in too many instances to a collection. . . . The original intention of the offertory and its place in the liturgy is quite different: it is the symbol of the response and dedication of the people and in its earliest times consisted not only of cash, but also of the elements of communion presented at this point by the members of the church . . . at this point there stands before God his own chosen people, newly summoned forgiven and dedicated and therefore ready to fulfil their priestly function.[20]

20. Gilmore, "Baptist Churches Today and Tomorrow," 121–22.

There is no hesitancy here about the place and function of the offertory prayer. It is cast in sacrificial and consecratory terms. But that was the early sixties. *Praise God* was penned nearly two decades later at a point when, Gilmore recalls, he was beginning to question his theology and practice of the Lord's Supper. Conceiving the meal in mystical language was not consistent with the necessity for plain speech. To this day he says:

> I am still troubled by the language we use around communion. I am not content just to say something is a mystery, and leave it at that, I want to know what we are talking about. We shouldn't get hung up about how bread and wine convey the mystical presence of Christ, rather we need to see how bread and wine point to the staple things of life; we need symbols that help us to make connections with life. In some ways the *agape* meal with its focus on generous hospitality feels to me to be more relevant and accessible.[21]

Ironically, perhaps, by virtue of Gilmore and Walker allowing each to do their task unhindered, the plain speech of Gilmore and more mystical sacramental language of Walker co-exist in *Praise God*. Gilmore's minimalist approach sheds the more archaic, exotic and mystical elements found in Payne and Winward but, at the same time, at key points in the text a generous cross-referencing system directs the reader to a rich feast of optional prayers, compiled by Walker, many of which are seasonal and more mystical in character. *Praise God* was a genuine response to the need of the time for more contemporary words in worship. It sought to encourage innovation and creativity but, at the same time, to reflect ecumenical consensus by further encouraging the integration of the Lord's Supper into regular worship and accentuating appropriate theological variations in the words used at the table according to the times and seasons in the year.

Despite the significant contemporizing that went into *Praise God*, the reception of the publication was mixed. Two factors may serve to explain this. The first factor, as the editor's had rightly perceived, was that the climate in the denomination at this time was not right for another book of orders and prayers. But the book was sensitive to the climate and progressive in its appeal for innovation and experimentation, so I would suggest that ambivalence about another book was not the only reason for its disappointing reception. The climate of ill-feeling and suspicion within the denomination at this time was intense, fuelled by a potent cocktail of "worship wars" and worries over charismatic splits and numerical decline. The charismatic movement was attracting a growing number of ministers, who believed

21. Myra Blyth, "Interview with Alec Gilmore" (March 2016).

that a more free-flowing style of Spirit-filled worship would be the answer to church decline. Given this climate of suspicion and division, I would suggest that a second factor contributing to the disappointing response to *Praise God* might have been more personal and political.

In an article entitled "Baptist worship in the 20th century," Michael Walker made clear his views on the charismatic movement. On the positive side, he noted approvingly that in Roman Catholic and Baptist churches alike: "there has been enrichment as the charismatic movement has gained ground and influenced many of our churches in different ways."[22] Among Baptists, for example, he cited the new interest "towards Catholic brothers and sisters who have embraced the second blessing and still cherish the Eucharist as central to their worship" and also "a renewed emphasis upon congregational participation in ways which reach far beyond the ordered responses of the earlier liturgical renewal movement."[23]

Alongside this appreciation, however, Walker presents a withering analysis of what he perceived to be the negative impact of the charismatic and church growth movements. He cited three problems in particular: "the rapid decline in biblical scholarship, formerly prized highly by evangelicals generally and Baptists in particular; the rise in authoritarianism and fundamentalism, and the uncritical adoption of a culture of consumerism which designs and measures worship according to feel good factors." Impassioned and frustrated as to the direction of the tide, he wrote: "The extent to which we have departed from the Reformation tradition was evidenced in the 1980 Nottingham assembly where, from the public platform, ministers were counseled to pay less attention to preaching and more to congregational management on the grounds that 'anyone can get up and spout.' From this astonishing description of preaching no one dissented."[24]

Given the tense climate of feeling and suspicion within the denomination at this time, Walker's strongly held views and the ecumenical sympathies of the editors of the *Praise God* publication probably did not bode well for its reception amongst the growing number of ministers committed to charismatic renewal and hungry for change in the leadership and direction of the Union.

---

22. Walker, "Baptist Worship in the 20th Century," 28.
23. Ibid., 28.
24. Ibid., 29–30.

Phase Three:
Reconciling Worship—Searching for Unity in Diversity

The appointment of Bernard Green as General Secretary in 1982 represented a move to build bridges within an increasingly fractious denomination. The backdrop to his term of office was an overwhelming preoccupation with numerical decline, complicated by multiple cross-cutting issues: social, theological, pastoral, and ecumenical. It was his pastoral and personal skills which helped to steer the Union into calmer waters.

The publication of *Patterns and Prayers* came near to the end of Green's term as General Secretary and, in terms of process and content, this project was paradigmatic of his leadership of the Union. Green was keen, along with others, to see a full replacement to the Payne and Winward edition, which increasingly felt dated and underused by ministers. Correspondence between Keith Jones (YBA) and Green suggests there was not just enthusiasm for, but increasing agitation for, a new manual to replace Payne and Winward.[25] *Praise God*, it was felt, did not sufficiently reflect the diversity of worship styles in the Union and, hence, a broad-based worship and comprehensive resource was mandated in 1988 by the General Purposes and Finance Committee and by the BUGB Council. A six-person editorial group convened by the General Secretary was tasked with the job. In the introduction to *Patterns and Prayers*, Green sets out clearly that the express hope was to create a book that would serve to bring together and unite the Union at a time when worship was increasingly diverse and at times divisive:

> There is now a wide variety of practice, from liturgical formality to charismatic exuberance, from reformed traditionalism to ecumenical experiment. In such a context and in response to widespread demand it has been judged that a new guide for leaders is needed.[26]

Commensurate with this aim, a significant feature of the publication is its pastoral, pedagogical and ecumenical spirit. It has a distinct conciliatory and inclusive tone. First, to bridge the divide between "liturgical formality and charismatic exuberance," it does not speak of orders and ordinances but of "patterns" and resources, stressing again and again the scope for choice, creativity and variation. Second, to win the confidence of a diverse constituency, the editorial process was extremely consultative, with all the material extensively field tested and revised in response to comments received.

---

25. Keith Jones, Letter to Bernard Green, 20th July 1987. Regent's Park College, Oxford: Angus Library and Archive.

26. *Patterns and Prayers for Worship*, v.

Third, whereas *Orders and Prayers* was subtitled a manual for ministers, and *Praise God* used the rubric of minister in the texts even while noting that this was for convenience and should not exclude others, the target audience for this book was explicitly "leaders of worship."

The introductory chapter, on Christian worship, strikes an optimistic note about the changes to worship in the late twentieth century. The developments in both the ecumenical movement and the charismatic movement are affirmed and celebrated as positively influencing Baptist life; the historical evangelical stance of Baptists is re-affirmed; and the urgent missional challenge to make worship socially and culturally relevant is boldly stated:

> The fact that at the present time the charismatic and ecumenical movements have influenced many Baptist churches has led to wide diversity of practice and preference. Indeed, it is true to say that Baptists historically represent an evangelical commitment to Word and sacrament, a catholic emphasis on tradition and fellowship, and a charismatic stress on gifting and participation. To that must be added the need for worship to be culturally relevant, since increased numbers of new adult converts have no previous experience of Sunday school or church.[27]

The section on planning worship places great emphasis on basic patterns and much less stress on content and text. In the section on the Lord's Supper the word "sacrament" is avoided and three patterns, rather than three orders, are offered to resource diverse stances: the first pattern offers the most basic minimalist outline; the second reflects the ecumenical pattern adopted in previous manuals; and the third seeks to give an outline shape to a more free-flowing charismatic approach.

In the first pattern, words of invitation and words of institution are offered, followed by the distribution of bread and wine. In the skeletal outline of this service, there is a note about the prayer of thanksgiving just before the distribution in which the content it should include is sketched, but in the full script for this pattern neither a sample prayer of thanksgiving nor even the rubric reminding of the content and purpose of this prayer is offered. This is indicative of the compromise sought in *Patterns and Prayers*, where the basic objective was to establish a pattern, and this took precedence over some of the liturgical details like the thanksgiving prayer. The second pattern, uses modern language and offers examples of thanksgiving prayers while still encouraging extempore prayer at every point. The goal of the editorial team, to achieve "charismatic exuberance and liturgical formality," was arrived at through a meticulous balancing of patterns.

---

27. *Patterns and Prayers for Worship*, 4.

A point of innovation in the second pattern, is the sharing of the peace. This is today a regular feature at the Lord's Supper but was novel at this point. In the text, the act of sharing the peace begins with words from the Didache, the same words that inspired Chris Ellis's communion hymn: "As the bread once scattered over the hills, was brought together and became one loaf, so Lord may your church be united and brought together from the ends of the earth into your Kingdom."[28] This is followed with three optional responses for leader and congregation before the one presiding invites members to take time to greet one another.

The act of sharing the peace is perhaps the most innovative development in the Communion text in *Patterns and Prayers*. It is a good example of the way freedom and order embrace one another and, whilst not uncontroversial across the Union, it is now a regular feature in the Lord's Supper which can take two minutes or twenty minutes, or anything in between! Peace within the denomination, like peace in the Communion, was being realized through a creative tension between order and spontaneity.

Phase Four:
Re-imagining Worship—Time to Play

Gathering for Worship, like its predecessors, is a product of its time. The mood in the denomination at the start of the twenty-first century, when work on this book began, was much more buoyant than ten years before when *Patterns and Prayers* was published. The Baptist Assembly—having grown to a three-day event with over 2,000 people attending—showcased the denomination to itself as well as to the world. There was a popular perception that things were on the up, even if numbers did not say more than decline was being arrested! Old tribal divides between evangelical and liberals, or conservatives and charismatics had little or no currency value. While traditionalists still grieved the loss of "treasured hymns" and "dignity in worship," the overall mood was mission positive and the approach to worship very eclectic. The editors of *Gathering for Worship* were keen to tap into this ethos and produce a resource that celebrated spontaneity within a framework.

The prevailing theological idea which undergirds the book, is that of worship as a journey in which God gathers us for worship (around word and table) and sends us out into the world refreshed and renewed for mission.[29] The core shape to the Lord's Supper texts, reflecting the ecumenical consen-

28. *Patterns and Prayers for Worship*, 84.
29. Ellis and Blyth, *Gathering for Worship*, 4–11.

sus, consists of four actions: receiving, thanking, breaking and sharing, but within that shape the seven Lord's Supper texts provide huge variations in style and thematic content. Including so many Lord's Supper texts was an intentional statement from the editors about the central place and meaning of Communion in worship. In contrast to *Patterns and Prayers*, and because the climate and context had changed, *Gathering for Worship* unapologetically offered many written prayers, either to be used as printed in the orders or, alternatively, taken as inspiration for those who want to offer prayer extemporaneously. In the years since *Patterns and Prayers* was published, considerable innovation and experimentation has occurred around the theology and practice of the Lord's Supper and, without making too many claims for the centrality of Communion in Baptist life, there are signs of more experimentation and more serious reflection in congregations on the meaning and practice of the meal.

New interest in written prayers and texts amongst Baptists noticeably grew during the nineties. In part, charismatic streams of renewal due to the enormous hunger for worship and prayer inspired this, but at the same time, a new hunger for prayer and spirituality drawing on ancient contemplative sources became popular in congregations and in private spiritual devotions. Movements like the Iona community and the Northumbrian community furnished this. Their ancient-modern contemplative style of prayer and worship offered a holistic approach, integrating prayer and praise with a strong passion for justice in the world and for ethical integrity in the life of Christ's followers. This fresh source of holistic renewal is very much reflected in the Lord's Supper texts, which explore the potential of the meal for nurturing justice, reconciliation, mission, and discipleship.[30] The meal is not a somber memorial, akin to a funeral, but a meal to re-member the events of Christ's death and to participate through his death in the re-membering of broken lives and relationships in the here and now. It is also a future-oriented eschatological feast, which celebrates God's kingdom of justice and righteousness. This present tense encounter with the Risen Christ avoids Reformation arguments about real presence and celebrates instead the promise of Christ coming to us in bread and wine through the ministry of the Holy Spirit. The meal is a dynamic place of nourishment, healing, reconciliation, and transformation. The texts enthusiastically draw upon ancient and contemporary ecumenical sources as well as upon Baptist tradition, past and present.

During the 1990s when David Coffey and Keith Jones provided a strong and dynamic leadership of the Union, there was considerable energy for ecclesial renewal motivated by the desire for the structures and

---

30. See ibid., 12–48.

activities of the entire Baptist Union to be "mission shaped." This process was accompanied at times by theological debate around Baptist identity and, particularly, the meaning and significance of covenant theology for denominational identity.

Covenant theology featured strongly in early Baptist life but faded from prominence between 1850 and 1985.[31] The language of covenant as used in early Baptist confessions reflected the separatist heritage, conceiving covenant in two dimensions, vertical and horizontal, a solemn agreement with God and with each other. Covenant making, rooted in the scriptural tradition, where God made a covenant with his people, found a fitting climax at the Lord's table where Christ identified the cup as the sign of the new covenant, sealed by his blood. According to his instructions the old covenant is remembered and replaced when—as he did with his disciples—we share bread and wine.

The covenant service in *Gathering for Worship* echoes the fourfold shape of worship, which runs as a leitmotif through the whole book: gathering, around word and table, and sending. The theme of covenant, or as Calvin called it "the eternal covenant of grace," is woven into each movement of the text reflecting both the unconditional and the conditional aspects of covenant making found in Scripture. Unconditionally, we receive the comfort and nourishment of bread and wine mediated to us by the Holy Spirit and experience the grace necessary to kindle and sustain covenant love. Conditionally, as the community of those baptized into the body of Christ, the church (local and universal; individual and corporate), we seek to re-member and embody his covenant love in all relationships, with those near and those far off.

This brief survey of Baptist Communion texts has revealed traces of continuity and innovation within the Baptist worship manuals produced over sixty years. While not used by all, these texts have had a pedagogical function, influencing many ministers and congregations as they gather around the word and table to be faithful witnesses to God's saving work. The communion meal is now integral to the service of the word in most if not all Baptist churches and is increasingly inclusive and celebratory in mood. The Lord's Supper texts in *Gathering for Worship* show a desire to draw on a range of communion themes from within Scripture that can build up the fellowship and lead to committed discipleship. The covenant service is one particular example of this. The orders also reflect the growing consensus

---

31. 1985 was significant because it saw the beginning of a recovery of covenant through the work of Paul Fiddes and others. See Fiddes (ed.), *Bound to Love* and then later documents, e.g., Kidd (ed.), *Something to Declare*.

ecumenically around the shape of worship, the development of Communion thanksgiving prayers, and the sharing of the peace.

THE IMPACT OF CHANGING COMMUNION THEOLOGY AND PRACTICE

In this section, the changing emphasis, over the last sixty years, in Baptist Communion theology and practice will be analyzed. It will become apparent that the developments have served the twin goals of mission and unity both within the Union and in relations with other Christian traditions. Three examples will illustrate this. First, current Communion practice has re-opened an old ecclesial question, namely who is welcome to the table? The gradual trend towards ever more open table fellowship has been supported by new insights into what it means to belong to the church. Second, Baptist identity has been enriched by re-discovering covenant theology as foundational to our understanding of what it means to be church. Congregations, associations and colleges covenanting within the Union do not behave as a secular voluntary organization, but an ecclesial communion, which, gathered by God, is blessed by the Spirit indwelling their words and actions in worship and in the world. Third, fresh thinking around *koinonia* (community) and communion has enabled two very different ecclesial bodies—Baptists and Roman Catholics—to speak as one.

Open Communion: A Generous Hospitality

The question, "how open is the table?" has long challenged Baptists. In 1949, the General Purposes and Finance Committee asked the Principals" conference to "draw up a statement concerning the Communion Service, what it means to us, what principles it involves and its proper observance in order that our churches may have some guidance on this very important matter." It directly addresses the questions of the relationship of the Lord's Supper to church membership and the question of open and closed communion, i.e., is the table open to those in membership of other churches who practice infant baptism? The statement is quite adamant that membership should precede participation because it is a meal "reserved for avowed Christians."[32] At the same time, the report advocates an openness to those in membership of other churches. It affirms the Baptist conviction about baptism of be-

---

32. Child, *The Lord's Supper*, 29.

lievers being the New Testament practice, but it appeals to those inclined to refuse Communion to those from other churches on the grounds that their baptism is not valid, with these words: "after 1900 years of Christian history it is impossible to maintain that God has owned and blessed only one particular type of Church order or one particular form of ministry. We know that is not so and that multitudes of Christian men and women who have not received believer's baptism but were christened in infancy have yet manifested in their lives those fruits of the Spirit which our Lord has told us are the real test of Christian discipleship (Mt 7:15–20)."[33] It likens the challenge facing the church today to that which Peter faced in Acts 10 when he discovered God bringing into the Church those whom he had been taught were unfit! Surely we ought, like Peter, to say now "the Lord's table belongs to Christ alone, . . . we therefore welcome to it in his name all who sincerely love him no matter to what branch of his church they belong."[34] In the late twentieth century, as the link between Communion, baptism, and membership further blurred, a much more generous and inclusive approach was increasingly adopted not just towards Christians of other traditions, but also towards children in the church and towards those seeking but not yet committed in the faith. In other words, the function of the meal was seen to be both pedagogical and missional; not just a meal for those who are mature in faith but also as nourishment on the way for the young and the enquiring.

A recent Baptist Union publication, *Gathering Around the Table*, seeks at a popular level to help congregations think through the place of children at the table, arguing from Scripture for a more open and inclusive approach.[35] Three main points are drawn from Scripture. First, the link between the Passover (a family gathering) and Jesus' last meal with his disciples, may suggest that the tradition is more family friendly than we have perhaps allowed. Second, the many meals Jesus shared with outcast and sinners challenges us to think again about whether table fellowship should be less bounded than formerly has been the case. Third, in the context of Paul's writings to the Corinthians, on the problem of eating unworthily, the authors note that Paul is specifically concerned about the manner in which the meal is conducted, accentuating divisions amongst people. In other words, for Paul, "right relationships is a fundamental basis for right participation in the Lord's Supper."[36] The issue today may not be between rich and poor, as it was in Corinth, but generational, between adults and children.

33. Child, *The Lord's Supper*, 33.
34. Ibid., 34.
35. See *Gathering Around the Table*.
36. Ibid., 19.

Add to this Jesus' teaching on the child as close to the kingdom, having a disposition that is open, vulnerable, and dependent on God, and the case towards greater inclusion has become compelling. Does our theology of the child and our practice of Communion accentuate division and, if so, does this constitute "eating unworthily"? With these arguments, we begin to see why the manuals have encouraged more careful thought and preparation for infant dedication or infant presentation services. If children are born into the kingdom, then their place in the church as children is not token but real. The journey from belonging in the church as a child of the kingdom to belonging as a committed believer is now conceived as a journey of initiation, which culminates in baptism and membership.

The pastoral outworking of this theology of initiation or Christian beginnings still leads Baptists to different conclusions. Some maintain that baptism, membership, and Communion should remain on a clear continuum, while others argue by degrees for Communion to aid the journey into committed discipleship.[37] The invitations to the table in the worship manuals show that congregational practice has become progressively more open. From Payne and Winward onwards, all stress that the table of the Lord is open to those who love him, but by the time of *Gathering for Worship*, the broadening tendency has moved towards including the inquirer who desires to know more and the child who has not reached a stage of committed discipleship.[38]

Covenant Communion:
Rediscovering the Nature of our Unity in the Union

During the final two decades of the twentieth century and up to the present day the Union has been in a process of radical restructuring, equal in scale, but opposite in design to the re-structuring instituted at the turn of the previous century by the then General Secretary, Howard Shakespeare. The current transition has significantly revised the way the Union feels and functions: de-centralizing the national structures, and investing in new ways of associating on all levels of the Union. In the course of this prolonged and sometimes painful transition, it was apparent that theological reflection on our identity and self-understanding as Baptists was required. So, with this need in mind, in 1997 four of the college principals collaborated together

---

37. See Goodliff, *To Such as These*.

38. See *Gathering Around the Table*, 31–51. Cf. Clarke, "A Feast for All?" esp. 94–99, 116.

to produce a document called *On the Way of Trust*.[39] It grew out of their personal commitment to one another and as representatives of their colleges to live out their covenant relationship with the Union. The publication set out a theology of covenant based on biblical and historical precedent, and argues that a covenantal approach—or the way of trust—is at the root of Baptist ecclesiology. Their appeal was for a renewal of covenant theology to revitalize the basis upon which the Union is held together.

The Union, they argued, should not be understood in simple sociological terms as a voluntary association of local churches, associations and colleges, but in biblical terms as a solemn covenant between God and his church, manifested through local churches, regional associations, and theological colleges covenanting together under the rule of Christ to walk with each other and to watch over each other.[40] Given the radical restructuring that has been pursued throughout the first decade of the twenty-first century their plea has proven to be prophetic. Partly in response to their appeal, a Lord's Supper text entitled *Covenant 21* was published by the Union in 2000.[41] It was used as the Communion text at the Baptist Assembly that year and then offered to churches and associations to encourage covenant renewal at all levels of Baptist life. The conviction of the college principals was that, just as God's covenant promise proved sufficient to renew and restore Israel in fragile times, so division within and between God's people today can be healed and restored through the bonds of covenant love.

Because unity today is less and less underpinned in the Union by the legal and financial models that were developed in the twenty-first century, the appeal to covenant faithfulness is crucial.[42]

Ecclesial Communion:
Speaking as One—Baptists and Roman Catholics

Baptist interest in covenant theology has also proven fruitful in recent Baptist-Roman Catholic dialogues.[43] A report published in 2015, *The Word of God in the Life of the Church*, points to the way communion ecclesiology (*koinonia*) and covenant ecclesiology (the way of trust) together provide rich language for Baptists and Catholics to speak as one. Communion eccle-

---

39. Kidd, *On the Way of Trust*, 18–19.
40. Ibid.
41. See *Covenant 21*.
42. It is encouraging to see the recent edition of Union's magazine *Baptists Together* (Spring 2016) dedicated to concept of covenant.
43. "The Word of God in the Life of the Church," 28–122.

siology, as the report acknowledges, is not a term with which Baptists are particularly familiar, and in truth the term has not really reached the grass roots in any tradition. On the level of theological dialogues, however, it has many advocates. In the early to mid-twentieth century, it was a particularly important concept for Roman Catholics and resulted, following Vatican II, in a renewal of lay participation in the worship and ministry of the Catholic Church. Since then, it has found a prominent place in ecumenical discussions and has been enthusiastically adopted by Western Protestant theologians. In essence, ecclesial communion understands the church in relational rather than structural or institutional terms. The stress on communion or fellowship is rooted in a theological vision of God as Trinity. God relates to God's self—Father, Son, and Holy Spirit—in community. The church, by the will of the Father, through the mediation of the Son, and in the power of the Holy Spirit, is drawn into the Divine movement of love that exists within God.

Critics of this theology consider the approach to be too mystical, remote, and detached from the church as a historical reality. Hans Küng has criticized Catholic theologians such as Mahler, Newman, de Lubac, and von Balthasar for their romantic portrayals of the church, accusing them of "idealizations, mystifications, and glorifications, which have no effect on the Roman system."[44] But supporters of this Trinitarian approach (including Orthodox, Catholics, and Protestants) insist that *koinonia* is a biblical term that holds apparent opposites in creative tension. The church is invisible and visible, local and universal, perfect and flawed, present gift and future promise. What we experience in the visible church is, therefore, an existing but imperfect communion. Christians in their divided and flawed state are bound together in an imperfect communion through their common participation in the life of the Trinity. The Baptist statement of 1949, quoted earlier, anticipates this idea of *koinonia* without using the term. It is also important—in the context of this article on Communion texts—to note how the report links *koinonia* to Eucharistic fellowship in the context of the Lord's Supper:

> Communion with the triune God and with the whole church of Christ is continually actualized in the Eucharist/Lord's Supper. In the celebration, those participating are sharing communion not only with each other in the local congregation, but with the whole church of Christ in time and space. "Because there is one bread, all of us share in one body" (1 Cor. 10:17). Because we hear the word of God in the Eucharist/Lord's Supper, this is a

---

44. Küng, *Christianity*, 4.

sharing in both word and sacrament (or ordinance) at the same time.[45]

While the notion of "actualization" might raise Baptist eyebrows and communion ecclesiology may be new and challenging language, the centrality of fellowship, which it affirms, is core to Baptist ecclesiology and to a Baptist understanding of the Lord's Supper.

The fruits of the journey toward oneness (*koinonia*) are sometimes frustrating but, as evidenced in the recent Baptist story of change and transformation, and in the recent ecumenical dialogues between Baptists and Roman Catholics, our oneness is real. In both stories, oneness is costly: it is not about bland uniformity, or opting for a "better together" survival strategy, it is about discovering deep respect for the other, through the bonds of fellowship and through shared mission.

CONCLUSION

While acknowledging the limited appeal of worship manuals to some Baptist ministers, this chapter maintains that their function has been and remains important on at least four levels. First, liturgically, they have functioned as a formative tool, offering guidance on good practice in the preparation and conduct of worship and a particularly helpful reference point where pastoral needs require special services. The comparative study of the manuals showed that practices have changed in response to prevailing theologies and cultures, and their interaction. There has been a dynamic and evolving understanding of the shape and content of worship. The word preached remains foundational to worship, but the proclamation of the word is not limited to sermon making alone; the word enacted in the breaking of bread has become integral to proclamation. Second, theologically, they have functioned like hymns, as a rich treasury of Christian wisdom on the Lord's Supper, shaped and tested by worshipping communities, which have ensured that received wisdom is not ignored or neglected. Third, pastorally, open and evermore generous invitations to the table supported the move towards more inclusive and hospitable practices, borne out of a greater recognition of the significance of the Lord's Supper pedagogically and missiologically. Fourth, ecclesiologically, undergirded by a theology of covenant trust, they have served the goal of unity both within the Union and in Baptists' relations with other Christians.

---

45. "The Word of God in the Life of the Church," 41–42.

God of Mission

God of mission, still you send us
To a world that needs your grace.
You have gone ahead to meet us,
You are waiting in each place.
Show us now your loving glory
In each child of every race.

God of hope, you call your people
To become the future now!
Help us see your will more clearly,
Grant us visions, show us how,
In your strength, despite our weakness,
We might live your kingdom now.

You have called us to be partners
In the mission of your son.
Black and white and male and female,
You have called us to be one.
Teach us how to serve together
That through us your will be done.

9

"To Become the Future Now"
Baptists Being Shaped by the Table

Ashley Lovett

BAPTISTS ARE A PILGRIM people and a missionary people. They have always understood that they are not at home in this world and yet at the same time they have been called to share in Christ's mission to see his kingdom come on earth as it is in heaven. Chris Ellis's hymn, "God of Mission," conveys well this sense of being missionary pilgrims. We are sent to a world that needs God's grace, sent to serve together as partners in the continuing mission of Christ. This much is readily affirmed by Baptist churches. Many Baptists long to see God's kingdom come, to see their neighbors, colleagues and friends have an encounter with Christ, to witness the transformation of their communities into places of light and hope. But Ellis's hymn does more than simply remind Baptists of their calling to be active in Christ's mission, it also hints at the importance of Christ-likeness in the character of the missionary people. We are not simply called to share a message of good news but we are called to be a people of good news. The church is both sign and foretaste of Christ's coming kingdom. Hence Ellis can write that God calls his people "to become the future now" and to be this by serving together in all our difference and diversity. Being more like Christ as individuals and as churches is at the heart of our calling as missionary pilgrims. We are to embody Christ in the world so that he is seen in us. Which is why we are called to regularly gather at the Lord's Table for it is here that God will, to pick up

Ellis's hymn again, "show us how, in your strength, despite our weakness, we might live your kingdom now."

The premise of this chapter then is that Christians are shaped by their participation in worship into people that more closely resemble Christ. This is particularly the case when we gather for the Lord's Supper. For it is when we share this meal that we are made into the people we have become in Christ.[1] Following the writings of Stanley Hauerwas and others, Baptist theologians Nigel Wright, Paul Fiddes, and John Colwell have offered different possibilities for how participation in worship within a British Baptist context might enable Christ's people to "take the right things for granted."[2] Whether by imitation of the Christian story, participation in the life and mission of God, or transformation by the mediating work of the Holy Spirit, they all suggest that sharing in the Lord's Supper is one of the primary ways for Baptist Christians to be written into the continuing story of God's mission in the world.[3] Having said that, the aim of this chapter is not to look in depth at what Baptists have written but rather to reflect on what British Baptist churches are doing when they meet at the Lord's Table.[4] We will do this by looking at three of the Baptist liturgies of the Lord's Supper in *Gathering for Worship* and reflect on what they tell us about the theology that has shaped them, and therefore how we might expect them to form Christians who share at the table in Baptist worship.[5] To give us some context, we start with a brief summary of the conclusions drawn by Ellis from his significant research into free church worship.[6]

BAPTIST PRACTICE PAST AND PRESENT

At the outset, Ellis observes that the "very fluidity of free worship means it will not be easy to determine how this tradition might best be allowed to speak."[7] Even so his analysis offers some particularly useful conclusions about the way that Baptists practice the Lord's Supper. He begins by not-

---

1. Colwell, *Promise and Presence*, 74.

2. Hauerwas and Wells, "The Gift of the Church," 25.

3. In particular see Wright, *Free Church*, Fiddes, *Tracks and Traces,* and Colwell, *Promise and Presence*.

4. Much of the material in this chapter is drawn from my unpublished MA Dissertation which does take a more considered look into what Wright, Fiddes and Colwell have written regarding the Lord's Supper.

5. Ellis and Blyth (eds), *Gathering for Worship*.

6. Ellis, *Gathering*, 21.

7. Ibid., 29.

ing that while most Baptist thinking has tended toward a non-sacramental view there is "a gathering momentum" towards using more sacramental language.[8] Ellis himself takes a sacramental view of the Lord's Supper, seeing it as a further outworking of the incarnation, in which God comes to us in the material of creation to enable the church to become his body.[9] While this opens up the possibility that all of creation becomes sacramental, it is only because gathered worship, water, bread and wine have given us a lens through which we might recognize God's presence in other things.[10]

> It is because the elements open us to God and enable us to participate in and receive grace that they also embody and disclose God's transformation of the whole of life.[11]

Looking at the way that Baptist practice has developed, Ellis suggests that the Lord's Supper is central to their worship but not normative.[12] What he means by this is that not all worship leads to the table but that it is nonetheless a regular practice of Baptist churches. From the historical record, Ellis draws attention to a number of features in Baptist practice. The most significant of these is the narrative framework, drawn primarily from the New Testament witness to the Last Supper that Jesus shared with his friends, and this reflects a Baptist preference for practices led by the witness of Scripture, and particularly the instructions of Jesus himself. In allowing the narrative to shape practice, he writes, the "drama is not primarily one of celebration but of a Bible story enacted in obedience to Jesus Christ."[13] For this reason the basic pattern Baptists follow when they come to the table has not changed much over time.

When it comes to the theological meaning of the Lord's Supper, Ellis identifies four aspects that summarize Baptist practice over the centuries. These are "found and united in its central meaning as the *Lord's* Supper," making it an essentially christological event.[14] The four aspects are: remembering Christ, led by careful attention to Scripture; communion with Christ, through personal prayer and renewed consecration; fellowship in Christ, which expresses the communal identity of the church; and, anticipating

---

8. Ibid., 178–81.
9. Ellis, "Embodied Grace," 6.
10. Ibid., 14.
11. Ibid., 15.
12. Ellis, *Gathering*, 183.
13. Ibid., 186.
14. Ibid., 198.

Christ's return, through kingdom living now.[15] We have already noted the significance of the narrative framework and the Baptist conviction that Scripture takes priority in shaping what they do in worship. Individual devotion is a common feature of Baptist practice and reflects a desire to meet Christ at the table in a spirit of confession and gratitude. The church's communal identity is not only in evidence in the sharing of a common meal, but also in other things that Baptists do when they come to the table, such as welcoming new members and offering prayers for the fellowship. Ellis regards the fourth aspect, anticipating Christ's return, as the weakest although he highlights how the Lord's Supper played a significant part in congregational discipline among earlier Baptists. James White argues that a weak eschatological focus is the reason for such limited attention to social justice in much Protestant practice of the Supper and attributes this to the church becoming too comfortable in Christendom.[16] To what extent has this changed? And are these four aspects of meaning still evident in the patterns offered to today's Baptist churches?

AN INTRODUCTION TO THE PATTERNS

In an introductory section, the editors of *Gathering for Worship* explain the underlying dynamic of gathering and sending that shapes the patterns offered throughout the book. This dynamic reflects the creative and redemptive movements of God's Spirit throughout history, centered on Christ, but now focused on the particular people known as the church.[17] While the editors emphasize the gathering and sending it is actually the middle movement, described as "shaping order and breathing life" and elsewhere as "transforming," that I want to scrutinize.[18] How do the words in these patterns for the Lord's Supper reflect that expectation? Is there a sense that the performance of these words, and associated gestures, intend to shape those who gather at a Baptist communion? And if so, in what ways? As we seek to explore these questions it should be noted that the editors describe the patterns as only indicative of "the core shape and dynamic flow of worship from which planning may begin."[19]

There are seven patterns offered in *Gathering for Worship*. This is a significant increase on the two in *Patterns and Prayers*, the book that

15. Ibid., 192–98.
16. White, *Sacraments as God's Self-Giving*, 129.
17. Ellis and Blyth, *Gathering for Worship*, 4.
18. Ibid., 4 and 7.
19. Ibid., 7.

immediately preceded it, and those that came earlier.[20] Three of these patterns are described as for general use and are identified as: A *Simple Pattern*, for use in Sunday worship and adaptable for various pastoral situations; the *Story-Telling Pattern*, which is a creative adaptation of the narrative in 1 Corinthians 11; and, the *Ecumenical Pattern*, which "draws freely upon prayers from" the wider church "whilst maintaining a free church structure."[21] Of these I have chosen to look more closely at the *Simple Pattern* because it is the one largely replicated from previous worship books and so most likely to be indicative of Baptist practice today.[22]

The remaining four patterns have "more specific thematic emphases"[23] and these are: *Hungering for Justice*, which "highlights the kingdom dimension of the Lord's Supper"; *Covenant-Making*, which brings out the Baptist emphasis on covenant relationships, with God and one another; *Re-Membering and Reconciling*, which imaginatively explores the holistic character of God's saving purposes; and, *Table Fellowship*, which is designed for a more intimate setting, and has a focus on confession and reconciliation. Each of these patterns suggests that there are ethical consequences for those sharing the Lord's Supper and for this reason I have chosen to explore two of them, *Hungering for Justice* and *Re-Membering and Reconciling*. My reasons for choosing these two is that they attempt to balance the transformation of God's people, into greater Christ-likeness, with the transforming effect that they might then have in the world.

For each pattern I shall give a summary of the overall shape, identify some of the key theological themes, and finally draw some conclusions about the ways in which the pattern might form those who come to share the Lord's Supper.

The Lords' Supper: A Simple Pattern

This first pattern is designated *Simple* and described as "for use in Sunday worship, or on other occasions such as with those who are sick." In an act of gathered worship it is suggested that this is preceded by "prayer, praise and the preaching of the word."[24] The pattern consists of eleven components,

---

20 Baptist Union, *Patterns and Prayers*, 67–91. Note the "Third Pattern" is just a list of items.

21. Ellis and Blyth, *Gathering for Worship*, 12.

22. See Baptist Union, *Patterns and Prayers*, 80–91, and Payne and Winward, *Orders and Prayers*, 9–21.

23. Ellis and Blyth, *Gathering for Worship*, 13.

24. Ibid., 14.

and these are: *Gospel Words* from the New Testament; an *Invitation to the Table*; a short confessional *Prayer*, after which it is suggested the church hear fellowship news and offer prayers for others; the words of *Institution* from 1 Corinthians 11:23–26; a prayer of *Thanksgiving*, either extempore or the one included, which can be followed by the Lord's Prayer; the visible *Breaking of Bread*; *Sharing the Bread*, by distribution; the *Lifting of the Cup*; *Sharing the Wine*, which is drunk together if using individual glasses; a period of silence followed by *Words of Acclamation and Prayer*; and, finally *The Grace*.[25]

The observation that Baptists have a preference for worship shaped by Scripture is very much in evidence throughout this pattern. We see it in the proposed use of *Gospel Words* at the start, the suggested use of the Lord's Prayer, and particularly in the *Institution* using 1 Corinthians 11:23–26, some of which is repeated when the bread and wine are shared. Even the prayer of *Thanksgiving* begins by recalling Jesus, his life as well as his sacrificial death, as the basis on which we come to the table. It appears that in identifying this pattern as a simple one the editors are inferring that little has been added to the tradition that Paul received from the Lord and then passed on. This dependence on such a tradition also serves to remind Baptists of their place within broader Christian history. While this might be regarded as a subtle pointer it is reinforced by the choice of a confessional prayer which has been part of the Anglican liturgy since the sixteenth century.[26] In this prayer we also see three of the meanings that Ellis identified, communion with Christ through prayer, fellowship with the body in shared confession and petition, and eschatological expectation turned towards faithful living: "cleanse the thoughts of our hearts . . . that we may perfectly love you, and worthily magnify your holy name; through Christ our Lord."

These themes have already been picked up in the words of the *Invitation* which strike a careful balance between the hospitality of Christ and our need for his grace. Each of the opening sentences juxtaposes two ideas—compulsion to come with freedom to do so, our hoped for strength with our true weakness, the right to come with the need to come, our lack of goodness with God's mercy, the poverty of our love with the lavish generosity of Christ's—and in doing so they point to the Lord's Supper as a meal that challenges preconceived ideas of what makes us acceptable. These simple words set us up for an encounter with Christ which offers to transform us from what we are, in our weakness and poverty, to what he can make us through his love, the body of Christ. Even if each use of *you* in the opening

---

25. Ellis and Blyth, *Gathering for Worship*, 14–17.
26. For current use, see Archbishop's Council, *Common Worship*, 168.

sentences is only heard in the singular, the concluding words remind us that God's intention is much bigger, for "we [who meet at this table] are his body." Crucially, though, the invitation is not simply to meet together but to "meet the risen Christ" and here we have the sense of the Lord's Supper as more than a memorial, but following Fiddes as a doorway between heaven and earth.[27]

This expectation of coming together to be transformed into the body of Christ is a reminder of the wider context of 1 Corinthians 11. In this part of the letter, the apostle confronts the Christians in Corinth for their failure to eat together as Christian brothers and sisters should, to the extent that their material differences were not only ignored but exaggerated. Paul's judgment was clear. Whatever they thought of their meal it was not, for him, the Lord's Supper.[28] From these words a greater sharing of material goods was evidently expected from those who had been brought together in this new body. For those who are aware of this context, the narrative should underline the implications of the invitation, that those who come do so together and to become one body. However, it is more likely that, shorn of this broader context, the use of such a simplified telling might have the opposite effect, and undermine this earlier emphasis on the table as uniting Christ's people.

This temptation to make the table a place of individual transaction is headed off to some extent by the prayer of *Thanksgiving* that follows, and again in the closing *Words of Acclamation and Prayer*. In fact I wonder if these prayers have been written in part to offer some balance. By recalling Jesus's life, as well as his death, the first prayer reminds us that the kingdom he came to establish is one that looks out towards others, and especially those who are most vulnerable. So we hear that he demonstrated the kingdom's power "in the lifting of the downtrodden, and the healing of the sick, and the loving of the loveless." The prayer then turns towards what we might hope for as we share bread and wine, and the emphasis is that our lives might become more like his. Similarly the final prayer contains the requests that "we who share Christ's body live his risen life; we who drink his cup bring life to others; we whom the Spirit lights give light to the world." This, the prayer concludes, enables us to hope beyond our own salvation, for a time when "we and all your children shall be free" and God's praise echoes throughout the earth.

From this analysis we might suggest that repeated practice of this pattern has the potential to shape Baptist Christians in at least two ways.

27. Fiddes, *Participating in God*, 281. See also Fiddes, "Ex Opere Operato," 227.

28. 1 Cor 11:20–22.

Firstly, in its dependence on Scripture, it will ground them in the story that is at the center of the church's faith, pointing to Jesus's life and death, and beyond that to the kingdom anticipated by both. The focus on his death, however, would still act as a sober reminder, that even our participation in this kingdom is not something to be taken for granted, but a gift of undeserved grace. Secondly, if the pattern is used carefully, it might also orient the church towards the kind of life that is in keeping with being the body of Christ. From beginning to end it reminds us of our shared responsibility to take Christ to the world, and so turns us towards others, with whom we are called to share his love in every possible way.

The Lord's Supper: Hungering for Justice

The second pattern "highlights the Kingdom dimension to the Lord's Supper—hungering and thirsting for justice."[29] It is a longer pattern than the previous one, with most of the material drawn from a liturgy prepared by the Wild Goose Resource Group (WGRG).[30] The components of this pattern are: *Gathering Sentences*, with responses, that indicate both who might come and what coming means; an *Invitation*; *The Story*, which is a composite based on the biblical narratives; a *Prayer of Thanksgiving*, either extempore or the one given, which includes the Sanctus[31]; *The Sharing*, of bread and wine; then *The Peace*, this time as a response to the meal; a choice of *Concluding Prayer*; and some *Closing Responses*, which point to the way that we should now live in the world.[32]

While the *Gathering Sentences* which begin this pattern identify its *telos* as the feast of the kingdom that is promised in Scripture, not least in the banquet parables, the focus is on the justice that anticipates this.[33] This is particularly evident when we come to the story which tells us of the Supper's origins and in which we find no reference to Paul's exhortation that we are to share this meal until Christ comes. Similarly, in the words of *Invitation* it is to the present table that we are invited, in the *Prayer of Thanksgiving* it is to this table that we are to look in wonder and praise, and when this prayer turns to confession it is the presence of bread, wine and others here that challenges our failure to act justly. In some ways this gives the pattern a greater sense of urgency, we are not to wait for this justice to come but to

---

29. Ellis and Blyth, *Gathering for Worship*, 30.
30. WGRG, *Wee Worship Book*, 93–102. See also pages 24 and 80–81.
31. On the "Sanctus" see Kreider, *Given for You*, 185.
32. Ellis and Blyth, *Gathering for Worship*, 30–35.
33. See Luke 14:7–24 and Luke 15, esp. 15:6–7, 9–10, 22–24.

pursue it actively, but it is surprising that there is not more emphasis on the coming kingdom given the intent signaled by the editors at the start.

The kind of justice expected is spelled out from the beginning in the *Gathering Sentences* which are not just asking God to gather us in but are a reflection of the divine mission to seek out and save all who are lost. The movement here is not so much of people coming to God, as in the story of the lost son, but rather of God going out to find them, even the poor, blind, and lame, as in the story of the great banquet. This is God's justice before it is ours, and it is surprising justice too, as we hear echoes of other biblical passages that remind us "we were nothing," we "had no name and no faith and no future," and yet God in his grace has "made us something," has "called us [his] children," and prepared "a table for us," offering us nothing less than himself.[34] All this prepares us for the words that precede *The Sharing* of bread and wine; "These are the gifts of God for the people of God." That God has done all this, for us but not just for us, is the basis for those who share at his table to remember the injustices that continue to spoil life and so to resolve to do something about them. This is, for me, the most poignant part of the pattern, as it points to the challenges that our presence at the Lord's Supper brings our way. Each challenge is met by a prayerful response to use what we have, or what we are, to do something to confront the injustice named. Thus:

> We cannot take bread and forget those who are hungry.
> Your world is one world and we are stewards of its nourishment.
> *Lord, put our prosperity,*
> *at the service of the poor.*

The choice of *Closing Responses* then reiterates that the justice of God, which has surprised us by making us welcome at his table, is the same justice that we must now go and practice in our daily lives. While the emphasis is on our actions—we pledge to take up the cross, we promise to go where we are needed—yet both sets of responses are clear that it will be God in Christ who makes the difference. He is the one who extinguishes the darkness, and he is the one who leads us on to the good things he has prepared.

Woven into the pattern are words which suggest that our sharing at the Lord's Table is a sacramental encounter, although the editors have cut out the reference in the source material to the bread and wine as a sacrament.[35] Even so we are left with the impression that there is more to what God has given his people than the symbols they are sharing; "Look, here is your

---

34. See 1 Cor 1; 1 Pet 2; Luke 15; 1 John 3.
35 WGRG, *Wee Worship Book*, 96, and 99–100.

Lord coming to you in bread and wine." The editors have sought to strike a careful balance here. God's gift to us is his Son, it is Jesus who meets us, not by transforming the bread and wine into his body, but by coming to us in these material elements. This comes close to Colwell's understanding of the Supper in which God mediates his presence through our sharing bread and wine.[36] Christ is not just recalled at this table, he is present here, as the Spirit takes bread and wine and turns them into a moment of encounter, in fulfillment of Jesus's promise. As we share this moment, we acknowledge in the *Prayer of Thanksgiving* that Jesus offers us himself "so that we may be filled, forgiven, healed, blessed and made new again," and so be able to put ourselves at the service of others, giving out of our fullness, transforming conflict through hospitality, and becoming together the one church of Jesus Christ.

While there is much in this pattern that has the potential to shape Baptist Christians towards lives that pursue justice and peace, the impetus for this comes less from the anticipated future and more from Jesus whom we see in bread and wine, and who is the surprising justice of God. Perhaps we might say, given the sacramental mood, that meeting Christ in the Lord's Supper and overwhelmed by such grace we will be reminded again of how far short we have fallen of showing the same justice to the hungry, the thirsty, those ravaged by war, and our own Christian brothers and sisters. This is where we are, but from the table, Jesus leads us on, "to refashion the fabric of the world until it resembles the shape of [his] Kingdom."

The Lord's Supper: Re-Membering and Reconciling

This third pattern is a creative engagement with Jesus's words to come to share bread and wine to remember him. The word remember is split and hyphenated to emphasize that this *re-membering* has past, present and future dimensions. The editors comment:

> When we re-member: broken damaged and dismembered aspects of our past lives are put together again; mind and body and soul in the present tense enjoy wholeness; and helplessness in the face of the unknown future gives way to resurrection hope.[37]

---

36 Colwell, *Promise and Presence*, 155–78. See also Colwell, "The Church as a Sacrament," 48–60.

37. Ellis and Blyth, *Gathering for Worship*, 40.

Of all seven patterns in *Gathering for Worship* this is the shortest and consists of only four components. These are: *Words of Approach,* which draw us to Jesus; *Words of Thanksgiving,* for the bread and wine to remind us of him, of who we now are, and of what that means; *The Sharing,* in which we find Christ as we eat and drink; and, a *Prayer after Communion,* that we might continue to re-member Christ in our embodied living.[38] The brevity of this pattern perhaps accounts for the surprising absence of any words of institution from Christ's lips in a pattern that emphasizes his physical humanity.

With its repeated mention of the human body, especially its emphasis on the parts that represent how we relate to the world, this pattern focuses on the way that Christians become the body of Christ. The *Words of Approach* set this dynamic in play as Jesus's life is retold through a series of simple statements about his flesh and blood encounters with others. While these are mainly general statements that point back to various episodes in his life, some can be related to specific events, such as the time that Jesus met with Martha and Mary and wept with them over the death of Lazarus. So, we recall, "the eyes that blazed against injustice, knew how to cry and saw the potential in everyone." Those who hear these words, about hands, feet, arms, legs, eyes, belly, and lips, are invited to step back into the stories the Gospels tell, to see God incarnate, fully human, and wonder again at the way he lived and revealed God's life. This simple telling then sets us up for the main focus of the pattern which is that his story continues but is now embodied in our lives, in our hands, feet, arms and so forth. In an echo of Ellis's hymn, the prayer is that we might "re-member [his] life in the world," that being re-membered by the Spirit we might be the body of Christ "living [his] life in this world." In the words of *The Sharing* we are reminded that this participation in Christ's life carries the same risks for our bodies as it did for his. The story of Jesus has a dark side and so the bread, we're told, "is a sign of all that we live and risk together as the community of Christ." Finally, the *Prayer after Communion* returns to the named parts of the body, and asks that our hands, feet, etc., might make Christ present to others.

In this pattern, then, there is a very strong sense that Christians who are shaped by Christ's story become the kind of people who live his way in the world. When we come to the Lord's Supper we enter this story at its most significant moment, not because this is all that matters, but because it signifies the whole of Jesus's life, from incarnation to resurrection. This is also what gives this practice political significance, not least in the observation that to live out Jesus's story invites the same confrontation with the powers

---

38. Ibid., 40–42.

that led to his death.[39] This emphasis on the Lord's Supper as the impetus to live differently, most evident in the words of the prayer which call on the Holy Spirit "to come alongside us, so that together . . . we may give ourselves afresh to the task of re-membering you," along with the reference to the bread and wine as a "timeless reminder," make this the least sacramental of the patterns. Whether this is deliberate or not it is certainly ironic given the emphasis on the way Christ is embodied in the person of Jesus and in the bodies of his people, the church. It is only in the words for sharing the bread that we find a suggestion of something more, but this is quickly eclipsed by the identification of the wine as that "of the kingdom of God" and not as the blood of Christ.

The focus on being re-membered has echoes of Fiddes's understanding of Christian life as making Christ visible by participation in God's life and mission.[40] However, this is clearly only possible as part of the church. The language of body echoes the Pauline usage and particularly his words to the Corinthians that they together are the body of Christ and each one a member of it. The context of those words is an argument that carefully emphasizes the value of each part in making up the whole body. All this, he writes, is because of the care with which God has arranged the members, to ensure the whole body is strong.[41] Thus, in the pattern there is a repeated stress on the words *we*, *our*, and *us* and no mention of *I*, or *me*. From the very beginning it is *we* who "gather at this table," *we* who "come to re-member," for it is *we* who "are called to be the body of Christ." The risen Lord is invited to "re-member our lives" so that "we embody [his] kingdom." It is *we* who "eat the bread and [drink the] wine," and so *we* who thank God for the way he has "loved us into life" and called "us to be partners." Even in sharing bread and wine it is *we* who do so and the risk signified is that faced by "the community of Christ" as a whole. Finally in the *Prayer after Communion* it is the hands, feet, and so forth, of all of us, that are to serve "where Christ leads."

Coming to the Lord's Supper using this pattern has the potential to shape Baptists as those who look away from themselves and towards participation in Christ's ongoing life through his body the church. Like the *Simple Pattern* the focus is more on looking back, to Jesus as the one whose embodied life revealed God's love for the world, and who is a pattern for the church to imitate in its own embodied life. At this table we are written again into the story of God's purposes for the world in such a way that Christ continues

39. The political significance of re-membering Christ is explored in Cavanaugh, *Torture and Eucharist*. On the Eucharist as the challenge to war that won't go away, see Schlabach, "Breaking Bread: Peace and War," 360–74.

40. Fiddes, *Tracks and Traces*, 67.

41. See 1 Cor 12:12–30.

to be re-membered both by us and through the way we live as his people in our worship and witness.

Each of the three patterns for the Lord's Supper in *Gathering for Worship* has much to commend it as a resource to help British Baptist churches as they plan for worship. There is a strong ethical character to the patterns that makes clear that the meal is not one for private consumption but is essential to the church's participation in God's life and mission for the world. Whether this character is strong enough is the question to which we must now turn.

DEVELOPING BAPTIST PRACTICE OF THE LORD'S SUPPER

Each of the three patterns has numerous strengths. In the *Simple Pattern* these include the narrative shape and strong Christological focus. This dependence on the Scriptures, on the life of Jesus, and particularly on the meal at which he first broke the bread and shared the wine is important for reminding those who come to the table of the one who meets us there, and of what life lived after him should look like. Not only does the pattern remind us that the Lord's Supper is a great leveler, that we come with the same need of mercy and grace, but it also points us outwards to a world that shares those needs, and to which we then go as Christ makes his appeal through us.[42] When understood from its context the narrative framework of 1 Corinthians 11, particularly if complemented by the words of the prayers, offers a strong challenge to the present-day cult of individualism. We have already noted that the narrative might also be the weakness of the pattern if the biblical text is read without knowledge of its stress on the church as Christ's body. That the pattern does not include any gestures, physical movements, congregational responses (meaning it is likely to be delivered by a solo voice) or the invitation to share a sign of the peace, misses the opportunity presented by the narrative focus and could adversely reinforce an individual-centered reading of the text.[43]

To talk about the gestures of worship is important because as Ellis reminded us Christian worship is embodied.[44] It involves words, and what we say or don't say is important, but it also involves movements, actions, silences, and other non-verbal participation. Sitting, standing, kneeling,

42. 2 Cor 5:11–21.

43. For more on "gestures" as an aspect of worship with formative significance, see Saliers, "Liturgy and Ethics," 15–35.

44. See also Haymes et al., *On Being the Church*, 143–47.

bowing heads, raising hands, looking towards or away from others, sharing a sign of the peace, and so on, are all gestures that both shape our practice of worship and illustrate how it has shaped us. E. Byron Anderson notes that what we are doing, our gestures, can either reinforce or undermine the words we use, pointing out for example that while our prayers at the table might emphasize thanksgiving our bodily posture of bowing our heads or kneeling speaks more of penitence and sobriety.[45] It is a weakness of all the patterns that there is little bodily participation encouraged and few opportunities for actual movement towards others. If as claimed the Lord's Supper "together with baptism is perhaps the most physical of all our activities in worship" then this is a sad indictment of the rest of Baptist worship.[46] As Colwell points out, it is "through our interaction with one another" at the table that we are formed into the habits of Christ-like living.[47] This gives us good reason, I suggest, to challenge our historic defiance and on occasion invite people to approach the table rather than have the elements brought to them. Going further, we might find ways to share the peace that not only take us out of our seats but also see us then serving one another with the bread and the wine. Such actions are necessary if we are to encourage people to "suspend a level of privacy and individuality."[48] We might also, following Wright, look to emphasize the celebratory aspect of the Supper, through the choice of a song not usually used, and by inviting people to stand to drink the wine and then respond to the affirmation that we drink until Christ comes with a shout of "Maranatha, come Lord Jesus!"[49] Having said all this, part of the problem is that the spaces we use have often been designed for an observer-model of church which limits the potential for movement. And so one of the key challenges, especially for those rebuilding or remodeling their church premises, is how space can be opened up to allow God's people to actually meet around the table and meet one another as they do so.

In *Hungering for Justice* the expectation that worship propels us into service is much stronger. This pattern is unequivocal about the challenge that confronts those who come to share at Christ's table. Of all the patterns it offers the clearest expression of the dynamic relationship between being gathered so that we might be sent, changed by our meeting with Christ, to share his grace with a broken world. While this emphasis reflects themes common in material produced by WGRG, it is to the credit of the editors

---

45. Anderson, *Worship and Christian Identity*, 78–79.
46. Haymes et al., *On Being the Church*, 142.
47. Colwell, *Living the Christian Story*, 162.
48. Butler, "Liturgical Ties of Community," 46.
49. Wright, *Free Church*, 103.

that they have included it in *Gathering for Worship*. The pattern achieves its aims by the use of simple phrases, especially the juxtaposition of "we cannot . . . and forget," and has the potential for drawing people into its movement through both well-placed responses and words that direct us to share a sign of the peace. Where it is particularly helpful in turning Christians outward to live justly is in keeping the onus on Christ as the one who brings about the transformation. At this table we meet Jesus, the emphasis is plural, and as we go from here it is Jesus who leads us, and who will be at work in what we do. While it has many references to Scripture these need to be decoded and so the risk is that younger Christians, or those with limited knowledge, might miss something of the depth of this pattern. At the same time, as with the other patterns, the limited use of gestures is a cause for concern, particularly as it appears that a couple of opportunities for participation found in the original have been taken out by the editors.[50]

The third pattern, *Re-membering and Reconciling*, also has much to commend it, despite what seems to be a fundamental flaw. Like both of the previous patterns the focus is on Christ and, once again, much is made of his life and the impact he had on others. Thus, the particular strength of this pattern is its focus on the incarnation, God has taken on a human body, and on how this embodiment continues in those who are the body of Christ today.[51] Even better in reminding us of this it points out gently but truthfully that an embodied church lives at risk of harm even to the bodies of those who are part of it. Given the tendency of some Christians towards forms of Docetism and Gnosticism, this affirmation of Christ's physical humanity and God's continued use of earthly bodies, including ours, offers a welcome corrective. Of all the patterns, then, this one cries out for physical gestures and movements towards others, but other than the breaking of bread and lifting of the cup none are suggested, and there aren't even any responses to bring voices together. To speak about being re-membered, put back together as Christ's body, but without any actual movements towards others threatens to undermine all the good that this pattern might do. Looking at the shape of the pattern and the words used I'd suggest it wouldn't be too hard to incorporate a range of voices and simple movements. While accepting that the editors cannot insist that the person presiding includes appropriate gestures and movements it seems a gross oversight not even to suggest sharing a sign of the peace.

50 See WGRG, *Wee Worship*, 95–96 and 98–99.

51. See also Bullard, "Communing Together," 104–5. Bullard highlights the subtle ways in which the market, by treating individuals as units of production, and the leisure industry, with all its demands on children and parents, are dismembering church members throughout the week.

Having said that no pattern can be expected to do everything, it is worth commenting briefly on the other four patterns offered in *Gathering for Worship*, particularly in regard to the criticism about the lack of gestures in the three we've examined. That all of them include an opportunity to share a sign of the peace further highlights its absence from *Re-membering and Reconciling*.[52] The *Table Fellowship* pattern also suggests that the bread and wine are shared by "everyone serving one another."[53] This is obviously more achievable in the smaller setting envisaged for this pattern but not impossible in a larger one. Two of the patterns, *Story-Telling* and *Ecumenical*, follow *Hungering for Justice* by suggesting the use of songs, which themselves have formative power, and so can move us towards a more perfect act of praise.[54] However this raises the question of appropriate choices with many designated communion hymns tending towards an individualized notion of salvation.[55] Other patterns include more responses and in the *Covenant-Making* pattern there is a notably long piece, which draws deeply on the Baptist heritage, for the congregation to say together.[56] One of the biggest surprises was that only three of the patterns use silences, which reflects a concern raised by Kreider that we tend to be overly wordy, and of these it is the one for *Table Fellowship* that does so most of all.[57] Silence at the table does more than slow things down, it gives us space to be attentive, to contemplate how God comes to us in earthly bodies and so remind us to be alert to meeting him in friend and stranger.[58] In terms of words the *Ecumenical* pattern is by far the longest but this is simply because it offers a greater selection of prayers from the wider church.[59] Unsurprisingly, all four of the patterns makes good use of Scripture, and similarly all retain the dynamic of gathering and sending, so that each ends with a commission to continue to live out Christ's life in the world.

---

52. Ellis and Blyth, *Gathering for Worship*, 19 and 44.

53. Ibid., 45.

54. Anderson, "O For a Heart," 122.

55. Good examples of songs that emphasize the corporate dimension of the table include "We Come as Guests Invited" by Timothy Dudley-Smith, "Behold the Lamb" by Keith and Kristyn Getty, and Stuart Townend, and another Chris Ellis hymn "The Communion of Saints."

56. Ellis and Blyth, *Gathering for Worship*, 37.

57. Kreider, *Given For You*, 180. See also her suggestion for "a communion without words," 179. Ellis offers a shorter pattern in Smith and Woodman, *Prayers of the People*, 224–5.

58. Fiddes, "Spirituality as Attentiveness," 46–49.

59. Ellis and Blyth, *Gathering for Worship*, 22–29.

One of the weaknesses in any set liturgy is that it cannot address the local context. In a sense this is inevitable, but if we follow Wells' suggestion that improvisation involves being faithful to two stories, Jesus' story as the foundational one but also our own local story, then we cannot be content simply to perform the patterns without some work to contextualize them.[60] While this may not be exactly what Wells had in mind, encouraging and facilitating local churches to improvise their own liturgies of the Lord's Supper might go some way to meeting the challenge raised by Scharen, who is critical of ecclesiology that does not deal with the church as it is but rather in idealized terms.[61] To do so would be wholly consistent with Baptist thinking about the local church as free to discern the mind of Christ for its own affairs. It might also help ministers who are trying to encourage their congregations to push out beyond their normal practice because it offers to involve them in the creative process. This may have been exactly what the editors of *Gathering for Worship* had in mind but in that case it would have been helpful to have some clearer guidance in the actual patterns.[62] Perhaps the only point at which those leading worship might move into other stories is when they use extempore prayer to name the hurts and needs of a broken world and of those in their church and wider communities. This is a shame because, as Kreider points out, telling our own stories and our local church's story in the context of telling "the big story which enfolds our local stories" has great potential to be transformative.[63]

That's not to say we don't have examples of Baptists doing just this. *Crumbs of Hope: Prayers from the City* is a book of prayers that was born out of the myriad of experiences "of a tiny and, by the world's standards, insignificant, congregation" in Higher Openshaw, Manchester. The authors describe these liturgies as coming "out of a particular time and place," one that involved real people, which means that from "time to time their names and stories creep into this book as a celebration of the Saints of Mersey Street, as the church is more commonly known." While the prayers have found their way into a book the authors are not precious about their finished form. In fact they encourage readers to use, adapt and re-write them for their own contexts.[64] One of their liturgies reflects the echoes of resurrection heard in the language of urban regeneration:

60. See Wells, *Improvisation*. On four possible stories, see Weaver, "Spirituality in Everyday Life," 144. On stories from church history, see Kreider and Kreider, *Worship and Mission*, 67.

61. See Scharen, *Public Worship*.

62. Ellis and Blyth, *Gathering for Worship*, xix–xxi.

63. Kreider, *Given for You*, 179.

64. McBeath and Presswood, *Crumbs of Hope*, 2.

> May the God who calls us to resurrection,
> > give us the courage to share our stories;
> May the God who calls us to recreation,
> > share our tears and heal our brokenness;
> May the God who calls us to remembrance,
> > stand alongside us in our struggle for justice and peace;
> May the God who calls us to regeneration,
> > work with us in making our dreams for this
> > community and this world into reality;
> In the name of the one who is love.[65]

In these few words we have a vision of the kingdom lived now that Ellis's hymn anticipates. This prayer is not dissimilar to those offered by *Gathering for Worship* but it is one which those in this small church are already working to bring about. The simplicity of this liturgy illustrates what is possible. And there are other possibilities for telling our stories in the Lord's Supper that go beyond using words. For example, one congregation in San Salvador worked together to create a mural to represent their church's pilgrimage. Not only did they produce "a striking banner of images" in which the church recognized its own life, but because the mural is hung at the front of the building they come to the Lord's Supper and see their story "framed by the bread and wine."[66] Such creativity gives us something more than just aesthetics, for Smith, who argues that to change us worship has to do more than convince, it has to move us.[67]

Having argued for a greater use of gestures, movements, silences, and now story-telling through other media, I want to return to words because words remain important to us. In fact, one of the risks of focusing on the Lord's Supper, is that of forgetting the other practices of gathered worship, including the sermon. Baptist preference for patterns shaped by Scripture arises from their commitment to the Bible and preaching as the ways in which God continues to speak to his church. My concern in this chapter has not been to take anything away from our attentiveness to the Word but to argue that Baptists need to spend more time around the Lord's Table lest we miss the richness of God's gift as both an encounter with him and one that transforms us for living Christ-like lives in the world. As such I want to conclude by suggesting two ways that Baptist churches might do this.

The first is simply to find more opportunities to share the Lord's Supper, whether on more Sundays in the month or more times during the

---

65. Ibid., 115.
66. Weaver, "Spirituality in Everyday Life," 146–47.
67. Smith, *Imagining the Kingdom*, 166.

week, in small groups or regular planned midweek meetings for the whole congregation. The second suggestion is that Baptists make their monthly communion a full Eucharist service, meaning that the Lord's Supper orients all the other practices, as we see in a typical Anglican service. This would probably mean shorter sermons and, more importantly, sermons that intentionally explore the breadth of themes that surround the Lord's Supper, not simply from Scripture but also as we explore how Christian tradition, our Baptist history and our local stories interact with it.[68] Many of the patterns that we have looked at could then be developed into fuller localized liturgies through which we might worship God and in our worship become what we already are, missionary pilgrims who make him visible and give him glory in the world.

---

68 Bullard, "Communing Together," 108.

The Communion of Saints

Jesus promises his presence,
We have nothing now to fear!
Come and gather round his table
For the Lord of life is here.

Though a hostile world should threaten,
He has promised to be near.
As we offer our thanksgiving,
Though our numbers may be few,

We are gathered with the millions
Who have known his word is true.
Come and celebrate forgiveness,
For God's grace is always new.

Come and look at one another –
In each other Jesus see.
Come and let his Spirit bind us
As his loving company.

Here in bread and wine he shows us
How his love can set us free.
So we bring our true thanksgiving:
All we are and hope to be.

Make us, Lord, your holy people
That the world may in us see
Glimpses of your kingdom coming
As each day love sets us free.

10

"We Are Gathered with the Millions"
Celebrating the Communion of Saints

Ruth Gouldbourne

"This is your fault," she said. I had seen her slip out as we were sharing communion, obviously in distress, and caught up with her at the coffee time after the service. "You're the one that taught me about sharing bread and wine with believers throughout time and space, and since my dad died, I can't bear it!"

I knew exactly what she meant; when my mother died it had taken many months before I could preside at the Table without tears. And yet it seemed to be ok; here where we had shared bread and wine through so many years, we were somehow still sharing, still together because of the love that held us and all in one community.

Within the same month as the event in the first paragraph, I was invited to share evening prayer with a Roman Catholic community, as part of the week of prayer for Christian Unity. There were only a few of us, and we simply read in turn through the set prayers—which resulted in me, the only non Roman Catholic present reading both the Gospel for the day, and the bidding in the intercessions: "We pray for the faithful departed, asking that light shines on them." In the discussion afterwards, I commented that asking a Baptist to read the Gospel was always going to be fine, whereas inviting her to pray for the dead was not so straightforward. An interesting ecumenical discussion developed, since most of the community with whom

I was sharing that evening had not realized that the prayerful affirmation of the fellowship of the whole communion of saints was not part of our tradition or practice.

But it is of course, one of the things that we, as Baptists, have always been clear about; it is given to each to die once and then to be judged. Death is the great divide, and between the living and the dead there is no connection. We don't pray for the dead, nor do we ask the dead to pray for us. We might—indeed, we often do—give thanks for them, remember them with gratitude, celebrate their lives, the goodness of God to them, and give thanks that, whatever it means, after death, those we have loved are now held securely, and untouchably in the closer presence of God's love. That said, however, even in our very valuable book of resources, *Gathering for Worship*, we have no resource for an "All Saints' Day" type of service.

But the notion that there is some fellowship, some "communion" between the living and the dead, across the divide that is marked by the cessation of physical life is not a theology that Baptists have worked with. Except in our hymns. And in our intuitive, instinctive responses to the graced moments of the Lord's Supper.

As Chris Ellis pointed out in his important work on worship, if you want to know what Baptists believe, patterns of worship, and the content of prayers and hymns are an invaluable resource.

> How do we find out what Christians believe? Should we turn to a professional theologian, someone who spends their life researching, reflecting, analysing and explaining what various Christians down the ages have thought and said about what they believe? Should we approach a minister or priest, someone responsible for helping others understand the truths of the Christian faith? . . . But there is yet another way, the exploration of Christian worship which can lead us towards a rich appreciation of Christian faith. Worship will not only inform us about the content of Christian believing, but will demonstrate faith's embodiment in the prayer, proclamation and the patterns of community life.[1]

While the priority of extempore prayer means that much of what is expressed in prayer is not immediately available to us, we do have hymns, and for all that our patterns of singing and the material that is used has changed significantly within the last generation, still as part of an ongoing tradition, there are hymns that suggest that in our affective reactions, if not in our official pronouncements, we find it impossible to let go of a "sense" of

---

1. Ellis, *Gathering*, 1.

communion with the saints who have, in the old phrase, gone to glory. Thus, the power and longevity of *Blest be the tie that binds*, thus the importance of the hymn of Ellis's that precedes this chapter; somewhere, within our worship, our experience, our expression of longing, hope and faith, especially when we gather at the Table of the Lord, we deeply know that there is something that we cannot let go of. Our "official" theology may not be able to well accommodate it, but our expressed deeper theology of worship and experience still asserts it; in Christ, the people of God are united across all the apparent boundaries that appear to separate us.

James McClendon has argued that at the heart of the baptistic vision is the condition that "this is that"; and he explains it most directly with the illustration of the identity between the apostolic church and the contemporary church:

> So, the [baptistic] vision can be expressed as a hermeneutical motto, which is shared awareness of *the present Christian Community as the primitive community and the eschatological community*. In other words, the church now is the primitive church and the church on the day of judgement is the church now; the obedience and liberty of the followers of Jesus of Nazareth is *our* liberty, *our* obedience.[2]

McClendon goes on to demonstrate how, among baptistic communities, this identity of Christian gatherings across time (and space) is because, in the Spirit, within each community, each believer, is in the same relationship to Christ.[3] The relationship is not determined by time or geography—and, by implication, and central to this essay's thesis, it is not affected by death. He sums the whole argument up with the phrase "this is that" and then explains

> The baptist "is" in "this is that" is therefore neither developmental nor successionist, but mystical and immediate; it might be

---

2. McClendon, *Ethics*, 30.

3. It is of course important to note that this cannot be pushed too far. There is a difference created by history; we are not living in the first century, and we cannot behave as if we are. However, when we understand it to be the assertion that our relationship with the Risen Christ is not mediated through history only, but is also that made active by the activity of the Spirit, we can recognize that it is the same as the relationship of the disciples after the Resurrection. Thus, we cannot take refuge in the excuse "it was easier for them—they knew him." We and they only know Christ as the Risen One through the action of the Spirit, and the activity is the same. Indeed, we could argue that we are better off than the early disciples .We have both the encounter with the Risen One and the benefit of two thousand years of reflection, wisdom and creative theology. See also the discussion by Harvey, "This as That."

better understood by the artist and the poet than by the metaphysician and the dogmatist.[4]

The poet and the artist—and also, I suggest, those who seek the meaning of belief not just in propositional statements, but also in the lived experience of the people of God are good at understanding this. Our formal theology may pay no attention to communion and community of saints; but our worship and our experience reflects a different truth.

The woman in my first paragraph made reference to a phrase that had shaped her experience; "held together across time and space." Space we have had no problem with. The Baptist awareness of being united with fellow believers across borders, language and culture has been self-evident and deeply formative. Our historic commitment to religious freedom around the world, our involvement with activism on behalf of fellow-believers in situations of danger or persecution is a proud heritage. The witness of those who refused to be combatants, at least in part because they knew that some of those they would be fighting were fellow believers and so more closely related than simply by nationality was an important aspect of the witness to peace in the interwar years, and indeed, during the 1939–45 war. The rebuilding of ties between Baptists in the UK, and in Germany immediately after the war, and the importance of the work of J. H. Rushbrooke was a tangible reflection of this sense of being bound together across space—beyond loyalty to borders and nationality and state. The importance of the separation of church and state is bound up in this; we are not a church that is identified with any nation state. Indeed, we are in Europe at least, often at odds with a church that is identified with a national identity.

This is significant. It points to an understanding of being the people of God who are identified with a kingdom that is not determined by this world's rules. Of course we fail at it, and of course Baptists can be, too often are, as toxically nationalistic as others, especially in times of conflict. But it is not our only witness nor our only understanding of ourselves. I believe it would be possible to tell at least part of the story of the way Baptists have spread around the world, and in particular our commitment to mission, in terms of this experienced conviction that borders, languages, and cultures are secondary in the face of the call of Christ and the love of God. It would be possible to trace it because we have worked at it. We have written and argued and experimented and explored what it means not to be identified with nation, and so there is a body of teaching to reflect on, and a tradition and language in which to have the discussion.

---

4. McClendon, *Ethics*, 32.

But "held together across time" is not a notion that has the same resources. We have not spent so much time in discussing the "communion of saints" as binding us together, giving us an identity that transcends the ending of physical life. Our rejection of an older tradition which we regarded as deeply suspect, with a theology of a treasury of merit, the apparent compromise of purgatory, the profoundly economic transactional relationships, and our adoption of a theology of salvation by grace through faith alone, and personal encounter with the Risen Christ leading to believers' baptism rather than baptism in the faith of the church later to be appropriated individually at the age of discretion has led this thinking on a different trajectory.

The idea that somehow there is an explicit relationship between the living and the dead in Christ has been regarded as deeply suspect, as undermining something fundamental in our understanding of the nature of salvation, the meaning of Baptism and the existence of the church.

And yet we have written hymns containing lines such as "When for a while we part / this thought will soothe our pain / that we shall *still* be joined in heart/and hope to meet again."[5] And, today we can write, "As we offer our thanksgiving / though our numbers may be few / we are gathered with the millions / who have known his word is true."[6] And we can include in our hymnbook, "We thank you for those others /who lived in different ages / and thought in different ways / but whose Lord *is* the same as our Lord / to whom be all our praise."[7] One begins to suspect that we have an experience in need of a theology, and, just as Ellis predicted, we have expressed that theology in our worship, even when we have not yet found the language to explore it in our reflections and arguments.

Of course, it is worth noting that none of these hymns have been written within the last five years; and, though I certainly don't claim to be an expert on contemporary hymnody, and so may have missed something, the lack of very recent worship material including this aspect may be an important indication of something shifting, and I suggest, lacking, in our reflection and practice of worship.

The recent book *Baptists and the Communion of Saints* is an attempt to make good this deficit.[8] Exploring philosophy, understandings of memory, what content can be given to words dealing with "life after death," and per-

---

5. "Blest be the tie that binds," *Baptist Praise and Worship* 472, verse 4. My emphasis.

6. "The Communion of Saints," Chris Ellis.

7. "We thank you for the memories," *Baptist Praise and Worship* 491. My emphasis.

8. Fiddes, Haymes and Kidd, *Baptists and the Communion of Saints*.

sonal reflection, this is a highly creative, and deeply important consideration of how Baptists might find a way of taking part in the wider discussion of the theology of the communion of saints; a consideration of how a whole tradition of theology might be made available to us, and how we, in our identity as Baptists might contribute to that discussion.

I wonder if alongside what that study and experiment has led us towards, we might also take a lead from Ellis' work on worship, and offer our experience of what we find ourselves doing when we sing or pray. Fiddes, in his discussion of "Blest be the tie" says

> This hymn is not a religious version of "Auld Lang Syne," a nostalgic remembrance of past friends no longer present, but is about the reality of a covenant that persists through the ages, among the people of God in the past, present and future. This quintessentially Baptist hymn prompts the question . . . what dimension might a Baptist theology of covenant offer to belief in the Communion of saints?[9]

The importance of this question, and the creativity of the possible answer presented in this book, is, I suggest, one of the places in which Baptist theology, and the call to speak in our own language, not that borrowed from other traditions, is significantly explored. And because it is, I do not intend to try and do it again.

Rather, within that wider discussion, and drawing from it, I want to start my reflection with the experience that Communion and "the communion of saints" belongs together. It is significant that it is in a communion hymn that Ellis himself explores this theology. Although there has been a tendency to assume a very minimalistic Zwinglian position (one, incidentally, untrue to Zwingli[10]) as the Baptist theology of the Lord's Supper, it is clear, both experientially, and in the terms that appear in our hymns that "mere symbols" does not express our full understanding of the Lord's Supper.

Ellis' work on worship draws heavily on the conviction of the Spirit's presence as being at the heart of a gathering of believers. Our refusal to understand a congregation as needing the authority to be a sacramental community to be "transmitted" through a hierarchical and sacerdotal structure is the expression of this. We do not need "apostolic succession" passed through the laying on of hands from bishop to bishop to link us into the presence of Christ, since, by the Spirit, we are in the same relation to the

---

9. Fiddes et al., *Baptists and the Communion of Saints*, 129.
10. See Gouldbourne, "Encountering Christ".

Risen Christ as the first disciples. The church now, then and to come, stands always in the same relation to the Risen Christ—and therefore, together.

The sharing of bread and wine is, I suggest, one of the moments when, even if we do not have the words for it, we are particularly conscious of this. Drawn by the Spirit into the presence of the Risen Christ through the action and story of the Supper, we, like the first disciples, encounter him as Presence, Call, Blessing, and Healing. And if this is like the first disciples, then it is also like all disciples since; we stand with all the people of God throughout all time, in the present presence of the Risen Christ through the power of the Spirit. There is, in these moments, an encounter with the Eternal Now. It is not through generations past that we reach back to "remember" a dead hero, but in the activity of the Spirit, we are brought into encounter with The Risen One in whom is our life. And so there are no "generations past," there is only the people of God, all now, in Christ, being grounded in the love of God, and shaped by the call of God.

Such an understanding of the Communion of Saints does not require us to believe in purgatory, to feel convicted that we have a need to pray for the faithful departed, nor even to ask them to pray for us. Rather it is an expression of the conviction that we all, in this life and beyond it, look towards Christ and thus are united. Because we know that, in grace, they are held in God's love, we do not need to pray for them. But I suggest we can also know that we are praying with them, and they with us, because, in grace, we are all praying by the work of the Spirit, and the Spirit is not divided, or differentiated between those on earth and those in glory. There are fellow believers across geography whom we will never meet, and where language and custom preclude direct interaction. But this does not rule out the conviction that we belong together. In the same way the boundary of death may be such that though we cannot have contact with those who have died, this does not mean that we do not all stand in relation to the same Christ in the power of the same Spirit.[11]

There are three implications of this that I want to explore in the rest of this paper. Firstly the importance of conversations across the generations. Just as our worship is immeasurably enriched as we draw on words, music, and practices from the world church—learning to sing our worship in

---

11. There is, of course, also a cultural and historical factor in this; Baptists from African contexts will have more to say about the communion of saints and the impact, for example, of the Apology for Slavery issued by the Council of by the Baptist Union of Great Britain in 2007. This is beyond my competence to discus, but it is important to notice just how culturally determined our understanding and practice of theology is. There remains not only the communion of saints across time to explore, but also that across geography and experience.

rhythms and with images from other cultures, for example, or exploring ways of studying the Scriptures that draw on insights from other contexts—so our worship and understanding is deepened when we understand ourselves as part of and in communion with those of previous generations. We do this in some churches to some extent in the material that we sing; the use of hymns that were written in previous generations, and words with which Christians before us worshipped has been part of our experience. However, there are contexts today in which this is no longer part of the regular practice. This is not a rant about how terrible modern music is, nor a blanket condemnation of contemporary worship material. There are poor quality worship songs now, and there have been poor quality worship songs before (Charles Wesley wrote how many hymns, and we sing how many of them now?) It is clearly important that we are in touch with words and music that are part of our own culture and context.

But there is also an importance in staying in touch with not just hymns from our own Baptists past, but the older material from the wider church; the reminder and the experience that we are not the first or the only generation to worship God from the heart and with all that we are is significant. It challenges our capacity to absolutize our own experience and to dehistoricize our context.

Not absolutizing our experience matters as a question of humility—we are not the only ones to worship, to seek and to follow the way of Christ—and therefore, we cannot assume that we are right in all things, or have attained full wisdom. We are not all there is; the Church of God is much greater than we are and so we can take the risk of being humble—of being open to change and of accepting we are not entirely responsible; there have been believers before us and there will be believers after us, and it is not our responsibility to do and to be all that God is doing and will do in the world. We all, of course, know this in theory. But our society is already so profoundly dehistoricized that it is easy to forget. Our cultural context is in grave danger too often of treating the past as an interesting theme park to visit and marvel over: how could they think that, weren't they odd in their ways; or, in too many places of violence—they were wrong and messed things up, and we need to go in and sort things out—and all too often, we try to do that, by using the same tactics.

In such a context, we find ourselves even more driven into it in the church, especially in the church in the UK. There has been such profound cultural changes in the way that we do church in the last two generations—both in our worship culture, and of the place of church in society, that we can run a serious risk of forgetting we are part of a much larger whole, and feeling as if we are the ones who discovered how to worship, how to order a church, how to be disciples. While it is true that each generation needs to discover this for their own context and situation, to be the people of God for this time in this place rather than live only in dead traditionalism, there is also the anorexia that comes from not being in touch with the nourishment of being part of a wider whole. When we are enabled to worship with the generationally different as well as the geographically different, we are held in that relationship in ways that enable us to nourish a wider vision. I don't mean simply to "remember"—to visit the past by singing old hymns. Rather, it is the recognition that when we sing what they sang, because we and they are worshipping through the action of the same Spirit, we and they sing together in worship and praise. And as we share bread and wine as they shared bread and wine we do not "remember" as an exercise in nostalgia, but rather, we and they receive from the Lord what has been handed on, for we are all in the same relationship to the Risen Lord, who stands among us.

If, when we gather in worship, we actively seek to affirm the conviction that we are worshipping together with the saints (read here as all those who have gone before us in the faith!) then our experience of being the people of God is deepened and confirmed; for those who feel beleaguered and embattled, the recognition that we are part of a much greater whole is encouraging and empowering, while for those who feel self-sufficient and powerful, it is a reminder that we are not all there is, and that God can and indeed often does do great things without us.

And secondly, pastorally, I suggest this is a deeply important conviction. Our society has largely abandoned formal mourning rituals. But what is undoubtedly evident is that in having abandoned them, we have gone on to reinvent them in new ways; the overwhelming and very public grief at the death of Princess Diana is regularly cited as evidence of this, but there are the much more personal, much more recent evidences too—the flowers attached to a lamppost near the site of an accident, and reattached every year on the anniversary of that accident; the ghost bikes around cities; the crowds that lined the roads when bodies were brought back to Brize Norton. We need ways to mourn and to make sense of death. The move away from funerals and towards thanksgiving or memorial services may have all sorts of practical and even pastoral justifications. But it can minimize the contexts in which we assert both the reality of the separation that death brings and the reality of the communion of saints. A thanksgiving service and even more a memorial service focus on remembering and giving thanks. There are, because we are deeply shaped in our convictions about resurrection, usually words of faith and hope about life eternal—but a funeral service that allows time to include us all in the convictions about being united in the presence and activity of the love of God has a different center-point. Not just a focus on the deceased, and on telling the stories and giving thanks—all of which are goods in themselves, but are too thin, too minimized to tell the full gospel conviction of all life held in the eternal love of God. A funeral service can (when traditional words, or a contemporary version of words such as *Lord, you renew the face of the earth; gather to yourself N whom we have loved, and grant to her/him those things which the eye has not seen, nor the ear heard, nor the human heart imagined* are used) also affirm in the face of the pain of loss and separation the deeper truth of the continued unity, not as a promise of "he'll be waiting for me when I get there" pie-in-the-sky, but as a fundamental truth of the world; that in the love of God, we are all sustained in life, and that death does not change that. This truth, expressed alongside of—perhaps even in defiance of—the experience of loss and grief offers a depth of pastoral comfort that leave our remembering with thanksgiving, or even our "he'll be waiting for you" words looking thin and trivial.

And a third practical aspect that emerges from this conviction that our unity in the Spirit is not broken by death is that it offers us a way of understanding what it means to exist in community even when we disagree. Our unity across the boundary of death is rooted in the activity of the Spirit, bringing us into relationship with the Father; we live and live together because the life that is in Christ is also in us. Baptists have always had to work at how we relate across difference. With apparently nothing to hold us together except our willingness to be together, we can hit problems when that willingness becomes strained.

But what if it is not dependent on us? What if, discovering more of the reality of our unity with our whole community, rooted in the Spirit, in the Spirit's activity in bringing us into relationship to the Father, and therefore into relationship with one another despite the apparent separation of death, we can also begin to discover that our unity here and now, across seemingly impermeable boundaries of theological conviction is rooted not in agreeing, but in the Spirit?

If we dare to consider the possibility that McClendon is right in his assertion that "this is that" and that all the saints stand in the same relationship to the Risen Christ through the action of the Spirit rather than through temporal proximity or indeed theological correctness, then we take the pressure off having to attain our unity by agreeing, or submitting, and we allow the Spirit to create unity as we all look towards Christ.

> And we, and all the saints, being rooted and grounded in love, will grow to the fullness of the knowledge of the love of God that surpasses understanding; and to him who is able to do immeasurably more than all we ask or imagine, according to his

power that is at work within us, to him be glory in the church and in Christ Jesus throughout all generations, for ever and ever! Amen.

Made to be One

Made in God's image: woman and man;
Here is the wholeness: God's human plan.
Brother and sister, daughter and son,
   Here is a family made to be one.

Dappled creation, diverse its ways,
Colors and cultures offer their praise.
Gathered together under the sun,
   Here is a family made to be one.

Don't let divisions get in the way,
Listen to others, hear what they say.
Caring and serving—that's how it's done,
   Here is a family made to be one.

We need each other, old folk and young,
Sharing together life from the Son.
This is the meaning, prize to be won,
   Here is a family made to be one.

Praise to the Father and to the Son,
Praise to the Spirit—our God is one.
Here is our vision, new world begun,
   Here is a family made to be one.

11

"We Need Each Other"
The Ecumenical Engagement of European Baptists

Tony Peck

I AM DELIGHTED TO contribute to this honoring of my friend and colleague over many years, Chris Ellis. We have worked together in regional Baptist life, as colleagues in ministerial formation, and we have shared several interesting journeys together that have taken us to different parts of the world in the work of the Baptist World Alliance. As well as his generous friendship and personal support I have learned much from his theological vision, his ecumenical commitment, and his seminal work on another interest of mine, worship in our free-church tradition. The hymn that prefaces this chapter is one of two, from the many fine hymns written by Ellis, that were included in what may well turn out to be the last denominational hymnbook of British Baptists, *Baptist Praise and Worship*.[1]

AN ECUMENICAL VISION

The words of the hymn celebrate a rich diversity held together by an underlying unity; in creation, in humankind, in society and in the community of the church, all undergirded with praise to the God who in Godself embraces

---

1. *Baptist Praise and Worship*, 633.

unity and diversity. The repeated line, "Here is a family, made to be one," has the elements of both God's promise and God's persistent challenge to our life in the world and our life as the church of Jesus Christ; to truly experience and embrace this aspect of God's "new world begun."

It is an all-embracing vision that Ellis has lived out in his varied ministries as local pastor of Baptist churches and a Local Ecumenical Partnership, and as a college principal in a context where much of ministerial formation was shared with Anglicans. He has sought to bring the breadth of ecumenical vision together with his own experience of the renewal of the Holy Spirit to enrich and illuminate the Baptist and Free-Church tradition in which he so clearly stands.

Ellis was also the author of the last book to be published by the British Council of Churches before it gave way in 1990 to the national ecumenical instruments in the different parts of the British Isles such as Churches Together in England, ACTS in Scotland, CUTYN in Wales and also to the Council of Churches in Britain and Ireland. Entitled *Together on the Way: A Theology of Ecumenism* it articulates, like his hymn, a theologically anchored vision of the visible unity of the church, which then reaches beyond itself into the wider *oikoumene*, in a concern for reconciliation and unity in the world as a whole.[2] In some respects it is a book of its time, when perhaps there were higher hopes about what was possible in terms of action to express visible unity in the churches of the UK. What is enduring, and resonates well with Baptists, is its theological emphasis on the prior calling of God to unity in the church, and that unity having as its foundation the one confession of Jesus as Lord.[3]

> If we ask whether there is a basic unity that encompasses Christians in their diversity and divisions we must reply that it is a unity "in Christ." Without him we are nothing. That does not mean that as human beings we cease to count, but that as a church we would cease to have meaning. Here is the strongest and gentlest argument of all in the cause of ecumenism. We have one Lord Jesus Christ and in him we are one. In him God loves us and saves us. In him God gives us hope. In him God calls us to follow.[4]

This chapter seeks to reflect on some recent developments with regard to the way in which one Baptist grouping, the European Baptist Federation (EBF), of which I have been privileged to be the general secretary since

2. Ellis, *Together on the Way*, 13–15.
3. Ibid., 125.
4. Ibid., 79–80.

2004, has attempted to live out something of this vision, however partial and incomplete, in its ecumenical involvement. I will argue, as others have done before me,[5] that more than any of the other five regional bodies that relate to the Baptist World Alliance (BWA) the EBF has been enabled to be more ecumenically committed as a whole because this has been undergirded theologically by a broader and richer ecclesiology than is often found among Baptists, and one that always seeks to put Baptists in the context of a *koinonia* (fellowship) with the wider church.[6] So far as the EBF is concerned this vision was founded on the contribution of certain key British Baptists to the early development of the EBF, and has informed both the shape of the "ecclesial" life of the EBF itself and its ecumenical involvement. This has been strengthened by some recent developments that I will describe.

FACING THE CHALLENGES OF UNITY AND DIVERSITY IN THE EBF

The EBF, consisting (2016) of fifty-nine member bodies—Baptist Unions, Conventions, networks of churches, and a few individual churches—is found in almost every country of Europe, the Middle East, and Central Asia. Founded in 1949 it consists of 13,000 churches and around 800,000 members with a community considerably larger than that. Baptists are one of the most widely represented Christian denominations in the region, though in each country they exist as a minority free church.

The unity in wide and rich diversity that is the subject of Ellis's hymn is certainly found in the life of the EBF itself. There is much greater linguistic, cultural, and theological diversity than is found in most other Baptist groupings. This presents its own challenges, especially on questions of theology, ethics, gender issues such as women in ministry, and in the diversity of "ways of being Baptist." But in what can perhaps only be attributed to a shared striving to "maintain the unity of the Spirit in the bond of peace,"[7] this diversity has gone alongside a high level of commitment to staying together in a unity based on *koinonia*.[8] This is evidenced by the high commitment

---

5. In writing this paper I acknowledge my considerable debt to the work of my former EBF colleague, Keith Jones, who has examined the "ecclesial" reality of the EBF in depth, including its ecumenical involvement, Jones, *The European Baptist Federation*, esp. 61–106.

6. Ibid., 59–60, 76.

7. Eph 4:3.

8. Translated fellowship, communion, participation, sharing: in the deepest way in Christ and with one another. *Koinonia* "has become central in the ecumenical quest for a common understanding of the church". See *The Church: Towards a Common Vision*,

of leaders of member Unions to meet together, so that at the annual EBF Council it is usual that forty to forty-five of the fifty-nine member bodies will be represented by their presidents and/or general secretaries.

In more recent years the EBF Council has achieved the level of mutual trust to be able to discuss such issues as questions of human sexuality, women in ministry, and responses to the current migration crisis in Europe, all from differing perspectives but without breaking fellowship.[9] It has also engaged in decision-making together about the future life of the EBF as a whole, recognizing the *episkope* (oversight) of its leaders to carry this forward. As we shall see, this is also true of the EBF's ecumenical commitments. Based on these observations I want to argue that the EBF indeed is in some way an "ecclesial" reality that has been very helpful in its relationship with other Christian denominations, and also with ecumenical bodies in its region.

For European Baptists there would be a wide diversity of responses to ecumenical co-operation, whether at local, national, or international level.[10] For those who are suspicious of all things ecumenical, some of this is down to a concern for what is seen as biblical truth and the danger of compromise, or the perceived lack of priority given to mission and evangelism. In some countries in Eastern Europe there is a legacy of "the ecumenical movement" during the Cold War being seen in the years since, rightly or wrongly, as a tool of the state control of the churches.

EUROPEAN BAPTIST ATTITUDES TO ECUMENICAL ENGAGEMENT

The situation of many European Baptists regarding the wider ecumenical scene is well summed up by the comment of Ian Randall, who in referring to the experience of the English Baptists of the twentieth century, states that "the ecumenical and the evangelical vision have seemed to some Baptists in the 20th Century to be in opposition to one another. Indeed, some Baptists have accused the ecumenically minded of abandoning evangelicalism."[11]

10–15.

9. The exception would be the Baptist Unions of Kazakhstan and Kyrgyzstan who in 2005 withdrew from both EBF and BWA, citing a number of issues about which they were not prepared to be in fellowship with those who took a different view, including that of the EBF's ecumenical involvement. However good informal relationships between these Unions and the EBF leadership have continued since then.

10. Green, *Crossing the Boundaries*, 224.

11. Randall, *The English Baptists of the 20th Century*, 6.

However, in the twenty-first century it could be argued that these distinctions have become more blurred, with some welcome new developments so far as Baptists are concerned. These would include the broader evangelical vision of the Lausanne Movement for World Evangelization that also espouses a commitment to unity in life and mission with other Christians;[12] the coming together to work on issues of contemporary mission by the World Council of Churches (WCC), the World Evangelical Alliance (WEA), and the Roman Catholic Church;[13] and the recent formation of the Global Christian Forum to seek to foster a better mutual understanding and fellowship between "traditional" Churches represented by the WCC and the Roman Catholic Church, and evangelicals represented by the WEA and the Pentecostal World Fellowship.[14] All of those developments have been important to, and in some way involved, European Baptists, broadening their vision of the church and Christian unity.[15]

Nevertheless, the contours of what many European Baptists understand by unity with other churches of other Christian traditions are as described by John Briggs:

> It sometimes seems as if the claims of unity and fellowship are set over against faithfulness to the truth as we see it. There are compelling arguments on both sides because the differences separating churches can be very great. How far do we go and when does it become a compromise too far? On the other hand do we not find ourselves in situations where, although the formulas seem all wrong, there is a perception deep down inside us of the spirituality of another tradition which witnesses something of Christ to us?[16]

What is remarkable is that, despite what appears at times to be the almost bewildering diversity of the EBF and a lot of hesitation, suspicion and sometimes downright hostility among individual European Baptists towards wider ecumenical involvement, nevertheless from the beginning

12. *Cape Town Commitment* (2011).

13. WCC et al., *Christian Witness in a Multireligious World*.

14. The most recent Conference of the Global Christian Forum, on the subject of the Persecution of Christians today, was held in November 2105 in Tirana, Albania.

15. EBF member Unions, and the EBF itself, were well represented at the Third Lausanne Congress in Cape Town, South Africa 2010. The EBF has officially adopted the agreed Statement on *Christian Witness in an Interreligious World*; and the EBF through the Baptist World Alliance is involved in the Global Christian Forum, with the EBF General Secretary being a speaker at the GCF Conference in Tirana, Albania in 2015.

16. Briggs, "Baptists in the Ecumenical Movement," 11.

of the EBF there has been a concern amongst its leaders that there should be a "connectedness" and where possible a working together with other Christian traditions in Europe.[17] And on the whole they have managed to carry the EBF with them, through the decisions of its Annual Council of the leaders of its member Unions and Conventions.

It remains true that in European Baptist discussions about our relationships with the wider church, even from those who are not enamored by "the ecumenical movement" there are inevitably testimonies given of what Briggs refers to here as "the spirituality of another tradition which witnesses something of Christ to us." Indeed, as we shall see, in more recent ecumenical discussions about the basis of unity, Baptists have been able to contribute their conviction that rather than it being on the basis of "our common baptism," which is problematic for us, it is rather that we see in a believer from another Christian tradition the clear evidence of the gifts and graces of the Holy Spirit in her/his life; and that in another church we see the marks of the true church of Jesus Christ. In his own ecumenical theology, Ellis expressed it this way:

> Ecumenism begins with encounter. . . . It is only when we hear the account of another's faith from that other person that we begin to understand another's faith as something which is alive. It is in the personal encounter that prejudice and ignorance are surprised and persuaded to listen.[18]

ECUMENICAL COMMITMENT GROWS OUT OF ECCLESIOLOGY

The central argument of this chapter is that the extent of ecumenical openness of the EBF as a whole, despite diversity on ecumenical issues among its members, has been undergirded by an ecclesiology that has seen a body such as the EBF not just as a convenient pragmatic way to organize Baptist life in Europe (and later also including the Middle East and Central Asia). But, as described earlier, the EBF is rather seen as a body having some degree of *ecclesial* significance based on a *koinonia* that enables a deep level of spiritual fellowship, but also the necessary mutual trust to act *together* as the EBF.

Keith Jones has explored this aspect in depth and traces its origins to the influence of British Baptists such as Ernest Payne on the early development

---

17. This is very well documented in Jones, *European Baptist Federation*, 61–106.
18. Ellis, *Together on the Way*, 130.

of the EBF in the 1950s, something in which Payne was actively involved.[19] He had already outlined his own ecclesiology in his influential book *The Fellowship of Believers*, stressing the interdependency of local churches in wider Baptist groupings having some kind of ecclesial significance, based on relationships founded on *koinonia* between its members, and on what Payne saw as the necessary connectedness of Baptists to the worldwide church.[20] He described "Associations, Synods, Unions and Assemblies of churches" not as "optional and secondary" but rather "the necessary manifestation of Christian fellowship, a necessary manifestation of the church visible."[21]

These convictions found expression in the 1948 Baptist Union of Great Britain Document, *The Doctrine of the Church*. It was published against the backdrop of two ecumenical developments, the formation in the same year of the World Council of Churches, and closer to home, renewed official Conversations on possible "intercommunion" between the Anglican Church and the Free Churches in England.[22]

The Doctrine of the Church states at the outset that "although Baptists have so long held a position separate to that of other communions, they have always claimed to be part of the one Holy Catholic Church of our Lord Jesus Christ."[23] This claim is echoed in the opening words of the 1993 EBF document on Baptist identity, *What are Baptists?* written at a time of seismic change in Europe after the ending of the Cold War. The document seeks to explain European Baptists, especially to state churches, and for Baptists to place themselves in the context of the worldwide Christian church. It begins, "We are part of the whole world-wide Christian church and we confess faith in one God as Father Son and Holy Spirit."[24]

In the 1948 Statement Baptist ecclesiology is set in this wider context, that "it is in membership of a local church in one place that the fellowship of the one Holy Catholic Church becomes significant."[25] A picture of a local church emerges in which its members, gathered by God in covenant with him and with each other, meet to discern the mind of Christ for its life together, to recognize "*episkope*" amongst them, and to be open to the counsels of the wider church. The document goes on to draw from early English Baptist writings about the church in order to emphasize this neces-

---

19. Jones, *European Baptist Federation*, 25–60
20. Payne, *The Fellowship of Believers*, esp. 120–21 and 126–30.
21. Ibid., 31.
22. Cross, *Baptism and the Baptists*, 139–42, 152–58.
23. "The Baptist Doctrine of the Church," 5.
24. EBF, *What are Baptists?*
25. "Baptist Doctrine of the Church," 2.

sary, rather than optional, connectedness to the wider church, both Baptist and beyond. The relevant paragraph is worth quoting:

> Although each local church is held to be competent, under Christ, to rule its own life, Baptists, throughout their history, have been aware of the perils of isolation and have sought safeguards against exaggerated individualism. From the seventeenth century there have been "Associations" of Baptist churches which sometimes appointed Messengers; more recently, their fellowship with one another has been greatly strengthened by the Baptist Union, the Baptist Missionary Society and the Baptist World Alliance. In recent years, General Superintendents have been appointed by the Baptist Union to have the care of churches in different areas. *Indeed, we believe that a local church lacks one of the marks of a truly Christian community if it does not seek the fellowship of other Baptist churches, does not seek a true relationship with Christians and churches of other communions and is not conscious of its place in the one catholic Church.*[26]

British Baptists picked up this thinking in the 1990s as they reflected on the "ecclesial" role of their Council and Assembly.[27] The primary ecclesial reality of the local church in affirmed but nevertheless is seen as somehow incomplete without its active participation in regional, national and even international grouping of both Baptists and other church bodies. These bodies have the potential to be "ecclesial" in some way, centered on a group of representatives coming together to seek the mind of Christ and electing those who will exercise *episkope* over them.

There was some hesitation about describing international Baptist groupings, especially the Baptist World Alliance in this way.[28] However, the criteria outlined there for a body to be considered in some ways "ecclesial"—"covenant responsibilities for making decisions and prophetic criticisms, for exercising oversight (*episcope*) and sponsoring mission"—would all find some expression in the current life of the EBF.[29]

In summary, Randall is surely correct in his judgment that "this view of Baptist ecclesial life as 'more than local' was influential in the establishment of the European Baptist Federation in 1950" only two years after the publication of the British Baptist document, and with one its architects,

---

26. "Baptist Doctrine of the Church," 8. My italics.

27. See *The Nature of the Assembly and the Council of the Baptist Union of Great Britain*.

28. Ibid., 13.

29. Ibid., 10.

Payne, being very involved in the early shaping of the life and structures of the EBF.[30]

THE EARLY YEARS OF THE EBF

What effect did this "more than" ecclesiology have on the beginning of the EBF form 1949 onwards? First of all it served as an impetus to gather European Baptists together in a way that was more than simply organizational but instead based on a deep sense of solidarity and *koinonia*. This happened first of all with the help and support of the Baptist World Alliance to bring together European Baptists whose nations had been in conflict with each other, in the era of reconstruction and reconciliation after the horrors of the Second World War. So the formation of the EBF was a response to a divided continent with so many displaced people; and also a coming together to support the situation of Baptists after the rise of the Warsaw Pact countries, with the most severe repression of the churches taking place in many of them during the years 1945–55.[31] But secondly, this ecclesiology also influenced the development of the EBF's ecumenical relationships.

Immediately we note once more that such a statement has always to be set against the hesitations and concerns of those Baptists who viewed the development of the World Council of Churches (WCC) and the Conference of European Churches (CEC) with suspicion and were not sure that Baptists should be involved at all. In reflecting in 1972 on the relationship between European Baptists and CEC, the first General Secretary of CEC, Welsh Baptist minister Glen Garfield Williams, made the very valid observation that in most of the continent of Europe Baptist history was only around a century old and "you can still talk with people who knew the founding fathers." In almost every country in Europe Baptist churches were born into a situation of persecution of them by state churches and governments influenced by them, and "the wound has by no means healed yet." And as a result Baptists have had to struggle with being referred to as a "sect" rather than recognized as a community of sister churches.[32]

The legacy of these issues and especially variable relationships with State Churches and governments in Europe remains with the EBF today. But despite these and other hesitations on the part of Baptists, there have always

---

30. Randall, "Counsel and Help," 34. See also Jones, *European Baptist Federation*, 37–41.

31. These issues are highlighted in, e.g., Kucová, "Pastors in the Dock, 127–45.

32. Williams, "European Baptists and the Conference of European Churches," 52–58.

been EBF leaders who have being willing to represent Baptists in ecumenical gatherings, and from the beginning the EBF council has welcomed ecumenical guests to address its meetings. The EBF also took an interest in the early years of the World Council of Churches (WCC) and whilst only a very few EBF member Unions have sought membership of the WCC there were several significant European Baptist responses to the key WCC "Lima" convergence document, *Baptism, Eucharist and Ministry* published in 1981.[33]

But the EBF's more significant ecumenical involvement has been with the Conference of European Churches (CEC) and, more recently the Community of Protestant Churches in Europe (CPCE).

THE EBF AND THE CONFERENCE OF EUROPEAN CHURCHES

The Conference of European Churches (CEC) was founded in 1959 in Nyborg, Denmark. It now consists mainly of Protestant Churches, both state churches and minority churches, together with the various autocephalous Orthodox Churches in Europe. The Roman Catholic Church has not been part of CEC but has related closely to it through the Association of the Catholic Bishops' Conferences in Europe (CCEE).

At the outset European Baptists were generally cautious about such a pan-European ecumenical grouping, though individual Baptist leaders, especially from Scandinavia, were more positive. The EBF at that time drew back somewhat on seeing itself as in some way "ecclesial," emphasizing that it was not a church, nor a "super-Union" but a Federation of Unions.

At first sight this seems somewhat paradoxical, and it illustrates a tension that continues to this day. On the one hand, there is the emphasis on the EBF as a "federation" that suggest members covenanting together for specific purposes rather than being in total union with one another. This is an important aspect because it avoids drawing the boundaries too tightly and definitely in a way that might well have the potential to exclude rather than include. On the other hand there is no doubt that in the way the EBF has lived out its life in such a "federation" there has developed a certain "ecclesial" character as described in this chapter. Perhaps these should be thought of as two poles of the same reality, and they probably represent a creative tension that is to some extent characteristic of all trans-local Baptist life, whether in national or international Baptist bodies.

So in responding to the emergence of CEC the EBF first encouraged individual member Unions to join. Nevertheless the EBF itself sent observers

33. Jones, *European Baptist Federation*, 71–76.

to the early Assemblies of CEC. It helped to boost Baptist involvement when a Welsh Baptist, Glen Garfield Williams, was appointed as the first General Secretary of CEC in 1962.[34] (A second British Baptist, Keith Clements, became the third CEC General Secretary from 1997 to 2005.) Post 1989 and the emergence of new nations and Baptist groupings in eastern Europe, the EBF leadership encouraged a more active participation *as the EBF* in CEC, believing that it could be a forum to address the issues of the relationships between state churches (especially the Orthodox churches) and minority free churches such as Baptists.[35] In 2016, there are twelve EBF member Unions that are also members of CEC.[36]

But a further step was taken in the 1990s when CEC opened a category of Associate Membership to pan-European organizations like the EBF. The EBF took some years to determine this, but after the Council agreed it in 1996, the EBF was formally accepted as an associate (non-voting) member in 1998.[37] It was now easier for the EBF as a whole to be actively involved in CEC, and successive EBF General Secretaries Theo Angelov and Tony Peck were elected by CEC as members of its Church and Society Commission. This proved to be a very valuable forum for building contacts and friendships with representatives other denominations, especially on issues of human rights, religious freedom, and relations with the European Institutions. Part of the fruit of this can be seen in the contribution of European Baptists to the significant 2012 CEC publication on human rights;[38] followed by a Human Rights Training Event for European Baptists jointly sponsored by CEC and the EBF in 2014. It remains true that EBF support for CEC is strongest for CEC's ability to provide a forum to discuss religious freedom, the relationship between majority and minority churches, and human rights.

A further deepening of the relationship with CEC came in an unexpected development in 2012 when CEC abolished the category of Associate

---

34. Jones, *European Baptist Federation*, 78–83.

35. Ibid., 83.

36. The Baptist Unions of Bulgaria, Croatia, Denmark, France, Georgia, Germany, Great Britain, Hungary, Italy, Poland. Also the Euro-Asiatic Federation of the Unions of the Evangelical Christians-Baptists (includes most of the Baptist Unions that were part of the former Soviet Union), and the Uniting Church of Sweden (that from 2013 brought together into one church the former Baptist Union of Sweden churches together with Methodist and Mission Covenant churches). Together these bodies account for about two thirds of the total EBF membership.

37. Green, *Crossing the Boundaries*, 227–28.

38. Conference of European Churches, *European Churches Engaging in Human Rights*, articles by Tony Peck, Theo Angelov and also British Baptist, Professor (now Sir) Malcolm Evans.

Member during proposals for major structural change.[39] The EBF immediately raised the question of its continuing membership of CEC and in the ensuing negotiations the "ecclesial" character of the EBF became an important factor. Somehow, though not without some questioning, CEC managed to live with the "untidiness" of twelve of the EBF member Unions belonging as full members in their own right, and now the EBF seeking full membership. At the CEC Assembly of 2013, and thanks to the persistent advocacy of the Baptists present and others supporting them, the EBF was enabled for the first time to make application to be a full member of CEC. The EBF is now placed in a membership category termed "International Areas" that also includes such bodies as the Ecumenical Patriarchate of Constantinople, The Evangelical Lutheran Church in Russia and other States, the Moravian Church in Continental Europe, and two United Methodist "Areas."

The EBF representative at the 2013 CEC Assembly commented that "CEC does very important work which the EBF is very interested in. Now it is possible for the EBF to be a more active participant by having full membership *as an ecclesial body*."[40] It is too early to say how this will work out in practice, but perhaps it is a good sign of the acceptance of the importance of CEC to European Baptists that the formal proposal to seek full membership was agreed almost unanimously by the EBF Council.[41] Involvement in CEC as a means to contribute to the voice of the churches in an increasingly secular Europe will continue to be important for European Baptists.

SEARCHING FOR A COMMON UNDERSTANDING OF BAPTISM AND THE BASIS OF UNITY

The other main involvement of the EBF ecumenically has been with the Communion of Protestant Churches in Europe (CPCE—formerly known as the Leuenberg Church Fellowship). Here it was the *process* leading to the EBF's first official ecumenical dialogue that shows most clearly its ecclesial character.[42]

---

39. This resulted in the "Uppsala Report" to the 14th CEC Assembly, Budapest, 3–8 July 2013. Accessed: 27.2.16 at http://assembly2013.ceceurope.org/fileadmin/filer/cec/2013_Assembly-Documents/Reports/The_Uppsala_Report.pdf

40. Keith Jones, unpublished Report to the EBF on the 14th Assembly of the Conference of European Churches, Budapest, 3–8 July 2013. My italics.

41. Minutes of the EBF Council, Bratislava, Slovakia, 26–28 September 2013, 22:2.

42. What follows is a summary. A much more detailed account up to the point when the results of the CPCE-EBF Dialogue were published is given in Jones, *European Baptist Federation*, 95–104.

CPCE sees itself as a "church fellowship," founded on theological agreement concerning the gospel and the sacraments/ordinances of baptism and the Eucharist. The original Leuenberg Agreement (1973) resolved historic differences (mainly concerning the Eucharist) between Lutheran and Reformed Churches, especially in Germany. Other Lutheran and Reformed Churches in Europe joined the Leuenberg Church Fellowship (LCF)[43] in succeeding years, and most European Methodist Churches became part of LCF via a separate Agreement. As well as its theological discussions and agreements, increasingly the LCF wanted to see it itself as a Protestant Voice for Europe on a range of social and political issues, and to that end wished to have dialogue with other "Protestant" groups in Europe, such as the Baptists, who were not part of LCF.

After initial theological conversations with German Baptists a report was brought to the EBF Council in 2000. Whilst the EBF Executive had thought that perhaps a theological dialogue could be possible with a group of Unions who would be interested in closer links with the LCF, the EBF General Secretary took the lead in proposing that the EBF itself, on behalf of all its member bodies, should be the dialogue partner, and this was supported by influential Baptist leaders from both West and East Europe.[44] The Executive was then entrusted to put together the Baptist "delegation."[45]

Jones describes this as "a significant development," marking "a whole new era,"[46] that "the EBF was given ecclesial authority to represent even those not formally committed to the ecumenical community and certainly was able to offer real representation on behalf of many Baptist Unions who might have struggled to engage in such activity themselves."[47]

The resulting Dialogue focused on the issue of baptism in the context of the LCF basis for church fellowship, namely theological agreement on the Gospel and the Sacraments. The three sections of the Report that was issued in 2005 were under the headings of "Gospel, Christian Faith and Baptism, and The Church."[48] There is agreement between CPCE (LCF) and EBF on the nature of the gospel and some substantial convergences about

---

43. Renamed "Community of Protestant Churches in Europe" in 2003.

44. Especially significant was the support for EBF to enter doctrinal conversations with the LCF by Gregori Kommendant, then President of the Baptist Union of Ukraine and an influential figure among the Baptists in the whole Euro-Asiatic Region, a region not known for its enthusiasm about official ecumenical relationships. (Author's personal recollection).

45. Minutes of the EBF Council, Riga, Latvia, 21–24 September 2000, XIX: 4.

46. Jones, *European Baptist Federation*, 95–96.

47. Ibid., 106.

48. Hüffmaier and Peck, *Dialogue between the Community*, 9–29.

the *meaning* of baptism. However, unsurprisingly the Report identifies from the CPCE side that "an important barrier to the full realization of church fellowship remains concerning the "proper administration of baptism."[49] The concern was with those baptized as infants in CPCE churches who later on might also be permitted to be baptized as believing disciples in Baptist churches.

The dialogue had greatly benefited from the contribution of British Baptist ecumenical theologian, Professor Paul Fiddes, who here, and in other ecumenical dialogues involving Baptists,[50] proposed a model of a "common process of Christian Initiation," completed when an individual disciple owns faith for themselves that sees infant and Believers baptism testifying to different parts of that process, with Baptists preferring to leave baptism until the interplay between grace and faith can be most clearly seen.[51] This is a Baptist and ecumenical response to the concept of "our common Baptism," widely accepted in ecumenical theology post-Lima, but problematic for most Baptists. Ellis has also entered this debate and after listing some of these problematic areas for Baptists asks:

> So how can we move towards a form of mutual recognition which takes seriously a diversity of baptismal practices and provides a bases for visible unity? The most promising way forward is to broaden our focus from baptism to the whole process of initiation.[52]

However, the idea of a "common process of Christian initiation" can be controversial amongst both CPCE and Baptist churches, for different reasons. Lutherans in particular have some difficulties with the language of a *process* to describe Christian initiation, seeing the grace conferred at infant Baptism as being in some way complete in itself.[53] Many Baptists are concerned about giving some validity to infant baptism as part of this process, especially as a majority of European Baptist churches practices closed membership. But the point to note here is that the EBF delegation in the

---

49. Ibid., 26–27.

50. See *Pushing at the Boundaries of Unity* and "The Word of God in the Life of the Church," 28–123.

51. Fiddes, Baptism and the Process of Christian Initiation," 48–65. For a recent assessment that includes the highly significant contribution of Fiddes in this area, see Blyth, "The Meaning and Function of "Dynamic Equivalence"."

52. Ellis, "A View from the Pool," 107–20.

53. Interestingly, the concept of "a common process of initiation" seemed more acceptable to Roman Catholics involved in the later dialogue between the Baptist World Alliance and the Pontifical Council for Christian Unity. See "The Word of God in the Life of the Church," Sections 101–6.

Dialogue felt that it was important to put the idea of a "common process of Christian Initiation" to the European Baptist community, challenging member Unions on issues such as closed membership, "rebaptism" and individual churches that are sometimes prepared to admit new members without any form of baptism. This was the EBF "providing leadership in the matter of ecumenical development beyond the safe territory of formal exchange of positions"[54] and indeed reception of it in some Baptist Unions has provoked some lively debate.

On the matter of church unity, the EBF diverged from the CPCE concept of unity based on their conditions to enable "church fellowship," namely agreement on the gospel and the sacraments. The latter condition could not allow full unity with Baptists because of the differences over baptism. The Baptists, for their part declared that

> ... being in the Body of Christ, and not Baptism is the basis of unity. This recognizes the evidence of the work of the Spirit in other believers, in terms of gifts and fruits of the Spirit.[55]

However, both groups were able to affirm that "despite differences of interpretation we recognize the presence of the true church of Jesus Christ in one another," able to share in one another's Holy Communion and "acknowledge" one another's presbyteral (pastor) ministries.[56]

The Report was commended by the EBF Council for study by its member unions, and some at least have taken it up. After a rather disappointing response from CPCE about the possibilities of future working together, there was an initial decision by the EBF to express its gratitude for the dialogue but proceed no further with developing the relationship. But for some member Unions, especially the German-speaking ones, some relationship with CPCE was important in their ecumenical context. So there followed some years of further conversations about what shape such a relationship should take, and again it was the EBF on behalf of all its Unions that was party to an Agreement of Mutual Cooperation setting out areas where the two bodies can work together. It was signed at the EBF Council in 2010 by the EBF General Secretary, Tony Peck, and the CPCE General Secretary, Bishop Michael Bünker.[57]

Since then there have been annual meetings of the EBF and CPCE leaders, CPCE participation in EBF Councils, and an EBF presence at the

54. Jones, *European Baptist Federation*, 103–4.
55. Hüffmaier and Peck, *Dialogue between the Community*, 25.
56. Ibid., 25.
57. Minutes of the EBF Council, Rome, Italy, 21–24 September 22–25, 2010, Section 16.

CPCE Assembly. The EBF has been invite to nominate members of CPCE Expert Groups, and the presence of Bulgarian Baptist Dr. Parush Parushev on the Bioethics Group has been especially noteworthy. There has also been an invitation to the EBF to contribute to the CPCE activities to mark the 500th anniversary of the Reformation, from 2017 onwards. It is hoped that areas of cooperation will grow in the future.

CONCLUSION:
THE ECCLESIAL CHARACTER OF THE EBF

Set in the context mentioned earlier of the great diversity of views and responses to all things ecumenical among the EBF Unions, these developments have been truly remarkable. An EBF Council of leaders representing the majority of EBF Unions has agreed to go a stage beyond celebrating a spiritual unity with Christian believers of other traditions, to making such unity visible, even in partial and limited ways, through the EBF involvement in CEC and CPCE. There has been level of trust given to those who represent the EBF that in turn has engendered a sense of responsibility to represent Baptists faithfully in ecumenical discussions and working together. There has already been at least one example (in Armenia) of how the nurturing of relationships by EBF leaders in CEC through the involvement of the EBF general secretary has helped a lessening of tension between Baptists and a state church and enabled the growth of friendship between individual senior leaders of the two churches.

POSTSCRIPT: RECENT DEVELOPMENTS

Two other developments are worthy of mention. When the Baptist Union of Sweden was contemplating entering a new church, uniting existing Swedish Baptist, Methodist, and Mission Covenant churches, the EBF was formally invited by Swedish Baptists to be active partners with them contributing to the process of discernment on the different stages of the journey towards union. The resulting Uniting Church of Sweden finally came into being in 2013 and the EBF General Secretary represented the wider Baptist community at its inauguration. Later the EBF Council agreed to admit the whole Uniting Church into membership, knowing that the great majority of members were originally from the other two denominations. Since then Uniting Church leaders have been very committed to involvement in the life of both the EBF and the Baptist World Alliance.

The other development takes us back to Ellis's vision of an ecumenism that leads on to that wider *oikoumene*, especially characterized by churches working for peace, justice, and reconciliation in the world. At the 2014 EBF Council in Bucharest a whole session was taken up considering the situation of the Middle East, first of all listening to Baptist leaders of Israel, Jordan, Lebanon, Syria, Iraq, and Egypt, and then reflecting and praying together for this strife-torn region, scene of so much recent human tragedy. These Middle Eastern Baptist leaders spoke powerfully to the EBF, urging its members not to see Christians as a beleaguered minority but as part of a "silent majority" of people of all faiths who desire to live together in peace in the same geographical space. This theme has been well articulated by Martin Accad who, based at the Arab Baptist Theological Seminary in Beirut, Lebanon, is a key theologian and prophetic voice in the Middle East situation today. He spoke of a "network of sleeper cells" made up of peaceful and loving religious people around the world, who need to rise up and neutralize the effect of a "reckless minority" who would promote violent fanaticism or a view that painted entire religions in the hues of violence and terror.[58]

This is all the more telling coming from a Middle East situation where ecumenical relationships between evangelicals such as Baptists and the "traditional" churches are often strained, something that the EBF takes up with these churches whenever it has the opportunity. Martin Accad and others play their part in not only working for the unity of Christians in the Middle East but by embracing this wider *oikoumene*. Baptists, especially in Lebanon and Iraq have provided some remarkable examples of initiatives for peace and reconciliation in the wider society and between the faiths. They have helped European Baptists as a whole to increase their vision of what Christian "witness" means in such a challenging situation as the Middle East. Our brothers and sisters in Christ there live out the truth articulated much earlier by Ellis in his own ecumenical vision:

> Shalom is [God's] will for the world he created and continues to sustain. In Christ he has announced forgiveness and acted for the redemption of the sin that distorts and destroys the world's peace. The church is called to be a community of peace, embodying shalom and living and acting as a sign and foretaste of the shalom God wills for the whole cosmos. The *being* and *doing* of the church cannot be kept apart—we are all called to be ministers of peace.[59]

---

58. See *Ethics Daily* article accessed on 28.2.16, at http://www.ethicsdaily.com/the-silent-majority-in-middle-east-seeks-peace-cms-22230.

59. Ellis, *Together on the Way*, 123.

This is but the latest staging post in a continuing journey of the ecumenical engagement of the European Baptist Federation. It illustrates the simple yet profound truth of Chris Ellis's hymn, that in the complex social, political and religious world of contemporary Europe and the Middle East we indeed "need each other" as together we bear witness to the continuing presence of the risen Christ.

Living God

Living God, we come to worship
trusting in your power and love.
All the earth is your creation,
you have stretched the sky above.
Awesome and majestic maker,
we have seen how much you care;
here is love and here is glory:
life of God for all to share

Living God, yours is the power
making worlds from empty space;
out of silence, out of darkness,
yours the word and yours the face.
In the telling of your story
servant saviour, gentle Lord:
here is love and here is glory
for a needy world outpoured.

Living God, life-giving Spirit,
surging wind and fluttering dove;
you equip your saints for service
sharing joy and growing love.
You create a kingdom people,
lead us on, our spirits feed:
here is love and here is glory
flowing out through heart and deed.

Living God you overwhelm us
with the wonder of your grace:
flood us with the joy of loving,
fold us in your strong embrace.
Father, Son and Holy Spirit
form our minds, direct our ways;
here is love and here is glory:
hearts and lives that live your praise.

12

"Father, Son, and Holy Spirit"
The Triune Creator in Hymn and Theology

PAUL S. FIDDES

WHY IS "LIVING GOD, we come to worship" such a good hymn? I am delighted to pose and try to answer this question in honor of its author, my friend Christopher Ellis. With a distinguished course of life as pastor, theologian, liturgist, ecumenist, college principal, and skilled artist, he has poured his rich experience into the writing of hymns. That is, without doubt, the basic answer to my question "why?" But I nevertheless want to go on and ask, "*What makes* this a good hymn?" Answering this question will give the opportunity to develop a doctrine of God as triune creator, exploring some of the theological depths that Chris himself plumbs in his hymn in such an accessible way, as well as making some reflections from a Baptist perspective.

1. GOD AS TRINITY

The first reason why this is such a good hymn is that it is truly trinitarian, or enables worship of a God who is Trinity, living in eternal relations of love. It is not as easy to write a properly trinitarian hymn as some have supposed. In an attempt to capture the mystery that the one God exists in three modes of being, some writers are content to repeat essentially the same affirmations about Father, Son, and Holy Spirit in turn, simply changing the names in each verse. The song, "Father, we adore you" readily comes to mind, where the same words of adoration are applied to Jesus and the Holy Spirit, the three verses confessing in turn that the singers lay their lives before, and love, each of the three persons.[1] Similarly, "Precious Father, how I love you" asks each of the three divine persons, in consecutive verses and identical terms, to bless, cleanse, and re-create the worshipper.[2] The result is to celebrate one God with three names.

These samples belong to the early stages of the modern "spiritual-song" writing movement, and more recent instances show a much greater awareness of relations between Father, Son, and Spirit.[3] We still find, however, songs which are helpful in a number of ways but are limited in effectively referring to one three-named God. One song, "Oh sovereign God," addresses a divine king, whom the saints and angels adore and before whose throne they fall; this is the one, it affirms, whose great descent from heaven has made the worshippers whole. It is thus unclear what distinction is being made between God the Father and the Son. The chorus then calls on the singers to praise Father, Son, and the Spirit as three persons in one God, and affirms that *this* is the God whose name is above all other names, an ascription usually made to Christ on the basis of Philippians 2:9.[4]

More traditional hymns can follow the same paradigm of a three-named God, such as the long-established "Holy, Holy, Holy, Lord God Almighty." In that hymn, based on Isaiah's vision of Yahweh, despite the threefold cry of "Holy" (traditionally called the "trisagion") and the orthodox formula "God in three persons," the impression is worship of a single divine Being, effectively the Father who is hidden in darkness and has a glory that cannot be seen.[5] By contrast, other writers are so anxious to affirm the distinct identity of the three persons that they seem to be celebrating three individual gods, perhaps one for each verse, hoping to affirm the unity with a flourish in a final verse which hymns the "most glorious Trinity."[6]

---

1. "Father, we adore you," by Terry Coelho, Copyright © Word Music (UK) 1972.

2. "Precious Father," by Susie Hare. Copyright © Thankyou Music 1984.

3. See, for example, "We believe in God the Father," by Lou Fellingham & Nathan Fellingham, Copyright© 2014 Thankyou Music, though it is still difficult to work out whom "Yahweh" refers to. See also "There's a dance" by Geraldine Latty (lyrics), Busbee (music) Copyright© 2005 Kingsway's Thankyou Music/The Livingstone Collective.

4. "Oh sovereign God, Oh matchless King," by Chris Tomlin and Ed Cash Copyright© 2008 Sixsteps Music.

5. See v. 3 of "Holy, Holy, Holy" by Reginald Heber (1783–1826).

6. An example is the unfortunate modernization of John Mariott's hymn "Thou whose almighty word" into "Father whose mighty word . . ." in *Baptist Praise and Worship*, no. 591.

The hymn by Chris affirms the "Living God" at the beginning of each verse, and the theme is the activity of this one God in creation and re-creation. Towards the end of each verse we repeat the same line, "Here is love and here is glory," giving the sense that we are worshipping the one God without labouring the point. Yet there is a real diversity of experience of this one God. In the first verse we sing of the "awesome and majestic maker" of heaven and earth, and we receive the impression that this is a life-giving God, full of "care" that all should flourish. In the second verse, the theme of a creator God continues, but now—without explicitly naming the Son—a distinction in persons begins to emerge. The living God is "word and face." The first image here is a traditional ascription for God the Son— the "Word"—and the second recalls a more modern Christology of Jesus as "the human face of God,"[7] but the metaphors still work for a singer who has no theological background. They evoke a personal reality who is being spoken out from the origin of a creative mind ("word"), and who makes the source of all life and love visible ("face"). The lines do not require knowledge of Scripture to make their effect, but in singing "making worlds from empty space . . . out of darkness" those who are familiar with John 1 will recognize the divine Word, "through whom all things were made" and the one whom "the dark could not overcome." That there is some loving reality distinct, while not separate, from the creator God being hymned in the first verse is underlined by the affirmation that this "word and face" has a story that is known in the history of "needy" humanity, and that it is a story about a servant and a savior.

In the third verse, the living God is named as "Spirit," but this does not require any theological acquaintance with the third person of the Trinity. "Spirit" appears first as an image, accompanied by the new metaphors of wind and dove in flight, and yet the singer quickly feels that these fresh images evoke nothing less than a third personal reality distinct from the first two, since the work of creation by this Spirit is the making of "a kingdom people" and an "equipping" of the saints, ideas that have not been mentioned so far. We do not have to be familiar with the occurrence of the metaphors of wind and dove in Scripture for them to have their impact, though for those who do recall them they come with the pleasure of recognition.

Thus, when we arrive at the fourth and final verse where "Father, Son, and Holy Spirit" are named for the first time, we have already experienced in our imaginations a God of tri-personal reality. Underlined by the repetition of "here is love and here is glory" this is no mere tying together of three beings (as often-supposed) in a paradox. Without resort to the traditional

---

7. For example, Robinson, *Human Face of God*, 180–211.

language of "three persons in one substance" we have been exploring a mystery which is manifest in our midst, gradually becoming aware that there is a threefold, relational way of being to the love which is the ultimate creative reality of the universe.

2. PARTICIPATING IN GOD

Here, then, is a second reason why this is such a good hymn. In singing it we have *engaged* in a triune God rather than merely *describing* God. The hymn exemplifies, that is, the point of the doctrine of the Trinity, which is not to attempt to observe God (claiming—"this is what God looks like") but to be enabled to participate in God (confessing, "this is what it means to share in God"). To understand the effect of the hymn, we must recall that early Christian theology never conceived of the three "persons" in God as three individual beings with their own centres of consciousness, somehow reconciled in *one* individual being. This would be a mere projection of our human understanding of persons, and would anyway rely on a modern psychological understanding of personality. The Greek word for divine "person," *hypostasis*, signified a "distinct reality," and this reality for the early theologians could only be understood in terms of a relationship of love. Augustine explained that "the names, Father and Son, do not refer to the substance but to the relation,"[8] and confessed in wonder that "we only say three persons to avoid saying nothing."[9] Neither is the one God an individual being, or even the "disembodied supra-being" beloved of philosophers of religion. Rather, the one being of God is a *communion* or fellowship of love which is supremely "beingful."[10]

It is not possible to *observe*—even in our mind's eye—three personal realities entirely constituted by their relationships with each other. In vain we ask how we might represent the triune God on a canvas, in a stained-glass window or through computer-generated avatars. God is not an object in the world to be scrutinized and analyzed. But as we pray, according to the New Testament bidding, "to the Father, through the Son, and in the Spirit," we find our prayers—and so our hymns—fitting into a movement which is like that of speech between a son and a father. Our response of "yes" ("Amen") leans upon a movement which is like a filial "yes" of humble obedience, glorifying the Father, a response which is already there before us. At the same time, we find ourselves involved in a movement of self-giving

---

8. Augustine, *De Trinitate* 5.6; translation from *The Trinity*, 180.
9. Augustine, *De Trinitate* 5.10.
10. See Zizioulas, *Being as Communion*, 33–48.

like that of a father sending out a son on a journey, a movement which the early theologians called "eternal generation" and which has its outworking in the mission ("sending") of the Son by the Father in history to achieve the reconciliation of all things.[11]

As we participate in God like this, we discover that these movements of response and mission are undergirded by movements of suffering, like the painful longing of a forsaken son towards a father and of a desolate father towards a lost son. More, these two directions of sending and response, are interwoven by a third movement, as we find that they are continually being opened up to new depths of relationship and to the new possibilities of the future by a momentum for which Scripture offers impressionistic images—a wind blowing, breath stirring, wings beating, oil trickling, water flowing, fire burning.[12]

The hymn prompts us to share in the triune God like this. Its language is one of dynamic movement, full of verbs rather than abstract nouns. In the first verse we come "trusting" to "share" in the life of God who stretches out the heavens. In the second we engage in the "telling" of a story in which love is "outpoured." In the third verse the images of movement multiply: the Spirit is like the "surging" of wind and the "fluttering" of wings, and we experience the Spirit as "sharing," "feeding," "leading," "growing," and "flowing." In the final verse, we find God to be "overwhelming," "flooding," "embracing," "forming," and "directing." Even without our being consciously aware of it, the language of the hymn is enticing us into participating in a movement which is already going on beyond us, but at the same time is catching us up into its flow. The ancient word *perichoresis*—intertwining and interpenetrating—is appropriate for this complexity within the life of God which draws us in. God is making room within God's self for us to dwell, or—to use another metaphor—to join the measures of the divine dance.[13]

So the theologian Karl Barth insists that "with regard to the being of God, the word 'event' or 'act' is final."[14] Barth's thinking goes like this. God's revealing of God's self is not a proposition but a "happening," and so—since God always speaks the truth about God's self—God must "happen" in God's own self. If God unveils God's self in an event, then in an *eternal* event of self-repetition, God is "thrice the divine I." Mathematics has no place in a

11. So Fiddes, *Participating in God*, 36–38.
12. See Matt 6:6; John 14:16; Heb 7:25; Eph 6:18.
13. The Greek term *perichoresis* cannot, however, simply be translated as "dance": on this, see Fiddes, *Participating in God*, 72–81.
14. Barth, *Church Dogmatics*, II/1, 263.

doctrine of God. God cannot be reduced either to an "I" which is a single numeral, or to three individual "I"s which are numerically plural.[15] Barth avoids using the term "person" to denote what are thereby distinguished in God as Father, Son, and Spirit, as he believes the word to be inevitably bound up with modern notions of an individual self-consciousness and so the term is an undermining of the one Lordship of God.[16] He prefers to speak of three "modes (or ways) of being" (*Seinsweise*), and this has opened him to the accusation of presenting God an Absolute Subject who diversifies himself.[17] In my view this is an unfair accusation, as it is clear that Barth conceives the "ways of being" to be always defined by their relationships.[18] But it would be better to take up his insight into the event character of God by speaking of three "*movements* of being characterized by relationship," or more simply "movements of relationship" which happen in one divine event. Robert Jenson has a similar intention when he speaks of God as "an event constituted in relations and personal in structure."[19]

Many theologians will think of the three "persons" in God as being three agents or actors, who are nevertheless inseparable from the relationships in which they live, so that there is no question of there being a divine person who first exists and then "decides" to be in relationship. I myself prefer to say that we can only think of the persons *as* relations, and I have argued this in a number of places.[20] The analogy between ourselves and God is not, I propose, between human *persons* and divine persons, but between human and divine *relationships*. For the purposes of appreciating Chris' hymn, I do not think the difference between these two approaches finally matters. The hymn assures us that as we "share" in the life of God (first verse) we can identify three distinct movements which are all like speech, emotion, and action; they are like movements within relationships "from a father to a son" and "from a son to a father," together with a movement of "deepening relations." They are mutual relationships of ecstatic, outward-going love, giving and receiving.

So far in describing these relationships I have followed the form of address that Jesus himself taught his disciples, "Abba, Father" (Matt 6:9), offering the image "from son to father" for the movement of response that we ourselves lean upon. His way of speaking is indispensable for us, since

---

15. Barth, *Church Dogmatics*, I/1, 394.
16. Ibid., 355–59.
17. So Moltmann, *Trinity*, 142; LaCugna, *God for Us*, 252–53.
18. Barth, *Church Dogmatics*, I/1, 364–67.
19. Jenson, *Triune Identity*, 161.
20. See Fiddes, *Participating in God*, 35–46; Fiddes, "Relational Trinity," 159–71.

we rely on his relation to God for our own "adoption" as daughters and sons of God. But these movements of giving and receiving in God cannot in themselves be restricted to a particular gender, as is quite clear with the images for the movement of Spirit. It is not that the Spirit is feminine where the other persons are masculine; the fact that the Spirit eludes gender alerts us to the same situation with the other persons. They will also, in appropriate contexts, give rise to feminine images; for instance, the experience of our participation may require us to say that we are engaging in a flow of relationships like those originating in a mother (cf. Isa 49:14–15), especially in experiences of being spiritually nurtured and fed. Or the experience is like human relations which we can only say are characterized by the response of a daughter, so that in some circumstances we can *recognize* the same kind of "daughterly" response in God as we know in human life. In Chris's hymn, by holding back the words "Father" and "Son" until the last verse, he enables us in the first three verses to develop various imaginative ways of conceiving the relations within the "Living God." "Father" and "Son" are appropriate images here, but not exhaustive.

3. THE OBJECTIVE AND THE SUBJECTIVE

Now I want to suggest a third reason why this is a good hymn which is rather different from the first two. The hymn combines the subjective and the objective in our worship of God. The hymn is, objectively, about the character and the acts of God. It affirms a God whose "power" is only to be understood in the context of love and servanthood. The acts of God in creation are alluded to in ways that neatly re-use metaphors from both the biblical account and from modern science: the living God "stretches out the heavens" (Isa 42:5) and at the same time, in a hint of the "big bang" and expanding universe, "makes worlds from empty space."

I must confess that I would myself have liked the hymn to be a little more explicit about the costliness of this creative activity of God. If God allows a creation to exist with its own freedom, then this is bound to cause God pain and suffering. The freedom of created beings to go their own way is likely to result in decisions that damage them and this in turn will hurt God who has the loving care for all things that the first verse celebrates. Moreover, it seems a moral requirement that if God gives created beings the freedom to inflict destruction on themselves and others, the creator should share in the risk of this venture and its consequences. There is, to be sure, a long Christian tradition of maintaining the impassibility of God in an attempt to establish the difference between the created and the Uncreated, but I suggest that God as uncreated being can freely and without external constraint will in love to be vulnerable. We see the truth of this unveiled in the cross of Jesus, and the hymn does hint at it in the lines "servant saviour, gentle lord . . . for a needy world outpoured." Not everything can be expressed in one hymn!

An objective declaration of the creative and redemptive acts of God continues in the next verse, where the living God as Spirit is hymned as "equipping saints" and "creating a kingdom people." But in approving the objectivity of the hymn, I do need to make clear that there is a difference between two kinds of objectivity. On the one hand there is the "objectivity" of God and divine activity in the sense of a reality existing "over against us," while on the other hand there is knowing "God as an object." The first kind of objectivity asserts that God is not merely a projection of our own minds, but it often confused with the second, which I reject. I have already insisted that God *cannot* be known as an object, as other objects in the world are known, and that our awareness of God always takes the form of participative knowledge.

Here I venture to take issue with Barth when he tries to combine participation with objectification by proposing that God is an "object" of our knowing in so far as we share in God's own knowledge of God's self, which is supposedly objective. "God offers Himself to man [sic] as the object . . . of the knowledge of his faith," Barth affirms, because "we receive a share of the truth of His knowledge of Himself."[21] But this assumes that God knows God's own self as an object, in the way that we know ourselves, and this imposes on God, who is the Uncreated, a model of consciousness that belongs to created beings. If we participate in God then we are indeed being given a share in God's own self-knowledge, but if God is really uncreated reality, then God can never be an object of our knowing. We certainly know things in the world in a subject-object way, and so there is always the temptation for us to try and manipulate and abuse people and nature for our own interests. We try to become dominating subjects, simply using others as objects to fulfill our desires or lust for power. While we cannot avoid experiencing things in the created world as objects, as we share in the triune God's knowledge of God's self, and so experience a relationship which is free of the subject-object structure, we can begin to treat objects in the world in a new way, allowing them to be truly themselves.

God, then, exists "objectively" over against us, in the sense that God confronts us with a demand to live in a way that has renounced domination.

---

21. Barth, *Church Dogmatics* II/1, 43, 51. This is a development from Barth's *Epistle to the Romans* where God's "objectivity" is of the first kind I have identified.

Hymns that recognize this claim on our lives release us into a new way of being—in fact, into a new creation. Yet at the same time there is an essential subjective dimension in our relationship with God. Worship involves not only our minds but our feelings and emotions. There is a long Baptist tradition of cherishing "sincerity" in worship, a history that Ellis himself has written about. "Sincerity carries the soul in all simplicity to open its heart to God," writes John Bunyan in a treatise on prayer.[22] As Ellis summarizes the thought of Bunyan and others, inspiration and sincerity are the two main marks of prayer.[23] Our forebears assumed that use of written prayers inevitably inhibited the participation in God I have been celebrating, obstructing the sincerity of our response to the inspiring movement of God's Spirit that draws us to God's self and enables us to respond. The prayer-book imposed, they felt, a cold formalism, lacking the warmth of affections and emotions directed towards God. Bunyan sums up the two movements of inspiration and sincerity when he defines prayer as "a sincere, sensible, affectionate pouring out of the heart or soul to God through Christ, in the strength and assistance of the holy Spirit, for such things as God hath promised."[24]

Now that we are no longer *required* to use a prayer book validated by Parliament and monarch we are, perhaps, released to notice that the Spirit of God can use written as much as unwritten prayers, and can inspire prayers prepared in the study as well as uttered spontaneously in the assembly. The objection of Bunyan and others to written prayers they were being compelled to use by state powers was rooted in a passionate concern to respect the "rule of Christ" who called and enabled prayer, and they were resisting not so much the form of prayer as subjection to any authority in worship that was not Christ. Now we are liberated from this oppression, we are freed to notice that spiritual songs of the present day are so full of human feelings that they lose the objective worship of God, which was prompted in our ancestors's devotions by the echoes of Scripture that their prayers were evidently soaked in. Too many spiritual songs of the present day seem to assume that worship *depends* on the way that we feel, as if God will not come to a worshipping people unless they can first build God a throne,[25] in apparent ignorance that the God of the Psalms comes to demand that the door of the temple be opened whether people are ready or not (Psalm 24).

Yet there is a proper "affectionate pouring out of the heart," as Bunyan puts it, and Chris's hymn gives plenty of opportunity for worshippers to

22. Bunyan, *I Will Pray with the Spirit*, 237.
23. Ellis, *Gathering*, 119.
24. Bunyan, *I Will Pray with the Spirit*, 235.
25. See "Jesus, we enthrone you," by Paul Kyle, Copyright © Thankyou Music 1980.

express this subjective dimension. We come "trusting" in love, telling the story, "overwhelmed" by wonder, and "flooded" by joy. The hymn allows and encourages us to express our emotions, so that the final repetition of "here is love and here is glory" refers, subjectively to our own lives where before it had referred objectively to the triune God.

4. THE SHAPE OF THE STORY

A fourth reason why this is a good hymn is that it expresses a progression in thought. In fact, it tells a story in the way that the creeds of the church do. The great ecumenical creeds do not present Christian doctrine in the form of a list of propositions, as is the case with modern confessions of faith. They tell a story which begins in the work of God the Father in creation, proceeds through the making flesh of God in Christ and re-creation through his death and resurrection, and then concludes with the work of the Spirit in the life of the church, inspiring hope in a future new creation. Telling a story makes clear that God's acts in creation and history form a divine drama which contains the whole drama of human life,[26] and the very playing out of this drama in the creed draws us in to take our parts actively within it.

So this hymn is thoroughly credal, beginning with the act of creation of the living God, proceeding through redemption and the formation of the church. The verses could not be arranged in a different order, and the worship leader cannot (or should not) choose to sing only one or two verses. I detect also a theological instinct in the way that these verses are written. While they tell the story progressively of creation, redemption, and the church, they do not isolate one of the divine persons within each of these moments of salvation-history. Because the ascription "Father, Son, and Holy Spirit" is held back to the last verse, while there is an implicit emphasis on the work of each one in the first three verses, the carrying through of the appeal "living God" and the unifying theme of creation means that each person of the Trinity overflows into each of the credal episodes.

In playing a kind of "riff" or variation on the story set out in the ecumenical creeds, our author stands in the succession of former Baptists who, as James McClendon has affirmed, have allowed the narrative of the faith to shape their own story.[27] The Baptist Confessions of the seventeenth century are startling examples of an interweaving of the credal story with the everyday story of Baptists in the turmoil and stress of their actual historical situation. The Particular Baptist "London Confession" of 1644, for instance,

26. See Balthasar, *Theo-Drama*, I, 15–23.
27. McClendon, *Ethics*, 31–35.

was written to be presented to the "Long Parliament" in order to secure toleration for Baptists. It follows the dramatic outline of the so-called Nicene Creed (properly the Creed of Nicaea-Constantinople, 381), moving in the same way from confession of God the Father and creator (I–V), through celebration of Christ in his virgin birth, sacrificial death, resurrection and second coming (VI–XXI), to the coming of the Spirit (XXII–XXXII), the nature of the church (XXXIII–XXXVIII), baptism (XXXIX–XLI), and finally to the resurrection of the dead (LII, in 1646 revision). But this bare, Nicene structure is filled out with theological expansions from a Calvinist perspective, specific Baptist concerns, and references to the challenging context of the time in which Baptists were confessing their faith. There is no need to suppose that the Baptist writers, from seven London churches, were *deliberately* following the Nicene Creed; it is more likely that they carried in their minds the basic shape of the credal drama which they had inherited and absorbed from Christian witness over the years,[28] and which had already been reflected in the Separatist "True Confession" of 1596 which appears to have served as a model for their own confession. What is clear is that this inherited story of the acts of God is interacting throughout with their own story.

For instance, with the mention of Jesus Christ as the "only son of God the Father, the brightness of his glory, the ingraven form of his being" (echoing closely the Nicene Creed), there is introduced the place and authority of Scripture as witness to Christ, reflecting the centrality of reading and interpreting Scripture in the local congregation.[29] To mention of the resurrection, the second coming of Christ and his receiving of the kingdom ("his kingdom will have no end," according to Nicaea) there is added the necessity for faith in this gospel, aroused by preaching.[30] The confession of the Holy Spirit is amplified by more reference to faith as a gift of the Spirit, and to power from the Spirit for leading a holy Christian life "through all duties, temptations, conflicts, sufferings,"[31] described shortly afterwards as "all manner of afflictions, tribulations and persecutions."[32] The Nicene clause on "one holy, catholic and apostolic church" is replaced by the bold announcement that "Christ hath here on earth a spiritual kingdom, which

---

28. See Harmon, *Towards Baptist Catholicity*, 77–80.

29. "The London Confession 1644," chapters VII–VIII; in Lumpkin, *Baptist Confessions of Faith*, 158.

30. "The London Confession 1644," chapter XXI; in ibid., 162.

31. "The London Confession 1644," chapter XXVI; in ibid., 163.

32. "The London Confession 1644," chapter XXXI; in ibid., 165.

is the Church,"³³ recalling the many Baptist protests against the false pretensions of royal and civil powers to exercise authority in "the spiritual kingdom of Christ," such as appointing its leaders and legislating for forms of prayer. Rather, the confession affirms that every congregation has power to choose "pastors, teachers, elders, deacons" for themselves, recognizing their appointment by Christ.³⁴ The Nicene clause on baptism is framed as participation in the death and resurrection of Christ to be "dispensed only upon persons professing faith, or that are Disciples," and this leads into the obligation of all baptized disciples—in church meeting—to "watch over" each other, complementary to Christ's appointing of officers in the church to "oversee, visit, watch."³⁵ The particular crisis of the time is further reflected in a totally non-Nicene clause added to the end of the confession, on the proper authority of civil magistrates, and their duty "to tender the liberty of men's consciences."³⁶

By 1660, after the Cromwellian Protectorate, England was anticipating the restoration of the monarchy under Charles II, and Baptists were being regarded as dangerous political plotters, seditionists, and heretics. Thirty General Baptists drew up a confession of faith to be presented to the new king, refuting slanders against them and rejecting any intention to use violence. Their "brief confession" (later called the "Standard Confession") was not as neatly constructed as that of the Particular Baptists, but once again follows the familiar Nicene drama of the triune God. Beginning with "One God the Father" (I–II), it moves to "One Lord Jesus Christ" (III–VI) and then to "One Holy Spirit" (VII–IX), expanding into intertwined affirmations about church and baptism (X–XIX), and ending with the resurrection of the dead (XX–XXII). At least, the shape of the *creed* ends there, since the confession appends statements about the authority of the holy Scriptures, the "free liberty of conscience in matters of religion," and a denial of "devilish reports" that "some of us . . . had lately gotten knives, hooked knives . . . and a great store of arms."³⁷

In its more rambling treatment of subjects than in the 1644 Confession, there emerges even more vividly for us the story of the social situation of these Baptists in the 1660s. The expected affirmation of the saving death of Christ is followed by need for faith in this act of God (as in the 1644

33. "The London Confession 1644," chapter XXXIII; in ibid., 165.
34. "The London Confession 1644," chapter XXXVI; in ibid., 166.
35. "The London Confession 1644," chapters XXXIX–XL, XLIV; in ibid., 167-68.
36. "The London Confession 1644," chapter XLVIII in revised version of 1646; in ibid., 148.
37. "The Standard Confession 1660," chapter XXV; in ibid., 234.

Confession), and this leads in turn to the gifts of ministry given by the Spirit of God to those who do believe and who are baptized "for the remission of sins" after repentance and faith. Those who exercise gifts in the church like this are contrasted colorfully with those "only brought up in the Schools of humane learning, to the attaining humane arts, and variety of languages ... seeking rather the gain of large revenues, than the gain of souls to God."[38] Affirmation of the Holy Spirit leads to reflection that those who "breath out much cruelty, and great envy against the Liberties, and peaceable living" of the faithful have evidently not received the "Spirit of promise."[39] The clause on baptism makes clear that children dying in infancy do not need to be baptized to escape hell, taking issue with "the uncharitable opinion of others, who though they plead much for the bringing of children into the visible Church here on earth by Baptism, yet . . . . shut a great part of them out of the Kingdom of Heaven for ever."[40] The section on the church commends spiritual leaders ("officers") who are "not greedy of filthy lucre as too many National Ministers [i.e., of the Church of England] are," and rejects "tithes, or any forced maintenance" of ministry.[41] "Poor saints" should likewise be supported in a voluntary way, without need of compulsion by magistrates,[42] and the Nicene affirmation of the resurrection of the dead is followed by the reflection that the bodies of the saints who "suffer here for Christ" shall inherit the kingdom, doubtless having in mind the saints of the writers's own congregations.[43]

While Baptists have explicitly affirmed that the ecumenical creeds and the Definition of Chalcedon are faithful witnesses to the truth of God in Scripture,[44] they have not regularly recited the creeds in worship. Rather, allowing the drama of God attested there to influence the shape and language of their confessions, prayers and hymns has enabled them at the very same time to bear witness to their own story. This is what our author does in his hymn, where the story reaches an emotional and conceptual climax in a deliberate prayer of petition, prayer flowing out of confession, in a way

38. "The Standard Confession 1660," chapter V; in ibid., 226.
39. "The Standard Confession 1660," chapter VII; in ibid., 227.
40. "The Standard Confession 1660," chapter X; in ibid., 228.
41. "The Standard Confession 1660," chapters. XV–XVI; in ibid., 229–30.
42. "The Standard Confession 1660," chapter XIX; in ibid., 230–31.
43. "The Standard Confession 1660," chapter XX; in ibid., 231.
44. See the General Baptist "Orthodox Creed 1678," article 38, in ibid., 326–27 (affirming the Apostles', Nicene, and so-called "Athanasian" Creeds). The German-language Baptist Confession used in Germany, Austria, and Switzerland affirms the Apostles' Creed, and the Norwegian Baptist Confession affirms the Apostles' and Nicene Creed: see Parker, *Baptists in Europe*, 57, 111.

which is only implicit in the creeds themselves: we pray, "flood, fold, form, direct."

5. THE TRIUNE CREATOR

Finally, and perhaps fundamentally, this is a good hymn because it seamlessly combines Trinity and creation. If a hymn book is organized thematically, it could be placed in either section, and it prompts the singer to hold the two doctrinal themes together. This has not always been the case in the history of Christian thought. There has been a habit of thinking about God as creator as if God were a single, superior divine being, and thought about God as Trinity has only entered at a later point as a kind of development. Sometimes it has even been imagined that the existence of a creator God can be demonstrated by human reason ("natural theology"), from observing certain proofs of design or cause in the world, while the belief that God is Trinity is supposed to be a kind of second stage where revealed truths are added to human reason. While not holding it in a crude form, courses and textbooks in theology can encourage this two-stage view by discussing the existence and attributes of God as creator in an opening section without any reference to trinitarian theology.[45] But if the Christian vision of God is triune, it is the triune God who creates.

How, then, shall we hold together the two doctrines, especially where the ecumenical creeds begin by affirming the Father as "maker of heaven and earth"? Some have supposed that we can distinguish three kinds of creativity—the Father through "making," the Son through "speaking" and the Spirit through "inspiring." This, however, seems to reduce the persons to functions of God's activity. Irenaeus among the early fathers gives us the picture of the Father creating with "two hands," the Son and the Spirit, but this leaves us with essentially a poetic image.[46] A favorite answer in the early days of the church was that of cosmic "mediation." I mean that the figure of Christ, in whom the New Testament writers find God to be uniquely disclosed and who certainly acts as a mediator in *relationship* between a righteous God and sinful human beings, was reconfigured as a mediator between God the Father and a physical creation. As early as Justin Martyr we find the assumption that there are two spheres of reality —a world of unchanging, intellectual Being, and a world of transient, material becoming where everything passes away.[47] This was effectively a re-writing of the bibli-

---

45. See the criticism of Rahner, *Trinity*, 15–17.
46. Irenaeus, *Against Heresies*, 4.20.1 in *Ante Nicene Fathers* 1:487–88.
47. Justin Martyr, *First Apology* 60 in *Ante Nicene Fathers* 1:183; *Dialogue with*

cal "heaven and earth" within a Platonic worldview. It was almost irresistible for early Christianity, moving out from Palestine into a Graeco-Roman milieu, to take up these popular philosophical ideas and put Christ into the available role of the Logos or World Soul, mediating between two ontological realms, or bridging an abyss between two completely different worlds which otherwise could have no contact with each other.

The assumption in this way of thinking is that God the Father is too transcendent to have dealings with the messy world of nature (what is "becoming") and employs the Son instead. This not only raises doubts about the full divinity of such a mediator in creation—a doubt exploited by the heretic Arius—but seems to make the Holy Spirit redundant as only one mediator is needed. This image has persisted in Christian thinking ever since, and has simply been assumed to be biblical. In the Bible, however, the "Word" of God (which this hymn mentions in the second verse) does not express the absence of a God-the-Father who has to send a representative in place of himself, but underlines the presence of a speaking God (John 1:14–18). The idea of a "cosmic mediator" not only results in an absent Father but in a God who must be impassible and immutable in order to conform to the rules of a sphere of Absolute Being, and who can only be involved in the suffering of creation through the narrow bridge of the human nature of Jesus Christ.

I have urged that our knowledge of the triune God is by way of participation, and so the relation of God to the world is always to be expressed as participation rather than mediation. There is no gulf that needs to be crossed. God as uncreated is of course infinitely *different* from what God has created, but not *separated* from it. The divine act of creation may be understood in the same way, as the bringing of reality other than God into being *by* God to participate in God's life, and then to be shaped through engagement in the interweaving relations of love and justice in God that we call Father, Son, and Spirit. God acts in the universe in continuous creativity wholly as Trinity, not as separate persons "in turn." God acts through influence and persuasion on the created materials that are immersed into God. When we are involved in the movement of triune relations, we are moved to certain ends, caught up in their momentum. We are incited to follow patterns of love and sacrifice like relations between a father and a son, and we are constantly opened up to new levels of being by the disturbance of Spirit.

These are divine actions which are not characterized by domination, but cooperation. There is an attractiveness of *movements* of love, patterns of the dance into which we are swept up, so that our actions follow the same divine aim. If *we* experience this creativity as persons, and human persons

---

Trypho 60–61 in *Ante Nicene Fathers* 1:227–28.

have emerged from the wider natural world through the urging of the Spirit of God, we may expect all created reality similarly to have a capacity to respond to God. This will not be exactly the same as the human potential, but in its own way, at every level, nature will be able to develop in tune with God's aims or to resist them.[48]

I do not suggest that this hymn by Chris Ellis directly sets out this theological exposition of creation. But it is a vision to which we may well be led if we ask to be "formed" and "directed" by the triune God (verse 4) who is making and re-making us. *Lex orandi, lex credendi*—"the rule of prayer is the rule of believing"—and no less is the effect of singing such good hymns as this.

---

48. Further on this, see Fiddes, *Participating in God*, 131–38, 144–47.

God of Power

Lord God of power, we celebrate your presence,
You are at work in atom and in star;
Yours is the strength in growing limb and landscape,
You are the life renewing all we are.

You are the rock, foundation of our living,
You are the ground on which we dare to build;
You are the walls which buttress all our hoping,
You are the strength with which our plans are filled.

Yet, powerful God, you come to us in weakness,
As our resources cease to be enough.
Help us to trust in you with all our being,
That all we are might be transformed by love.

Lord God, our strength, you come to us in Jesus,
Your power is focussed in a cross of shame:
Help us to stand as faithfully we witness,
Help us to make the power of love our aim.

13

"The Ground on Which We Dare to Build"

Putting Calvinism to Work

NIGEL G. WRIGHT

CHRIS ELLIS'S HYMN "LORD God of Power" comes as close as any other within his hymnody to a statement of divine sovereignty. It chimes well with the philosophical and biblical statement that, "In him we live and move and have our being" (Acts 17:28). God here is imagined as the vivifying power that infuses all things, the undergirding reality that gives shape and support to fragile created existence. Moreover divine power is seen above all in the person and career of Jesus in which, paradoxically through the weakness and vulnerability of the cross on which he died, God's purposes of love are powerfully and graciously accomplished. The cross is not an abdication of divine power but a manifestation of it. Where the Ellis conception of sovereignty might differ from traditional accounts is in its avoidance of the language of "over-ruling" in favor of that of depth and interiority. It achieves the same end. The power that ultimately triumphs is that of love.

The Reformed tradition out of which the Baptist expression of Christianity has primarily emerged, and to which Ellis is heir, is well-known for its emphasis on divine sovereignty. God is all-powerful and reigns over all things. In particular, God is the author of salvation such that human beings contribute nothing to their salvation other than the sin from which they need to be redeemed. All is of God. There is therefore no room for human boasting. We have nothing that we did not first receive (1 Cor 4:7). Yet divine sovereignty remains for us a mystery and we are most certainly in the realm of the inscrutable when it comes to tracing the purposes of God within cruel and chaotic history. How are we to interpret these things? And how are we to help people draw strength from the confidence that "all shall be well"?

It is not insignificant that the first English-speaking Baptist church was established in 1609 at the end of the very decade in which the legacy of John Calvin (1509–64), one of the founding fathers of Reformed Christianity to emerge at first in Switzerland was being vehemently debated, and in the Dutch homeland in which one of its bold re-interpreters, Jacob Arminius (1560–1609), lived and taught. Although the distinction between General Baptists and Particular Baptists, the two original Baptist proto-denominations of the early seventeenth century, may not have been as stark as we retrospectively imagine, the fact remains that differences of understanding surrounding doctrines of predestination, atonement, and final perseverance have played a significant part in shaping Baptist history. This remained the case well into the nineteenth century when the debate began to run into the sand,[1] and concern to adopt a more inclusive evangelical, rather than Calvinist or Arminian, identity came to the fore.

In the twentieth century, in which both Ellis and I have lived the majority of our lives, the Christian churches of the United Kingdom for the most part experienced steady loss. To be sure, there have also been times of refreshing and growth that have sweetened the pill of overall decline. Yet particularly disappointing for those who are conscious heirs to the Free Church tradition has been the steep decline of religious communities that at the beginning of the century were not only a power in the land (though the impact of the "nonconformist conscience" could be over-stated)[2] but also a wholesome presence in multiple local communities across the nation. The continuing visibility of so many church buildings in town and country, whether presently used for worship or not, is testimony to the one-time presence that Free Church Christianity previously enjoyed. Whatever signs of hope there may presently be, it is hard not to regret the degree and rate of the decline. Specifically to be regretted is the loss of a strong and informed sense of Free Church identity. To be sure, this is in part owing to the fact that the magisterial traditions have progressively adopted Baptist-compatible principles, so that what once was the preserve of dissenters has become more

---

1. Sell, *The Great Debate*, 89–98.
2. Pope, "The Nonconformist Conscience," 454.

mainstream. Yet most Baptist church members exist in relative ignorance of the theology and principles that have defined their church life. Those few who do demonstrate an informed awareness of Baptist history and principles are apt to seem idiosyncratic in the current climate.

It is certainly worth celebrating when churches espouse and display a general evangelical character through the emphasis on living "under the Word of God" and the expectation of personal conversion. Yet within this, the lack of mention or even awareness of the doctrinal concerns that once preoccupied our forbears is quite striking. What place does Calvinism play within our contemporary church life?

BAPTISTS AND CALVINISM

It should of course be said that Baptists have never been orthodox Calvinists. This was certainly true of the General Baptists who from the beginning, either by virtue of their contact with the Waterlander Mennonites or with the theology of Arminius, held a variant approach to the question of predestination. Since Arminianism properly understood is an intra- rather than anti-Calvinist position this does not disqualify those who espouse it from standing in the general Reformed tradition. Yet both Generals and Particulars diverged from the teaching of Calvin's *Institutes of the Christian Religion* in ways that marked them out as Baptists rather than, say, Presbyterians. The most obvious disagreement was over the question of infant baptism, the rejection of which was integral to their espousal of believers' baptism. Calvin continued to argue for the validity of infant baptism in ways that Baptists have found unconvincing.[3] The persistence of the practice among Calvinists was undoubtedly related to their continuing adherence to the *corpus christianum*, the persuasion that the social and political order was under obligation to submit to godly rule. Civil government carried the responsibility of rightly establishing religion.[4] The positive result of this has been a Reformed concern for sober government, the education of the populace and the health of the people. Less welcome features have been a prurient concern for the private morality of the citizen and, most unwelcome, a mandate for the civil power to punish and eradicate heresy or theological dissent.[5] At this point

---

3. *Institutes* IV:XVI.

4. *Institutes* IV:XX, 3.

5. David Fergusson points out how Scottish Reformed Christianity had its own "Servetus moment" when it secured the execution on grounds of heresy of the Edinburgh divinity student Thomas Aikenhead in 1697, Fergusson, *Church, State and Civil Society*, 73.

the Baptist objection becomes clear, following the root conviction, that not only Baptists have shared, that coerced religion cannot be true religion. Given these divergences from characteristic aspects of Calvin's work, elements that are still widely insisted upon in large parts of the Reformed world, though the civil suppression of heresy has been largely dropped, it would seem incorrect to describe Baptists as Calvinists. They might accurately be designated as "Calvinian" in that, with the exception of the elements identified, they still follow the main contours of Calvin's theology in contrast to, for instance, Lutheranism or even Anabaptism. Indeed Baptists can be seen to stand somewhere between Calvinism and Anabaptism and to have their significant agreements and disagreements on both sides.

ELECTION AND PREDESTINATION

Seeing that Baptists are in disagreement with Calvin on some significant issues how far might their disagreements stretch? It is already clear, given the emergence of the General Baptists, that not all Baptists have felt obliged to follow orthodox Calvinism in its espousal of double predestination. In the seventeenth century the most significant Particular Baptist "London" confessions of faith of 1644 and 1677/88 (published after the Act of Toleration in 1689) respectively tracked (and repeated) the preceding Separatist confession of 1596 and the Westminster Confession of 1646, except that they modified the articles on baptism, church, and state in a Baptist direction. What is of further interest is that they also attenuated the articles on predestination in a more cautious direction, falling short of the affirmation of double predestination.[6] This established them in these doctrines as moderate Calvinists. To be sure, there have been later Baptist theologians who were persuaded that double predestination was a logical inference from other Christian doctrines and who gladly (and competently) advocated it, none more so than Dr. John Gill.[7] But overall, and once more, British Baptists, both General and Particular, have fallen short of being fully orthodox Calvinists while remaining recognizably Calvinian.

What is clear in the contemporary scene is that debates that once preoccupied Baptists have radically fallen into the background such that most Baptists are unaware of them except on the periphery of their understanding of faith and practice, perhaps indeed as subjects to be avoided rather than to be engaged, both because of their difficulty as well as their potential

---

6. See my contribution "Election and Predestination in Baptist Confessions of the Seventeenth Century," 16–32. See also Lumpkin, *Baptist Confessions of Faith*, 237.

7. Gill, *Gill's Complete Body of Practical and Doctrinal Divinity*, 130–32.

to evoke disagreement. Predestination, not for the first time, has become the doctrine that "dared not speak its name."[8] In some ways it is hard to regret this in that it makes for a less contentious atmosphere—these debates often make provoke more heat than light; in other ways it may be an indication that we have become less doctrinally serious than is good for us. The so-called "Five Points of Calvinism" asserted against the Arminian tendency and crystallized by the Synod of Dordrecht (Dort) in 1618–19, embrace the doctrines of total depravity, unconditioned election, limited atonement, irresistible grace, and the perseverance of the saints. When Baptists came to be, these debates were in the atmosphere and it is not surprising that they have played their part in the formation of Baptist church life. But how might they play their part in contemporary Baptist church life? I have four proposals to make.

CALVINIAN SPIRITUALITY

The first is to say that whatever questions we may have about the formulation of doctrines of divine sovereignty and predestination (on which see below), there remains much to be said for the cultivation of a Calvinian spirituality. By this we mean that the so-called "doctrines of grace" can be regarded not so much as a problem to be solved as a mystery to be adored. We may affirm that we are wholly unable to save ourselves from our own sin; that as a consequence we are utterly dependent upon the grace of God that precedes us and purposes our salvation from before our birth; that we find ourselves to have been chosen and called by God in a way quite contrary to our deserts and inclination; that Christ has died not only for all but also for me and indeed particularly for me;[9] that the grace and persistence of God have proven irresistible in convicting and regenerating us, and that the power that won us to faith in the first place is able to ensure that we persevere in the faith to the end. These distinct and characteristic elements of Christian experience are what lie behind a Calvinian faith position. They foster a spirituality that can be recognized by believers whether or not they endorse strict orthodox Calvinism. We have nothing that we did not first receive. More than that, this is a spirituality that should be promoted more

---

8. MacCulloch, *Thomas Cranmer*, 375.

9. I record here a piece of oral tradition: Canon Thomas A. Smail studied in Basel under Karl Barth and at a seminar at Spurgeon's College recalled Barth saying in a discussion: "Christus is für uns alle gestorben; und nicht nur für uns alle sondern auch für mich, und nicht nur für mich sondern besonders für mich"—"Christ died for us all, and not only for us all but also for me, and not only for me but in particular for me."

than it currently is. It is essential evangelical spirituality and we do not hear enough of, perhaps because, regrettably, those who represent it have not always displayed the grace of which they speak.

RESHAPING THE DOCTRINAL LANDSCAPE

Yet this does beg the question as to whether such a spirituality can be sustained without the doctrinal undergirding that gives rise to it, and so we return to the questions raised by traditional Calvinist doctrine. Specifically there is the need here to address the question of double predestination.

There is a logic to this doctrine. On hearing the gospel of Christ not all people believe. How is this to be explained? Is it because people have free will and choose not to believe, in which case salvation is in our own hands; or is it because God has previously decided from eternity past to save some and to condemn, or reprobate, others? The Arminian chooses the first option and the Calvinist the second. Calvin put it so: "We call predestination God's eternal decree, by which He determined with Himself what he willed to become of each man. For not all are created in equal condition; rather eternal life is foreordained for some, eternal damnation for others. Therefore, as any man has been created to one or other of these ends, we speak of him as predestined to life or death."[10]

The emphasis on divine sovereignty thus ascribes all outcomes to the will of God (Rom 9:14–21). This is sometimes portrayed as a "high doctrine of God": the more arbitrary the will of God is thought to be, the "higher" the doctrine of God. And it is hard to avoid the suspicion that this doctrine is indeed arbitrary. Persons are determined for salvation or reprobation from before the foundation of the world irrespective of how they live or what they do, since grace is not conditioned by human behavior nor based on foresight. What is described as grace is in truth hard to distinguish from what others would call luck. Being determined in eternity, election or reprobation bears no relation to what humans actually do so to be in one category or the other is a matter of divine decision without regard to anything other than internal considerations. It is no surprise that the doctrine has been subject to sharp criticism.

Arminius did not reject the doctrine of predestination (no Christian thinker ultimately can) and in fact maintained a high degree of agreement with Calvin on the doctrines of grace in general. But he did contest the interpretation of predestination advanced by orthodox Calvinists. In its place he proposed that *classes of persons* were predestined, those who believed to

10. Calvin, *Institutes* III:XXI, 5.

eternal life and those who did not to eternal death. Christ has died for all and not only for the elect and so potentially salvation is available for all. Yet it remained a choice of the human will which category to be in. Predestination thus depended on divine foreknowledge not divine determination. Ostensibly this is a more generous doctrine than that advanced by Calvin. But is it? A God who simply offers salvation rather than bestowing it is not fully sovereign. Salvation pivots on the human will rather than the divine. Furthermore, given that it was the misuse of the human will that has led to the sorry store of human sin and rebellion in the first place, why should we believe that any different outcome will be forthcoming if humans are left to choose life in the economy of salvation?

It is hard to avoid the conclusion that Calvin got this one wrong. In particular we find in Calvin a preference for safeguarding the will of God rather than divine love. This criticism was long since expressed by the Scottish Reformed theologian, James Orr:

> Calvin exalts the sovereignty of God and this is right. But he errs in placing his root idea of God in sovereign will rather than in love.... I do not, therefore, abate one whit from the sovereignty of God in election, calling and salvation of such as are called; but I do feel strongly that this election of God must not be disjoined from the context in which it is set in God's historical purpose, which, grounded in his love embraces the widest possible blessing for the whole world.[11]

Calvin's defenders are apt to claim that since his doctrine of double predestination appeared at the end of the *Institutes* rather than, for instance, within his doctrine of God, that it should not be seen as central to his thought. This was not, however, the judgment of his successors who elevated it to a primary place. On the other hand, the Arminian option, while affirming the love of God for all and the universal value of the death of Christ simply leaves us with a different set of problems. Calvin's doctrine is not one that most of us would be keen to preach. If anything it remains in the background as a teaching that might be shared with the advanced Christian but concealed from the rest.

That the doctrines of election and predestination should indeed be understood and proclaimed as good news and as "the sum of the Gospel because of all God's words that can be said or heard it is the best,"[12] was the intention that lay behind Barth's reconstruction. According to T. H. L. Parker, Barth has played the part of a landscape gardener, retaining all the

---

11. Orr, *The Progress of Dogma*, 292, 294–95.

12. Barth, *Church Dogmatics* II/2, 3. Barth's doctrine is set out in chapter 7, 3–506.

traditional elements of the doctrine but rearranging them in such a way as to transform the scene: "We can now see that in his landscape gardening Barth has transformed the scene from severity and even gloom into a joyfulness and light. He has brought about a miracle that even Capability Brown could not achieve—he has made the sun shine on the scene."[13]

Barth achieves this by insisting on a number of steps all of which emerge from his central theological proposition, that there is no God other than the God who is revealed in Jesus Christ. Consequently there is no election or predestination that is concealed in the divine eternity as though behind Jesus Christ there is a hidden God who is not revealed. What is known of God's election is made open and manifest in Jesus Christ, the Revealer of the Father; and what is made known is entirely good news. For this reason, all our thinking about God must first pass through the narrow defile which is Christ himself. Election begins with God in that God chooses to be God for us: "I will be your God and you will be my people" (Jer 32:38). Secondly, God elects Jesus Christ to be both the Elect and the Reprobate, and so a doctrine of double predestination is retained, but of a very different kind. In Christ all people are elect, but in bearing divine judgment and God-forsakenness in place of sinful humanity, Christ ensures that no human being need be reprobated. God's justice is vindicated in the death of Christ in such a way as to reveal the divine justice while making possible the salvation of all. Thirdly, it is the work of the Holy Spirit to expand the circle of those who are in Christ, and therefore actually elect, and no limits can be set to the extent of those who will finally be saved. All people are to be considered "Christians in hope." In this way the mystery of salvation becomes not one of a past eternity hidden in God but of the present work of the eternal God who in history chooses some and not others in the outworking of salvation. The verses that speak of the doctrine of election are to be interpreted, not as metaphysical or philosophically-derived statements but as expressions of the purposeful way God works in history. Moreover, election is not simply to salvation but to service and vocation.

Although Barth's construct has been criticized as an unprecedented novelty, it offers a coherent and persuasive interpretation of the biblical evidence, one that avoids the mournful suggestion that the Book of Life has a death column.[14] Moreover, as Parker suggests, it transforms the doctrine into one on which the sun shines, that can genuinely be preached, rather than kept under the counter, as good and affirming news. Had Calvin understood it this way the history of doctrine would have been markedly dif-

---

13. Parker, "Predestination," 272.
14. Barth, *Church Dogmatics* II/2, 16.

ferent. My second proposal therefore is that such a re-constructed doctrine should be embraced, thus restoring a positive doctrine of divine election to the church's regular proclamation.[15]

Are there implications here however for what is termed "universalism," a doctrine against which the majority of Baptists have wished to guard as presumptuous? Universalism has typically been regarded as a doctrine of theological liberalism, but in fact is well represented in some forms of Continental pietism, to which evangelicalism is related, and indeed in Calvinism itself. There is a logic here. If God's love is universal and God is able to save to the uttermost then what is to say that God will not finally save all? How can we conceive of an all-powerful and all gracious God *not* saving all? And how are we to understand those New Testament verses that point in the direction of universal restoration (for example Col 1:15–20, Rom 5:18–19, 11:32)? Gregory MacDonald has put the case for universal salvation in a persuasive form and from a decidedly evangelical perspective. He styles his position as "hopeful dogmatic universalism" or "non-dogmatic dogmatic universalism" since he both wishes to say that it is rooted in Christian doctrine, and therefore is "dogmatic," and yet is un-dogmatic in acknowledging that he may not have interpreted the biblical witness correctly, which is what any evangelical theologian ought to say.[16] Yet universalism was a conclusion that Barth denied drawing: "I don't believe in universalism, but I do believe in Jesus Christ, the reconciler of all."[17] His point is entirely consistent with his theological method in that strict logic is not the way in which theology is pursued. It is logic that led to the doctrine of double predestination in the first place. Rather, theology is pursued by means of ontology, that is by means of honest encounter with the God who has spoken objectively in Jesus Christ and who continues to address us in the one who is God's Word.[18] It is God who determines the final scope of salvation and not logic. We may follow the truth in the direction in which it seems to point but always in ways subject to who and what God is and always with respect for the divine freedom. God is the sovereign Lord who does what God chooses with that which is God's own.

---

15. Barth's proposals are constructively and creatively developed in Grebe, *Election, Atonement, and the Holy Spirit*. My own attempts to present election as the good news it is are found in *The Radical Evangelical*, chapter 3, "God's Universal Outreach"; and *Vital Truth*, chapter 11, "God's Gracious Election".

16. MacDonald, *The Evangelical Universalist*, 4.

17. As recorded in Busch, *Karl Barth: His life from letters*, 394. See also 426.

18. On Barth's theological method see Torrance, *Karl Barth: Biblical and Evangelical Theologian*, not least 46–47.

THE GREATER HOPE

Yet there is a third proposal here, which is to suspend judgment about the final scope of salvation. Even impeccably reliable orthodox Calvinists, such as Charles Hodge of Princeton, have wished to assert that in the end the majority of human beings would experience salvation.[19] Indeed, it is the Calvinist position rather than the Arminian that makes such a claim possible since it roots salvation in the will and power of an almighty and reliable God rather than the volatile and unreliable choices of human beings. It is generally believed that in the Old Testament the notion of a resurrection and a world to come emerged only slowly. When it did so it was under the pressure to account for how justice could be done in God's world in the face of the manifest injustice of the present age. A future resurrection of the just was projected in which the martyred righteous would be raised, vindicated and rewarded (Dan 12:1–7). We face similar moral pressure to account for how justice might be done in a world in which billions are apparently excluded from the very possibility of salvation. One answer is to project a future beyond death in which justice might be done as God's persistence in seeking the lost is pursued to whatever limit the sovereign Lord chooses. To characterize this as a "second chance" and to claim that it is "unfair" misses the whole point of grace. Salvation is undeserved whether it is realized in this life or any life which is to come and, as in the parable of the laborers in the vineyard (Matt 10:1–16), God is free to do what God wills with that which is God's, whatever constructs of "fairness" humans might operate with. God is more than fair. Although we rightly regard death as a boundary and should be swift to make life-transforming decisions in the face of it, there is every reason to believe that it is no kind of boundary to the God who triumphed over death in Jesus Christ.[20]

TRUST IN GOD

The three proposals that have preceded enable us to make a fourth proposal in the project of making Calvinism work for us. This is one that applies to all believers but most especially to those who bear, as Ellis has done, the burdens and joys of mission and ministry. It is all too true that "our resources

---

19. Hodge, *Systematic Theology* Volume III: "We have reason to believe, as urged in the first volume of this work, and as often urged elsewhere, that the number of the finally lost in comparison with the whole number of the saved will be very inconsiderable," 889–90.

20. For a thoughtful discussion of these issues see Jonathan, *Grace Beyond the Grave*.

cease to be enough." Pastors and evangelists in particular will identify with Jesus's parable of the sower and its depiction of the various responses following on from the sowing of the word of God (Matt 13:1–9, 18–23). Most of those responses are disappointing. But comfort can be taken from two aspects of the parable. One is that the fruit borne by those who do respond positively is so very considerable and worthwhile (v. 23). The other is that Jesus' own experience of the word of God apparently not bearing fruit is the same as our own; and if the Son of God endured such disappointment then our own is easier to bear. Ultimately the salvation of the world depends entirely not on human beings but on God.

Within the world of Christian discourse there is a trope that has long done the rounds. It pictures a vast multitude of human beings progressing *en masse* towards a cliff, heedless of the danger that lies ahead of them. Between the cliff and the crowd there is a group of Christians making daisy chains and making no effort, with the exception of but a few, to warn people of the danger that lies ahead of them. The lesson is that while people proceed in ignorance towards a Christ-less eternity, Christians make only small efforts to warn them of what is to come. For this reason they have blood on their hands.

The idea here is to motivate people to evangelism. Personally I find it a recipe for despair and paralysis. To imagine that the salvation of other people depends upon me and my efforts is a burden I am unable to bear. I find in myself neither the physical nor emotional energy to pursue this task to anything like the extent it requires. Even more seriously, there are lacking in me the considerable reserves of compassion that the task requires. I am left therefore with crippling feelings of guilt and inability. It is at this point that Calvinism rides to my aid and works for me. Ironically, and wonderfully, the freedom to trust God with the work of salvation has the power to stimulate a non-anxious mission that might finally prove more effective than one emerging from feelings of guilt. To this the words of the hymn can speak: "Help us to stand as faithfully we witness, Help us to make the power of love our aim."

I have declared myself to be Calvinian rather than Calvinist and have offered above, with the help of Barth, a way of reconstructing the biblical doctrines of election and predestination that establishes them in their proper light as good news. The upshot of this is to affirm gladly that "salvation comes from the Lord" (Jonah 2:9). It is the sovereign Lord who has purposed, enacted and established the work of salvation. It is God alone who will bring the divine purposes to their fulfillment and this God knows what is to be done with every single human soul. Nothing is left to chance. To be sure, this God also calls me to a life of grateful service, a "eucharistic" lifestyle in which I offer myself to work with God in those purposes. But with or without me the purposes of God will come to pass, and not one of us can set limits on how far they will reach. The persistence of God in seeking the lost is to be reckoned with. In this way the sovereignty of God that is able to make all things work for the good of those who love him rescues us from despair, assures us that nothing can finally stand in the way of God's purposes (Rom 8:28, 31–39), offers us a place of peace and grants us the joy of hope. Such is the power of love.

MISSIONARY GOD

Missionary God in our worship we give you
All that your Spirit through us might achieve.
Breathe into all of our praying and living
Life-sharing joy, that the world may believe.

Missionary God we exult in your Gospel:
Good news of Jesus for all to receive.
Help us to tell of your loving forgiveness,
Give us the words that the world may believe.

Missionary God, you have called as your people
Those whom the world would denounce as naïve;
Open our eyes to the world as you see it,
Open our hearts that the world may believe.

Missionary God, as we pray for your kingdom
Show us your truth where the world would deceive.
Give us the courage to speak out for justice,
Work through our hands that the world may believe.

Missionary God, how your love overwhelms us,
Richer and wider that we can conceive!
Remake our hearts and direct all our actions,
Fill us with love that the world may believe.

14

"Missionary God"
The Place of Mission amongst British Baptists

Andy Goodliff

WHEN CHRIS ELLIS WRITES a hymn you will often find he prefaces the word "God" with a word that names the kind of God we are singing to. A look through his hymns we discover God is addressed as Almighty, Forgiving, Redeeming, Living, Creator, Powerful, Gracious, Sharing, Loving, Passover, Reconciling, and—in the case of the hymn that begins this chapter—Missionary. Some of these words are unsurprising, others like "Passover God" describe God in a way that does not pepper our prayers or hymns. To describe God as "Missionary" is also to say that which has been rarely said about God. While it is now common to speak of the mission of God, mission as something that speaks of the way God acts; it is to say something different to speak of God as missionary, to say this is who God is. It is this distinction that I will explore in this chapter in honor of Chris.

The origins of the hymn "Missionary God" arose from the 200th anniversary of the Baptist Missionary Society in 1992. BMS asked Chris to write a hymn for that year's Assembly. The hymn as far as I know did not become widely sung outside of that Assembly,[1] but the phrase "Missionary God" became embedded in Baptist God-talk from the mid-1990s onwards when David Coffey, the then General Secretary of the Baptist Union began to use it. The question I want to ask is what does it mean for Baptist to sing and speak of the "missionary God"?

---

1. It is not part of any hymn book that I am aware of.

The phrase can be found once in the David Bosch's influential *Transforming Mission*, where he writes: "In the new image mission is not primarily an activity of the church, but an attribute of God. God is a missionary God."[2] It also appears in John Stott's *The Contemporary Christian*, where he says, "Christian mission is rooted in the nature of God himself. The Bible reveals him as a missionary God (Father, Son, and Holy Spirit), who creates a missionary people, and is working towards a missionary consummation."[3] It is likely that either Bosch or Stott, or both, are the source for Coffey's new expression. Coffey never unpacks what it means to call God missionary. This may reflect that he's a preacher foremost, not a theologian. For the most part the phrasing by Coffey reflected the desire to shift the Baptist Union in a more missionary direction, so alongside missionary God, the language of missionary people, missionary Union, missionary communities and missionary purposes through the 1990s becomes part of the Baptist shared vocabulary. The underlying argument being developed is the idea that if we can confess God as missionary, then the Union and churches must also be missionary. By 2005 *Gathering for Worship*, edited by Chris Ellis and Myra Blyth, uses the language of "Missionary God" as part of prayers offered for the commissioning of a missionary overseas;[4] for the celebration of Pentecost;[5] and in the introduction to the section on ministry where it is said that "all Christians share in the ministry of the missionary God."[6] Also in the mid-2000s "Missionary God" begins to find a theological rationale from the Baptist Union's leading theological voices: Paul Fiddes,[7] Stephen Holmes,[8] John Colwell,[9] and Nigel Wright.[10]

CONTEXT

At the beginning of the 1990s there was a belief that the Union and its structures were no longer fit for purpose and that they belonged to another era. This claim is most clearly made in Nigel Wright's *Challenge to Change*, to

---

2. Bosch, *Transforming Mission*, 390.
3. Stott, *The Contemporary Christian*, 325.
4. Ellis and Blyth, *Gathering for Worship*, 182.
5. Ibid., 392.
6. Ibid., 114.
7. Fiddes, *Tracks and Traces*, chapter 11.
8. Holmes, "Trinitarian Missiology," 72–90.
9. Colwell, "Mission as Ontology," 7–12.
10. Wright, *Free Church, Free State*, 16.

which Coffey wrote a foreword.[11] For example, Wright says "the cultural factors which have been added to our experience of faith are largely Victorian in nature.... These may have been all right at the time ... [but] if left unreformed, they assume a power they should not have."[12] Coffey himself shares Wright's view, though as general secretary, speaks about it in a less direct way.[13] Alongside the perceived inertia in the structures of the Union is the wider issue of decline in church attendance, and of the number of baptisms and those in local church membership.[14] This reflects the wider context of a post-Christendom, post-denominational, increasingly secular situation[15] in which the UK church has found itself in from the 1960s onward.[16] Coffey sets out to put mission and evangelism at the heart of the Union and every local church. Over the decades the Union had been engaged in seeking to encourage the churches in evangelism,[17] but what was different now was Coffey embodied a much more charismatic, visionary style and was more intentional about seeking to lead.[18] The reform of the structures is set in a missional direction. Coffey sought to remake the Union as a "modern denomination" ready for the new millennium, in the way that John Howard Shakespeare, one of his predecessors, had done at the beginning of the twentieth century.[19]

The context of this call for renewal and reform lies further back to the end of the 1970s and the creation of Mainstream, a broad evangelical Baptist network, with which Coffey and Wright were closely involved. Mainstream was a voice throughout the 1980s arguing for change in the Union's structures and for more emphasis on evangelism and church growth. The

---

11. Wright, *Challenge to Change*.

12. Ibid., 52.

13. *Baptist Times* 25th March 1992, 8.

14. Writing in 2008, Chris Ellis sounds a note of caution when he says "decline brings its own pathology, and one feature to which we must pay particular attention when considering mission is the matter of motivation," "Spirituality in Mission," 172.

15. The debate over secularization is contested. See Woodhead, "Introduction" for a brief overview of debate and links to various relevant literature.

16. Amongst Baptists the language of post-Christendom is most associated with Stuart Murray and his books *Post-Christendom* and *Church After Christendom*. For other reflections on post-Denominationalism see Wright, *New Baptists*.

17. See for example both *Call to Obedience* and *A Call to Commitment*, 4–7.

18. On Coffey as leader see Burnard, *Transformational Servant Leadership*.

19. The phrasing of this sentence borrows from the title of Peter Shepherd's study of Shakespeare, *The Making of a Modern Denomination*.

appointment of Coffey as General Secretary and the publication of Wright's *Challenge to Change* gave Mainstream a position to realize its ambitions.[20]

Coffey, with the Deputy General Secretary Keith Jones, began their new roles in 1991 with a series of Listening Days, which resulted in a Statement of Intent for the next ten years, in which mission and evangelism were priority number one.[21] At the same time as the Statement of Intent, the Council was presented with a National Mission Strategy to affirm, which centered on local church renewal in mission, church planting, engagement with rural and urban, and association's developing mission strategies.[22] By mission Coffey meant "church planting and evangelism, social action and prophetic protest, a world mission commitment and a Kingdom of God awareness of international affairs and environmental concerns."[23] This, as we will discuss below, is a largely functional description of mission; mission as an activity of the church. By the middle of the 1990s, Coffey and Jones called for a Denominational Consultation. This emerged out of what they perceived was "the challenge of being a missionary people to a needy world."[24] Mission, Coffey and Jones argued, was "the prime factor" and the Consultation was an opportunity to be a kind of "missiological prism" in which the structures of the Union might be viewed and challenged.[25] It is here that Coffey uses for the first time the expression "missionary God." The link is made that missionary activity must be judged in the light of the doctrine of God: "as a Union, surely we need a fresh vision of God."[26] An invitation is made to reflect on mission theologically.

EARLY REFLECTIONS ON GOD AND MISSION

The Union's Doctrine and Worship Committee prepared a set of bible studies called *Beginning with God* ahead of the Consultation. In the "Preface" Ellis, who was the then Chair of the Committee, argues that the Consultation

---

20. Alongside Coffey, the new Secretary for Evangelism for the Union was Derek Tidball, also closely involved in Mainstream. Tidball uses the language of "ambition" in his review of Mainstream, "Mainstream: 'far greater ambitions,'" 202–22.

21. The other three concerns we the development of a distinctive Baptist identity, the strengthening of associating and the promotion of a greater sharing of resources. See *A Ten Year Plan Towards*.

22. *A Ten Year Plan Towards 2000*, 22.

23. *Baptist Times* 25 March 1991, 8.

24. Coffey and Jones, "The Denominational Consultation," 1.

25. Ibid., 2. The other factors were financial, frustration and ferment.

26. Ibid., 2.

should not begin with problems or even vision, but with God.[27] *Beginning with God* makes it quite clear that this God is the "missionary God." The study concludes with the hymn "Missionary God" written by Ellis and first used back at the 1992 Baptist Assembly. Ellis in the "Preface" says that mission is God's and this appears to be the basis for naming God as missionary. Each verse of Ellis's hymn begins "Missionary God" but the rest of the verses speak more of asking God to breathe, help, open, give and remake and fill the church in God's mission. God has a mission, but the church carries it out. Is it appropriate then to call God missionary?

Also written ahead of the Consultation was *Something to Declare: A Study of the Declaration of Principle* jointly written by the principals of the four English Baptist colleges.[28] In his "Foreword" Coffey writes of the need for pastor-theologians who will "address how faithfully the Church of today is reflecting the nature and purposes of the missionary God."[29] In the introduction, Richard Kidd says that what the principals are doing in *Something to Declare* is a contribution "to think more deeply about the 'missionary God' and to focus our explorations through a so-called 'missiological prism.'"[30] In the third section of the study under the heading the "Question of Mission" which discusses the third clause of the Declaration of Principle,[31] the principals understand discipleship as "a participation in the energy and life of the missionary God."[32] This participation is made possible through baptism. They recognize the influence of David Bosch in the development of the theology of *missio Dei*. The principals make a helpful observation that the language of "mission of God" is ambiguous as it can mean that mission is what God calls us to go and effect and it can also mean that mission is that in which God is the chief player, not just that God sends, but that God is

27. *Beginning with God*, 3.

28. The four principals at the time were Paul Fiddes, Brian Haymes, Richard Kidd, and Michael Quicke. Fiddes, Haymes, and Kidd had been friends and theological collaborators from the early 1980s and had published three other publications with the involvement of others: *A Call to Mind* (1980), *Bound to Love* (1985) and *Reflecting on the Water* (1996). Fiddes, Haymes, and Kidd, with others, offered a different vision of the future of Union and Baptist life that whilst not being deliberately antithetical to Mainstream was intentionally different. It could be argued that if Mainstream had gain influential positions with the Union, the colleges, particularly in Fiddes, Haymes, and Kidd, also held significant positions of power.

29. Kidd, *Something to Declare*, 7.

30. Ibid., 9.

31. The third clause of the Declaration of Principle is "That it is the duty of every disciple to bear personal witness to the Gospel of Jesus Christ, and to take part in the evangelization of the world."

32. Ibid., 48.

active in mission.[33] It is the former that seems to lie behind most usages of "missionary God" by Coffey and Ellis. The principals argue that we should hold on to both, mission is both that which God does *and* that which God calls us to participate in. Through the "mission of God" prism the principals suggests three characteristics of what mission looks like: interactive, diverse, and corporate. The story of God's mission in Jesus is interactive, that is, it is a "venture of risky and vulnerable love" in which Jesus calls followers. The story of God's mission in Jesus is diverse, that is, Jesus's ministry sees each person as they are, in their particular need and context. The story of God's mission in Jesus is corporate, that is, mission flows both ways that there is no longer a clear sense of sender and receiver, as we see in Jesus, mission is shaped by weakness and vulnerability and as such this is "the measure for once and for all."[34] This leads to the conclusion that the mission of God must be "determinative" for the mission of the church, how we carry out mission should reflect the way God in Christ does mission.[35] The principals here embrace the "missionary God" but seek to begin to provide a thicker theological description that does not see mission as overly concerned with success or numbers, but with faithfulness to God.[36] In other words, the importance of mission is theological, not pragmatic.

A third piece of work that also contributed some reflections on God and mission is the report *Transforming Superintendency*. A group had been set up in 1994 to review the General Superintendency as one of the objectives in the section on associating from the Statement of Intent. In the terms of reference given to the group, they were asked to set their report "within the perspective of the Mission of God."[37] The group took this seriously and began the report with a theological reflection on the doctrine of God.[38] This report, in common with the others mentioned, is happy to describe God as the "triune missionary God." Like *Beginning with God*, *Transforming Superintendency* argues that "Christians must always begin with God."[39] To speak of God, they claim, is to speak of Father, Son, and Holy Spirit. The triune God is by nature relational and is "always 'going out' in love to others."[40]

33. Ibid., 49.
34. Ibid., 50–51.
35. Ibid., 51.
36. Ibid., 52.
37. *Transforming Superintendency*, 51, cf. 7.
38. The structure of the report, beginning with the doctrine of God, was probably due to the group's Chair, Brian Haymes, who went on later to write a book which made the same move: Haymes, Gouldbourne, and Cross, *On Being the Church*.
39. *Transforming Superintendency*, 9.
40. Ibid., 9.

This "going out" takes shape as "a will to save" and as a result restore relationship with humanity. The triune God through Jesus calls the church and this is an invitation to "share the life and mission of God."[41] The church is marked by fellowship with God and comprises those who are the body of Christ in the world.[42] The church is described as those who share in God's missionary purposes. One way God does is through the gift of ministry; ministry is defined as the "enabling of the Church in every place to be the Church."[43] The mission of God is made evident through the preaching of the gospel and the witness of the church.[44]

MORE RECENT REFLECTIONS ON GOD AND MISSION

It is not until the middle of the next decade that some more work was done, as mentioned above, to reflect further on the language of missionary God. Here John 20:21 is taken as the key biblical text by Fiddes, Holmes, and Colwell. We look first to Paul Fiddes's chapter on mission published in *Tracks and Traces* in 2003.[45] Fiddes begins with John 20:21 that he interprets as meaning the church shares in the mission of God. The church is "apostolic" because the church is "sent" and sent in the same manner and form of Christ: "*as* the Father sent me."[46] Fiddes goes further than simply saying that mission is the church imitating Christ to claim that mission is "a *participation* in the Father's own sending of the Son."[47] Mission is not a task but a call to share in God's work. The sending of the Son by the Father, according to Fiddes, was "God's mission from eternity."[48] Mission is the way the church is, because it is the way God is in himself. If the church is apostolic, it is also catholic says Fiddes, for it's the church's being-sentness that is an expression of it's catholicity.[49] Fiddes has already described mission in participatory language, before he also introduces another key word in his

---

41. Ibid., 10.
42. Ibid.
43. Ibid., 12.
44. Ibid., 13.
45. Fiddes, "Mission and Liberty." The origins of this chapter are a paper presented first in 1997 as part of conversations between the Baptist World Alliance and the Orthodox Ecumenical Patriarchate of Constantinople.
46. Ibid., 250.
47. Ibid., 251.
48. Ibid.
49. Ibid., 252.

theology, "covenant."[50] A theology of covenant lies at the heart of Fiddes's doctrine of God, developed from Karl Barth: the covenant God makes with us through Jesus is an expression of the eternal covenant between Father and Son and Holy Spirit. The covenant that God makes with us through Jesus is a missionary act—the Father sends the Son.[51] For Fiddes the missionary God is also the covenant-making God. This means mission must always be "relational" and focused on "making communion and community."[52] Furthermore, mission that is shaped by covenant must always be intentionally open, that is, a church participating in the mission of God, can never seek to create a homogeneous unit, because God seeks covenant with all people, not a select groups.[53]

Stephen Holmes's starting point is to test the claim that "a missionary church worships a missionary God." While the wider church has widely accepted the language of the *missio Dei*, that God has a mission, it has been more reluctant, or it is at least rarer, for the wider church to speak of God as missionary. Holmes seeks to provide a rationale for Baptists confessing God as missionary.[54] His paper also begins with John 20:21. A reading of John's Gospel demonstrates, says Holmes, that the sending of the disciples is linked, is continuous, with the sending of the Son by the Father.[55] The disciples and Jesus share in the same work. It is this point that gives scope to name God as missionary. The means of the church's participation in the mission of Jesus is through the Holy Spirit, which John's Gospel records Jesus breathing on the disciples. As Jesus is sent by the Father, there is a parallel mission or sending of the Holy Spirit that connects the church to Jesus. Having made these brief exegetical comments on John 20:21–23, Holmes turns to the theology of Augustine as "the *locus classicus* discussion of divine missions."[56] Holmes's engagement with Augustine raises the question of while we might say that mission belongs to the economic Trinity, (the means in which God acts), there remains a question of whether we can speak of mission belonging to the eternal life of God. The former means we can speak of God's mission, the latter would mean we can affirm missionary

---

50. I discuss Fiddes's theology of covenant in Goodliff, "Why Baptist Ecclesiology is Non-Voluntary," 3–8.

51. "Mission and Liberty," 252–53.

52. Ibid., 253.

53. Ibid.

54. Holmes, "Trinitarian Missiology," 72. Holmes paper was published in the academic journal *International Journal for Systematic Theology* which probably means it has not been widely read by many Baptists.

55. Ibid., 74.

56. Ibid., 76.

as an attribute of God. Augustine argues strongly for the *missio Dei*, that the Son and the Spirit are sent by God, but these are "anomalous events" and not integral to who God is in himself.[57] Augustine is concerned to protect the divinity of the Son from the suggestion that being sent implies ontological subordination and because he believes that we cannot divide the actions of God, it is God who acts, and so the Son is involved in his own sending.

In order to speak then of God as missionary, Holmes turns first to Basil of Caesarea. Basil argues that we can differentiate the acts of the Trinity on the basis of the relationships of origin. Basil says that each divine act has its origin in the Father, therefore we can say that redemption is initiated by the Father, carried out through the incarnation of the Son and brought to completion by the Spirit's work in the church.[58] If Basil is right, and Holmes believes that he is, this also helps us to see that it must be possible to speak of the Son and the Spirit "defer[ing] to the authority of the Father" and that this is a "necessary consequence of the particular relationships of origins within the Trinity."[59] Turning back to John 20:21, Holmes can see that there is room to claim that the sending of the Son by the Father is ontological, within God's own life, and not just economic. This is strengthened by the earlier conversations between Father and Son in John chapters 13–17 which many read as an intra-trinitarian conversation.[60]

On this basis Holmes argues his case for describing God as missionary. He goes on though to distinguish his claim from the likes of Jürgen Moltmann. Holmes says if the events of the Gospel story do reveal God's eternal life, it does not entail that these events are definitive of God's life. Where Moltmann argues that the crucifixion is definitive for God's eternal life, Holmes contends instead that the crucifixion is "a repetition of the pattern of God's eternal life."[61] At this point Holmes discusses the Fiddes paper explored above as an example of someone following the Moltmann line, but one alert to the theological pitfalls that Moltmann arguably falls into. That is, Fiddes is the best example of a Moltmannian theology, but Holmes argues that we do not need to follow this trajectory to enable us to say the triune God is missionary.[62] Holmes suggests that following Barth is more helpful. Barth takes the doctrine of election and places it within his doctrine

57. Ibid., 79.
58. Ibid., 80.
59. Ibid., 82.
60. Ibid., 82.
61. Ibid., 83.
62. Ibid., 84.

of God, which means the history of Jesus is not a separate act, but "part of who God is, not just what God has done."[63]

In the final sections of Holmes's article he draws his argument together. To speak of the missionary God is to say that the relations of Son and Spirit to the Father are not just a "movement of origination, but a movement of purposeful sending."[64] Holmes says the character of these relations according to John 20:19–23 are of "gracious generosity."[65] Jesus speaks words of peace over the disciples and speaks of forgiveness of sins. To attribute mission to God's character is also to suggest that God's own life is orientated outward, although Holmes is more cautious than Fiddes (in his view) to not give any ground that God needs something outside of himself. Yet in the way that love says something about how God relates to creation, so being missionary gives rise to a movement of God that goes beyond concern to action in order to realize his loving purposes.[66] Holmes's final observations are around how a doctrine of God that includes being missionary affects ecclesiology. If God is missionary in himself then the church cannot truly be itself without it too being missionary. The doctrine of God, as we explored above in the works from the mid-1990s, does shape what it is to be the church. Mission becomes a mark of the church, alongside one, holy, catholic and apostolic.[67] Holmes's final point says that for a missionary God mission never comes to an end, mission is not temporal, but eternal. Holmes finds no reason for this not to be the case, and some hints in the book of Revelation to support it.[68]

Holmes's article, while subtitled as only "towards a theology of God as missionary," remains amongst Baptists the most extensive argument thus far for the confession that Coffey, Ellis, and others have made, and continue to make, about the identity of God.[69]

Holmes's article was originally written for the Doctrine and Worship Committee in 2003–4. John Colwell's shorter paper "Mission as Ontology" originated at the same time. Colwell's paper covers similar ground to Fiddes and Holmes, but he makes his own argument. Colwell's concern is that

63. Ibid., 85.
64. Ibid., 86.
65. Ibid., 88.
66. Ibid.
67. Ibid., 89.
68. Ibid., 89–90.

69. Coffey continued to speak of a missionary God in his Dr. George Beasley-Murray Memorial Lecture delivered in 2006 and published in 2014 in Wright, *Truth That Never Dies*. Ellis also continues to speak of God as missionary in "Spirituality in Mission."

language of the church "doing mission" is theologically ungrammatical.[70] To talk about mission, we must, like others, begin with God. Following Bosch, he says that the language of mission was first used "exclusively" with reference to the doctrine of the Trinity. He refers to Bosch's claim that mission is an attribute of God and affirms this in terms of the economic Trinity, but *pace* Holmes, not with reference to God *in se*. Colwell is concerned that to make mission an attribute of God's nature is to ultimately make the object of that mission eternal too.[71] Therefore, Colwell steps short from speaking of God as missionary.

Colwell's constructive point is to argue that the Son and the Spirit's sending is ontological rather than functional.[72] Who the Son and Spirit are is defined by their being sent by the Father, not primarily by what they do. The same is true of the church, says Colwell and he supports this point with reference to John 20:21.[73] The church is sent as a witness to the Son and this corresponds to the sending of the Spirit. The mission of the church reflects more the mission of the Spirit than that of the Son. The sending of the Son is unique. The church does not continue the Son's sending, but is related to the Son through its witness to the Son.[74] The mission of the church, like that of the Son and the Spirit is ontological rather than functional. Colwell's point is that the mission of the church is not dependent on what it does, but on it's being sent into the world. Anything the church does is an outworking or an outcome of its mission, but its mission resides in who it is, those gathered and sent into the world by the Son in the power of the Spirit.[75]

Colwell goes on to comment that the language of mission has largely replaced the language of evangelism, and this points to a fresh understanding that evangelism, as in proclamation, must be accompanied by social and political action.[76] While on the one hand this might be applauded, Colwell expresses concern that this is probably more about evangelism becoming something the church is uneasy about. More importantly all the church's talk of mission as that which is done as activity creates a separation between the church and mission.[77] It creates an "and" where there should be

---

70. Colwell, "Mission as Ontology," 8.
71. Ibid.
72. Ibid.
73. Ibid., 9.
74. Ibid.
75. Ibid.
76. Ibid., 10.
77. Ibid.

no "and."[78] It identifies some of the church's life as mission and parts as nonmission, often what might be termed "worship." Colwell wants to stress that the church is a "missionary people," at no point does mission start or stop.[79] Mission is who the church is as it indwells the gospel story through baptism and the Lord's Supper.[80] As such it is itself a sign and a sacrament—a witness to the Son.[81]

Nigel Wright is the fourth Baptist theologian to think theologically about God and mission. In *Disavowing Constantine* he affirms the *missio Dei* and argues that "the sending of the Son and Spirit reveal God's self-giving love and expresses the centrifugal movement of God's being."[82] Mission defines God's being and as a consequence the church's. Like Colwell, he speaks of the church as a sign, sacrament, and instrument.[83] In Wright's later work *Free Church, Free State* he argues that mission is a priority of the church, it is the "defining essence of the church."[84] He then provides an extended quote from Daniel Migliore, in which Migliore says that "the triune God is a missionary God."[85] He returns to mission and the church towards the end of the book and describes the mode of mission as declaring truth through persuasion. The church's mission follows the pattern of it's Messiah and Wright suggests it is less the "agent" of mission, but the "locus," that is, where God is at work.[86] This echoes Colwell that the church does not do mission, but is mission, where the gospel is present. Stuart Murray is critical of Wright's theology of mission for its brevity.[87] Despite the language of the "priority of mission" and the church as a "missionary, messianic community," Wright does not include mission in his description of the "ecclesial minimum." Evangelism and mission are strangely muted themes in both Wright's key accounts of Baptist identity *Challenge to Change* and *Free Church, Free State*. They are present, but not upfront and central. Wright's shorter book *New Baptists, New Agenda*, which was written in between the

78. I borrow this point from a similar one Stanley Hauerwas makes in a paper called "Worship, Evangelism, Ethics," 155–61.

79. Colwell, "Mission as Ontology," 11.

80. Ibid. Colwell develops his argument around "indwelling" in *Living the Christian Story*.

81. For more on the church as sacrament, see John Colwell, "The Church as Sacrament."

82. Wright, *Disavowing Constantine*, 9.

83. Ibid., 10.

84. Wright, *Free Church*, 16.

85. Ibid., 16, quoting Migliore, *Faith Seeking Understanding*, 200–201.

86. Ibid., 234.

87. Murray, "Church Planting, Peace and the Ecclesial Minimum," 132.

other two mentioned, is where he offers some further comments on mission. Here he distinguishes evangelism as a subset of mission. Mission is the holistic action of God to seek and restore all that was lost.[88] Mission is the imperative of the church, that is, churches are, or should be, missionary congregations.[89] Mission is "participation in God's saving purposes for the world."[90] Mission is congregational says Wright, for conversion is a trinitarian and ecclesial experience, it is to be gathered into God and as such gathered into the church.[91] He does not say it, but the suggestion is that we must speak of missionary congregations, but not missionary associations or unions. The role of the association or union is to relate and resource the local church in mission (see *Free Church, Free State*, chapter 9).

To summarize we have seen that the confession of a missionary God is supported by Fiddes and Holmes, although in different ways. Colwell supports the concept of missionary God in terms of how God acts, but resists the move to say this of God's eternal life. For Colwell though mission is ontological rather than functional, such that to speak of a missionary church is not to speak of what a church does, but who the church is in God.

FOUR REFLECTIONS ON BAPTISTS AND MISSION

1. A Missionary Union Must Be Ecclesial

David Coffey wants to speak not just of a missionary God and a missionary church, but also a missionary Union.[92] To speak of a missionary Union is only possible if the Union is understand in ecclesial terms, that is, to see the Union as an expression of *being* church.[93] To speak of the Union in less than ecclesial terms, for example, as a "national resource agency"[94] is to treat it merely functionally. Mission, as Colwell, has argued is a matter of ontology rather than function. Coffey's description indicates that his use of missionary as a descriptor of God, church, Union is to emphasis what Union and churches should be doing. Mission is understood as a series of tasks that

---

88. Wright, *New Baptists*, 31.
89. Ibid., 65.
90. Ibid.
91. Ibid., 81–82.
92. Coffey, "A Missionary Union," 87–113. The lecture was originally given at the Baptist Assembly in May 2006.
93. See the Doctrine and Worship Committee report *The Nature of Assembly* for one account of seeking to define the Union theologically.
94. Coffey and Jones, "The Denominational Consultation," 1.

God calls the Union and churches to carry out in order to grow and build the kingdom of God. Coffey borrows from Bosch the language of "paradigm shift" in order to help Baptists see that the church exists for mission, that Baptists must have a "mission mentality" over maintenance.[95] The status of the Union found no clear consensus during the Coffey's tenure as general secretary, there remained a tension between those who argued for a covenantal view of the Union and those that saw it more in terms of a resource for mission and advice.[96]

It might be asked if it is the case that the Union must be ecclesial in order to be missionary, what about the Baptist Missionary Society? Here we should note that there have been attempts both in 2012 and during the Denominational Consultation in the late 1990s to see the Baptist Union and the Baptist Missionary Society (BMS) merge to become one body. How should we understand the theology of a missionary society? Is BMS merely functional and does it operate with a functional understanding of mission?

It is the view of the report *The Nature of Assembly* that the difference between the Baptist Union and BMS is that the former is an ecclesial body, while the later is a voluntary body.[97] They are different organizations. The Union is made up of the churches, associations, and colleges in covenant relationship. BMS is a separate organization from the churches, but with very close church links, seen in the financial support of BMS and it's sharing in Baptist life through the joint Baptist Assembly.[98] These church links are vital if mission is to avoid being separated from the church. Haymes argues that the "proper home" of mission is in the life and work of the church and to "locat[e] mission in a society leads to an impoverished understanding and practice of the church's calling."[99] A recent BMS document speaks of the "essential missionary nature of the church" and suggests that they understand the Society as an expression of that missionary nature, whilst describing themselves as a "Christian mission organization."[100]

---

95. In an interview with the *Baptist Times* on his appointment as General Secretary John Capon reports that Coffey's "chief passion is to ensure that the denomination develops a mission mentality, rather than a maintenance one," "New Man in the Baptist Hotseat," *Baptist Times*, 9th May 1991, 7.

96. The later is reflected in the renaming of the Mission Department as the "Department for Training and Research in Mission" in 1997.

97. *The Nature of Assembly*, 25.

98. Historically, Brian Stanley argues that, "during the nineteenth century, and arguably also for the first two decades of the twentieth, the BMS was the principal force unifying British Baptists," *A History of the Baptist Missionary Society*, 511.

99. Haymes et al., *On Being the Church*, 185.

100. See the document *For God . . .* (Didcot: BMS, 2010), 1–2.

2. Mission and Apostolicity

This emphasis on mission can be seen as the Baptist Union recognizing and realizing one of the traditional four marks of the church, specifically apostolicity. The history of interpretation concerning apostolicity in the Catholic tradition has predominantly seen it associated with some form of historic succession from the first apostles to the present through the laying on of hands to each successive generation of bishops. In this interpretation, apostolicity consists in the ability to demonstrate an unbroken link with the earliest church through the guarding of the *regula fidei* by the bishops in unbroken succession. In both cases apostolicity is understood as something received from the past and handed on. Since the Reformation, and its breaking with that succession, an alternative version has located apostolicity, not in the person of the bishop, but in faithfulness to the apostolic teaching and witness. In both cases apostolicity is understood as something received from the past and handed on. This is primarily about the preservation of doctrine, a contention that the church's identity and beliefs resembles that of the church at its beginnings. In the former, historic succession affirms those appointed bishops, in the latter, adherence to the apostle's teaching is the meaning of the mark. More recently apostolicity has been understood in terms of the practice of witness. As the early church witnessed to Christ and the gospel, so the church which is apostolic also bears witness to Christ and the gospel. Apostolicity is a matter of mission.[101] As Colwell says "the apostolicity of the church is surely a matter of its 'being-sent-ness,' its being sent into the world as the Son was sent into the world."[102] Apostolicity is about *where* the church is—in the world—as much, if not more, than conformity with apostolic teaching. It can be argued that this is not new for Baptists. The Baptist understanding of church, seen most clearly by its practice of believers' baptism means Baptists have always been apostolic. It is essential to a Baptist ecclesiology. It is evident in the theology of Andrew Fuller and in the third clause of the Declaration of Principle. However, a reading of W. M. S. West's *Baptist Principles*[103] and Gordon Martin's *The Church: A Baptist View*[104] find no discussion of evangelism and/or mission in their account. West's *Baptist Principles* was first published by the Baptist Union in March 1960 and revised and reprinted four times, the last in 1986,

---

101. This is the argument made by the Faith and Unity Executive of the Baptist Union in the joint report with the Church of England, *Pushing at the Boundaries of Unity*, 108.

102. Colwell, "The Church as Sacrament," 59.

103. West, *Baptist Principles*.

104. Martin, *The Church*.

so it has claim to be a key little text for twenty-five years. Evangelism is at best a muted form. There are chapters on the Bible, the church, baptism, and church membership. West speaks of "an inescapable responsibility for evangelism"[105] and later "Baptists have always been recognised at the forefront of evangelism,"[106] but this is not given further description or explanation. What makes the reforms in the 1990s different was an attempt to intentionally shape the structures of the Union and the life of local churches with mission as their priority, to make mission a definitive and explicit Baptist principle alongside others. Of course, we might ask whether this was out of panic at falling number or from beginning with the doctrine of God. The clearest example of the desire to make mission definitive is the report *Five Core Values* which emerged out the Denominational Consultation. A task group was asked to draw up a statement of core values reflecting a Baptist commitment to "the poor and marginalized and issues of equal opportunities."[107] The report was presented and accepted at Council meeting in March 1998 and published in 1999 as *Five Core Values for a Gospel People*. The five Core Values identified contended that the church was to be a prophetic community, an inclusive community, a sacrificial community, a missionary community and a worshipping community.[108]

There was a sense by some that the way the Union had been organized did more to hinder the church in being missionary.[109] It is questionable whether the new structures set in place from 2002 were ultimately any more missional. One of the changes was to provide more focused regional ministry that could help enable mission with associations and amongst local churches. However, the associations moved from twenty-six county associations to thirteen regional associations and in many places the already weak associating was arguably weakened further, rather than being strengthened as had been the intention behind the report *Relating and Resourcing*. The language of mission and being missional is now part of everyday speech,

---

105. West, *Baptist Principles*, 5.

106. Ibid., 38. In Martin's *The Church* he says the church is shaped by worship, teaching and fellowship. Witness, he says, is "engaged in at personal level in secular situations by individual Christians," 29.

107. Baptist Union Council Minutes, November 1996, 16.

108. *Five Core Values*, 3. The section describing missionary community might be better headed being evangelistic communities and together the five values together reflecting what it is to be a missionary people.

109. It can be heard in Rob Warner's question, "Do we have the courage to reinvent an ageing denomination as a contemporary missionary movement," "Ageing Structures and Undying Convictions," 16.

but I suggest this remains in many ways at the level of talk and statement rather than practice.

3. Mission and Faddism

Ian Stackhouse identifies faddism as an issue amongst evangelicals, especially of the charismatic variety.[110] An emphasis on revival and church growth, sees the church always looking for the latest "fad" which will bring that growth. Baptists are not immune from this faddism and continual reports, projects and calls to prayer can be seen throughout the second half of the twentieth century and into the twenty-first. Underlying this again is a functional understanding of mission, where the Union is a resource agency generating ideas for mission, creating a need for the latest and most novel, that which will "work." It might be argued that when Baptists began speaking of a "missionary God" this reflected the latest fad rather than something intrinsically theological.

However, what Fiddes and Holmes begin to explore is what might be described as the character of mission, the virtues of mission over against the pragmatics of mission. If mission is a participation in the missionary God, it will reflect the mission God makes in Jesus and the Holy Spirit. Holmes argues that the church is sent "in a cruciform, purposeful and self-sacrificial way" as this reflects who God is.[111] *Five Core Values* makes a similar argument, although not in the language of participation, but in the language of following Jesus. *Five Core Values* describe not what the church should do, but who the church should be: "these values are an embodiment of the gospel in communal form."[112] A missionary Union would not mean necessarily one involved in church planting and evangelistic and social action projects, but one that enables the growing of churches in missionary virtues, that is, a Union that is focusing on growing missionary communities of character. In 2007 the Union began to speak of "encouraging missionary disciples,"[113] but this is something of a tautology, for there is no kind of disciple that is not missionary, and this applies equally to the church, and of course, also to the Union. Mission is not about engaging in the latest fad, it is a participating in the life of the missionary God and so embodying the character of God. The church as an instrument (the activity of mission) of the missionary God is

---

110. Stackhouse, *The Gospel-Driven Church*, 3–42.
111. Holmes, "Trinitarian Missiology," 89.
112. Ellis, "Spirituality in Mission," 180.
113. This was the strapline of the Union's Strategy agreed at the Council in November 2007.

a consequence of its participation in God (its being-sent-ness); *who* it is has priority over *what* it does.[114]

4. Mission and Discipleship

At the end of the reflections on mission *Something to Declare* wonders whether alongside an emphasis on evangelism, Baptists need an equal emphasis on evangelization: that is proclamation must be joined with discipleship.[115] Again an analysis of Baptist life in the 1990s could claim that there is an over-emphasis on mission to the detriment of creating communities of character.[116] A functional understanding of mission that views it as activities or projects or as a matter of personal witness fails to view the "church is mission."[117] *Transforming Superintendency* recognizes this when it argues that superintendency should be focused on the care, encouragement and development of local ministers, for the minister or ministers are those that enable the church to be the church. Mission is not second step,[118] something that can be separated from other things the church does, the church is missionary in how it lives out its life as Christians together. Coffey writing at the end of his period as General Secretary acknowledges this when he identifies that "the fifth mark of a missionary Union is a commitment to intentional discipleship."[119] Roger Standing argues that the separation of "maintenance" and "mission" can create a "false juxtaposition,"[120] which perhaps is an argument to see apostolicity as both about maintaining community identity (through a handing on of tradition) as well as a community that recognizes its being-sent-ness, it's communal witness. *Something to Declare* is helpful here again by outlining a link between the second and third articles of the Declaration of Principle—the meaning of baptism and the emphasis on

---

114. Colwell, "The Church as Sacrament," 59–60.

115. *Something to Declare*, 52.

116. This is of course is a deliberate borrowing from the title of Hauerwas's *A Community of Character*.

117. As Hauerwas says of the church: "it is not merely the agent of mission or the constituency of a mission agency. It is the mission," "Beyond the Boundaries," 167.

118. The language of "second step" I borrow from John Flett, *The Witness of God*. He is critical of theology of the doctrine of God which separates God's being from this act. The mission of God becomes a "second step," rather than who God is. This plays out also in the church. For example Flett is critical of Miroslav Volf's book *After Our Likeness*, which offers an ecclesiology in which Volf says "the church's mission are only in my peripheral vision," 7.

119. Coffey, "A Missionary Union," 106–7.

120. Standing, "Missional Church," 10.

evangelism. Baptism is a disciples" baptism and participation into the life of God, who is the missionary God.[121]

CONCLUSION

The last twenty-five years have seen Baptists attempt to make mission an organizing priority and at the same time, in some quarters, to be a place of theological reflection. There remains a tension between those for whom the drive to mission is a context of decline and those who for whom the centrality of mission is fundamentally theological. The former continue to push the latest fad or for greater activism, the latter focus more on the character and life of the church as being mission. There is something perhaps of the economic versus the ontological in play, in which, if held in conversation, might enable Baptists to not only speak but live out what it is to worship a missionary God as a missionary Union.

---

121. Kidd, *Something to Declare*, 48.

Bibliography of the Writings of Christopher J. Ellis

———. "Relativity, Ecumenism and the Liberation of the Church." *Baptist Quarterly* 29 (1981) 81–91.

———. *Together on the Way: A Theology of Ecumenism*. London. British Council of Churches, 1990.

———. "On Personal Renewal." *Mainstream Magazine* 52 (1995) 7–11.

———. "Believer's Baptism and the Sacramental Freedom of God." In *Reflection on the Waters: Understanding God and the World through the Baptism of Believers*, edited by Paul Fiddes, 23–45. Regent's Study Guides 4. Macon, GA: Smyth & Helwys, 1996.

———. *Baptist Worship Today. A Report of Two Worship Surveys Undertaken by the Doctrine and Worship Committee of the Baptist Union of Great Britain*. Didcot, UK: BUGB, 1999.

———. "A View from the Pool: Baptists, Sacraments and the Basis of Unity." *Baptist Quarterly* 39 (2001) 107–20.

———. "The Baptism of Disciples and the Nature of the Church." In *Dimensions of Baptism: Biblical and Theological Studies*, edited by Stanley Porter and Anthony R. Cross, 333–53. London: Sheffield Academic Press, 2002.

———. "A Little Child Shall Lead Them." The 2002 David Jellyman Lecture. Unpublished.

———. "Duty and Delight in Baptist Worship and Identity." *Review and Expositor* 100.3 (2003) 329–49.

———. *Gathering: A Theology and Spirituality of Worship in Free Church Tradition*. London: SCM, 2004.

———. "Baptist Worship." In *New SCM Dictionary of Liturgy and Worship*, edited by Paul Bradshaw, 53–55. London: SCM, 2005.

———. "Who Are the Baptists? A Study in Worship." In *Baptist Faith & Witness. Book 3. Papers of the Study and Research Division of the Baptist World Alliance 2000–2005*, edited by L. A. (Tony) Cupit, 78–90. Falls Church, VA: Baptist World Alliance, 2005.

———, and Myra Blyth, eds. *Gathering for Worship: Patterns and Prayers for the Community of Disciples*. Norwich, UK: Canterbury and the Baptist Union of Great Britain, 2005.

———. "Baptists in Britain." In *The Oxford History of Christian Worship*, edited by Geoffrey Wainwright, 560–72. Oxford: Oxford University Press, 2006.

———. "Gathering Struggles: Creative Tensions in Baptist Worship." *Baptist Quarterly* 42.1 (2007) 4–21.

———. "Understanding Worship: Trends and Criteria" and "Worshipping at the Heart of Life." In *Currents in Baptistic Theology of Worship Today*, edited by Keith G. Jones and Parush R. Parushev, 25–39. Prague: International Baptist Theological Seminary, 2007.

———. "Spirituality in Mission: Gathering and Grace." In *Under the Rule of Christ: Dimensions of Baptist Spirituality*, edited by Paul Fiddes, 169–87. Macon, GA: Smyth & Helwys, 2008.

———. "Embodied Grace: Exploring the Sacraments and Sacramentality." In *Baptist Sacramentalism 2*, edited by Anthony R. Cross and Philip E. Thompson, 1–16. Milton Keynes, UK: Paternoster, 2008.

———. *Approaching God: A Guide to Leading Worship*. London: SCM, 2009

———. "Being a Minister: Spirituality and the Pastor." In *Challenging to Change: Dialogues with a Radical Baptist Theologian. Essays presented to Dr Nigel G. Wright on his Sixtieth Birthday*, edited by Pieter J. Lalleman, 55–70. London: Spurgeon's College, 2009.

———. "Who Is Worship For? Dispatches from the War Zone." *Perspectives in Religious Studies* 36.2 (2009) 179–85.

———. "Written Prayers in an Oral Context: Transitions in Baptist Worship." In *The Collect in the Churches of the Reformation*, edited by Bridget Nichols, 139–56. London: SCM, 2010.

———. "Prayer and Theology." In *Baptist Faith & Witness Book 4: Papers of the Study and Research Division of the Baptist World Alliance 2005–2010*, edited by Fausto A Vasconcelos, 85–96. Falls Church, VA: Baptist World Alliance, 2011.

———. "Gathering Round the Word: Baptists, Scripture and Worship." In *The "Plainly Revealed" Word of God? Baptist Hermeneutics in Theory and Practice*, edited by Helen Dare and Simon Woodman, 101–21. Macon, GA: Mercer University Press, 2011.

———. "Out of a Believer's Heart: Orality and Text." In *Wrestling with a Godly Order: Encounters with the 1662 Book of Common Prayer*, edited by James Steven, 49–66. Salisbury, UK: Sarum College, 2015.

General Bibliography

Ahl, Diane Cole. *Fra Angelico*. London: Phaidon, 2008.
Alison, James. *Broken Hearts and New Creations: Intimations of a Great Reversal*. London: DLT, 2010.
Allison, Elizabeth J. *A Feminist Discussion of "Complementarian" Arguments for Women in Ministry, with Particular Reference to the Baptist Union of Great Britain*. MTh diss., University of Oxford, 2015.
Allmen, Jean Jacques Von. *Worship: Its Theology and Practice*. London: Lutterworth, 1965.
Ante-Nicene Fathers, The, Translations of the Writings of the Fathers Down to AD 325. Edited by Alexander Roberts and James Donaldson. 10 Vols. Grand Rapids: Eerdmans, 1956.
Anderson, E. Bryon. "Linking Liturgy and Life." In *Worship Matters: A United Methodist Guide to Ways of Worship, Volume 1*, edited by E. Byron Anderson, 63–69. Nashville, TN: Discipleship Resources, 1999.
―――. "O For a Heart to Praise My God": Hymning the Self Before God." In *Liturgy and the Moral Self: Humanity at Full Stretch Before God: Essays in Honor of Don E. Saliers*, edited by E. Byron Anderson and Bruce T. Morrill, 111–25. Collegeville, MN: Liturgical, 1998.
―――. *Worship and Christian Identity: Practicing Ourselves*. Collegeville, MN: Liturgical, 2003.
Augsburger, David. *Dissident Discipleship*. Grand Rapids: Brazos, 2006.
Augustine, Saint. *The Trinity*. Translated by Stephen McKenna. *The Fathers of the Church*, Vol. 45. Washington, DC: Catholic University of America Press, 1963.
Balthasar, Hans Urs von. *Theo-Drama: Theological Dramatic Theory. I: Prolegomena*. Translated by Graham Harrison. San Francisco: Ignatius, 1988.
―――. *Truth is Symphonic: Aspects of Christian Pluralism*. San Francisco: Ignatius, 1987.
"The Baptist Doctrine of the Church: A Statement Approved by the Council of the Baptist Union of Great Britain and Ireland, March 1948," In *Baptist Union Documents 1948–77*, edited by Roger Hayden, 4–11. London: Baptist Historical Society, 1980.
Baptist Praise and Worship. Oxford: Oxford University Press on behalf of the Psalms and Hymns Trust, 1991.

The Baptist Union Human Sexuality Working Group. *Baptists Exploring Issues of Human Sexuality: How Baptists Might Think Biblically and Theologically about Homosexuality.* Papers for the Educational Process, 2011. Unpublished.

Baptist Union of Great Britain. *Briefing Paper for the BUGB Faith and Unity Executive on the meeting on 31st July 2008, at IMC, Birmingham, of Representatives of the BUGB Women's Justice Group, the Regional Associations, the Baptist Colleges, the BUGB Staff, and Mainstream (North) on the Subject of Women in Leadership in the BUGB.* Unpublished.

Barth, Karl. *Church Dogmatics.* Translated and edited by G. W. Bromiley and T. F. Torrance. 14 vols. Edinburgh: T. & T. Clark, 1936–77.

———. *The Teaching of the Church Regarding Baptism.* Translated by Ernest A. Payne. London: SCM, 1959.

Beale, G. K. *We Become What We Worship: A Biblical Theology of Idolatry.* Downers Grove, IL: IVP Academic, 2008.

Beasley-Murray, George R. *Man and Woman in the Church.* London: Baptist Union of Great Britain, 1983.

Bebbington. David. *Baptists Through the Centuries: A History of a Global People.* Waco, TX: Baylor University Press, 2010.

Begbie, Jeremy S. *Theology, Music and Time.* Cambridge: Cambridge University Press, 2000.

Beginning with God. A Guide to Prayer, Study and Reflection in Preparation for the Denominational Consultation of the Baptist Union of Great Britain 1996. Didcot, UK: Baptist Union, 1996.

Behm, Johannes. "ἀνακαλίζο." In *Theological Dictionary of the New Testament*, Vol. 3. Grand Rapids: Eerdmans, 1965.

Bell, John L. *The Singing Thing: A Case for Congregational Singing.* Glasgow: GIA, 2000.

Best, Thomas, and Dagnar Heller, eds. *Eucharist Worship in Ecumenical Contexts: The Lima Liturgy—and Beyond.* Geneva: WCC, 1995.

Blyth, Myra. "The Meaning and Function of 'Dynamic Equivalence' in Ecumenical Dialogues." In *For the Sake of the Church: Essays in Honour of Paul S. Fiddes*, edited by Anthony Clarke, 163–72. Oxford: Regent's Park College, 2014.

Bonhoeffer, Dietrich. *Ethics: Dietrich Bonhoeffer Works,* Vol. 6. Minneapolis: Fortress, 2005.

———. *Letters and Papers from Prison. Dietrich Bonhoeffer Works,* Vol. 8. Minneapolis: Fortress, 2010.

Bosch, David J. *Transforming Mission: Paradigm Shifts in Theology of Mission.* Maryknoll, NY: Orbis, 1991.

Briggs, John H. Y. "Baptists in the Ecumenical Movement." *Journal of European Baptist Studies* 6.1 (2005) 11–17.

———. "English Baptists and their Hymnody." In *Baptist Faith and Witness: The Papers of the Study and Research Division of the Baptist World Alliance, 1990–1995*, edited by W. H. Brackney, 152–59. Birmingham, AL/McLean, VA: Samford University/Baptist World Alliance, 1995.

———. "She-preachers, Widows and Other Women: The Feminine Dimension in Baptist Life Since 1660." *Baptist Quarterly* 31.7 (1986) 337–52.

Brueggemann, Walter. "Enough is Enough." *The Other Side* 37.5 (2001). http://liferemixed.net/2012/02/29/enough-is-enough/ (accessed 23rd June 2016).

———. *The Message of the Psalms: A Theological Commentary.* Minneapolis: Augsburg Fortress, 1984.
———. *Finally Comes the Poet.* Minneapolis: Augsburg Fortress, 1989.
———. *Journey to the Common Good.* Louisville, KY: Westminster John Knox, 2010.
Bullard, Scott W. "Communing Together: Baptists Worshipping in the Eucharist." In *Gathering Together: Baptists at Work in Worship*, edited by Rodney Wallace Kennedy and Derek C. Hatch, 94–109. Eugene, OR: Pickwick, 2013.
Bunyan, John. *I Will Pray with the Spirit.* In *The Miscellaneous Works of John Bunyan*, Vol. II, edited by Roger Sharrock. Oxford: Oxford University Press, 1976.
Burnard, Clive. "Transformational Servant Leadership as Exemplified in the Ministry of the Reverend Doctor David R. Coffey." DMin thesis, University of Wales, 2014.
Burns, Stephen. *SCM Study Guide to Liturgy.* London: SCM, 2006.
Busch, Eberhard. *Karl Barth: His Life from Letters and Autobiographical Texts.* London: SCM, 1976.
Busher, Leonard. *Religious Peace; or, A Plea for Liberty of Conscience, in Tracts on Liberty of Conscience, 1614–61*, edited by E. B. Underhill, 1–81. London: Hanserd Knollys Society, 1846.
Butler, Amy. "Liturgical Ties of Community." In *Gathering Together: Baptists at Work in Worship*, edited by Rodney W. Kennedy and Derek C. Hatch, 39–50. Eugene, OR: Wipf and Stock, 2013.
Caemmerer, Richard R. *Preaching for the Church.* St. Louis, MO: Concordia, 1959.
Calvin, John. *Institutes of Christian Religion.* Edited in two volumes by J. T. McNeil. Philadelphia: Westminster, 1960.
A Call to Commitment: Baptist Christians through the 80s. London: Baptist Union, 1980.
Call to Obedience: A Study in Evangelism. London: Baptist Union, 1969.
Cameron, Helen, and Deborah Bhatti, Catherine Duce, James Sweeney, and Clare Watkins. *Talking about God in Practice: Theological Action Research and Practical Theology.* London: SCM, 2010.
Campbell, Charles L. *The Word Before the Powers: An Ethic of Preaching.* Louisville, KY: Westminster John Knox, 2002.
Caputo, John D. *What Would Jesus Deconstruct? The Good News of Postmodernism for the Church.* Grand Rapids: Baker, 2007.
Carrell, Severin. "Alex Salmond Announces Scottish Independence Referendum Date." 21 March 2013. http://www.theguardian.com/politics/2013/mar/21/scottish-independence-referendum-date.
Cavanaugh, William T. *Torture and Eucharist: Theology, Politics and the Body of Christ.* Oxford: Blackwell, 1998.
Cavarero, Adriana. *Relating Narratives: Storytelling and Selfhood.* Translated by P. A. Knottman. London: Routledge, 2000.
Charon, Rita. *Narrative Medicine: Honoring the Stories of Illness.* New York: Oxford University Press, 2008.
Child, Robert L., ed. *The Lord's Supper: A Baptist Statement.* 1951. Reprint. London: Carey Kingsgate, 1961.
The Church: Towards a Common Vision. Faith and Order Paper No. 214. Geneva: WCC, 2013.
Church of South India. *The Service of the Lord's Supper or Holy Eucharist.* London: Oxford University Press, 1950.

Claiborne, Shane, and Jonathan Wilson-Hartgrove. *Becoming the Answer to Our Prayers: Prayer for Ordinary Radicals*. Downers Grove, IL: IVP, 2008.

Clark, Neville. "Baptist Praise and Worship." *Baptist Quarterly* 35.2 (1993) 95–100.

———. *A Call to Worship*. London: SCM, 1960.

Clarke, Anthony J. "A Feast for All? Reflecting on Open Communion for the Contemporary Church." In *Baptist Sacramentalism 2*, edited by Anthony R. Cross and Philip E. Thompson, 92–116. Milton Keynes, UK: Paternoster, 2008.

Coffey, David. "A Missionary Union: Past, Present and Future Perspectives." In *Truth That Never Dies: The Dr. G. R. Beasley-Murray Memorial Lectures 2002–2012*, edited by Nigel Wright, 87–113. Eugene, OR: Pickwick, 2014.

Coffey, David, and Keith Jones. "The Denominational Consultation." *Baptist Leader* 13 (1995) 1–2.

Coleman, Kate. *7 Deadly Sins of Women in Leadership*. Birmingham: Next Leadership, 2010.

Collicutt, Joanna. *The Psychology of Christian Character Formation*. London: SCM, 2015.

Colwell, John. "The Church as Sacrament." In *Baptist Sacramentalism 2*, edited by Anthony R. Cross and Philip E. Thompson, 48–60. Milton Keynes, UK: Paternoster, 2008.

———. *Living the Christian Story: The Distinctiveness of Christian Ethics*. Edinburgh: T. & T. Clark, 2001.

———. "Mission as Ontology." *Baptist Minister's Journal* 295 (2006) 7–12.

———. *Promise and Presence: An Exploration in Sacramental Theology*. Milton Keynes, UK: Paternoster, 2005.

Common Worship: Services and Prayers for the Church of England. London: Church House, 2000.

Conference of European Churches, *European Churches Engaging in Human Rights*. Bruxelles: Church and Society Commission of CEC, 2012.

Covenant 21. Didcot, UK: Baptist Union, 2000.

Cranfield, C. E. B. *Romans, Vol. 2*. The International Critical Commentary. Edinburgh: T. & T. Clark, 1979.

Cross, Anthony R. *Baptism and the Baptists*. Carlisle, UK: Paternoster, 2000.

Cunningham, David S. *These Three Are One: The Practice of Trinitarian Theology*. Oxford: Blackwell, 1998.

Dawn, Marva J. *Reaching Out Without Dumbing Down: A Theology of Worship for the Turn-of-the-Century Culture*. Grand Rapids: Eerdmans, 1995.

Dex, Shirley. "The Church's Response to Feminism." *Baptist Quarterly* 31.7 (1986) 320–25.

Douglas, Mary. *Purity and Danger*. 1966. Reprint. London: Routledge, 2002.

Eakins, Adam. "That Joke Isn't Funny Anymore." *Talk: The Mainstream Magazine* 7.2 (2007) 12–13.

Eckblad, Bob. *A New Christian Manifesto: Pledging Allegiance to the Kingdom of God*. Louisville, KY: Westminster John Knox, 2008.

Egner, Malcolm J. "Re-imagining the Covenant Community: The Church Meeting and Baptist Congregational Life." MTh diss., Spurgeon's College, 2007.

Electoral Commission. "Scottish Independence Referendum: Report on the Referendum Held on 18 September 2014." (December 2014). www.electoralcommission.org.

uk/__data/assets/pdf_file/0010/179812/Scottish-independence-referendum-report.pdf.

Ellis, Robert. "Where Two Or Three Are Gathered: The Church as Praying Community." *International Journal of Congregational Studies* 14.2 (2015) 85–106.

Fergusson, David. *Church, State and Civil Society.* Cambridge: Cambridge University Press, 2004.

Few, Jenny. "Hats and WI(w)GS: Personal Reflections of the Baptist Union Women's Issues Working Group." In *Theology in Context*, edited by Stephen Holmes, 33–46. Oxford: Whitley, 1999.

Fiddes, Paul S. "Baptism and the Process of Christian Initiation." *The Ecumenical Review* 54 (2002) 48–65.

———. "Ex Opere Operato: Re-thinking a Historic Baptist Rejection." In *Baptist Sacramentalism 2*, edited by Anthony R. Cross and Philip E. Thompson, 219–38. Milton Keynes, UK: Paternoster, 2008.

———. "Mission as Liberty: A Baptist Connection." In *Tracks and Traces*, 249–73. Carlisle, UK: Paternoster, 2003.

———. *Participating in God. A Pastoral Doctrine of the Trinity.* London: Darton, Longman and Todd, 2000.

———, ed. *Reflections on the Water: Understanding God and the World through the Baptism of Believers.* Regent's Study Guides 4. Macon, GA: Smyth & Helwys, 1996.

———. "Relational Trinity: Radical Perspective." In *Two Views on the Doctrine of the Trinity*, edited by Jason Sexton, 159–171. Grand Rapids: Zondervan, 2014.

———. "Spirituality as Attentiveness: Stillness and Journey." In *Under the Rule of Christ: Dimensions of Baptist Spirituality*, edited by Paul Fiddes, 25–57. Regent's Study Guides 14. Macon, GA: Smyth and Helwys, 2008.

———. *Tracks and Traces: Baptist Identity in Church and Theology.* Studies in Baptist History and Thought, Vol. 13. Carlisle, UK: Paternoster, 2003.

———. "'Woman's Head is Man': A Doctrinal Reflection upon a Pauline Text." *Baptist Quarterly* 31.8 (1986) 370–83.

Fiddes, Paul, et al. *Bound to Love: The Covenant Basis of Baptist Life and Mission.* London: Baptist Union, 1985.

———. *A Call to Mind: Baptist Essays Towards a Theology of Commitment.* London: Baptist Union, 1980.

Fiddes, Paul S., Brian Haymes, Richard Kidd, and Michael Quicke. "Doing Theology Together: 1979–99. A Shared Story." In *Doing Theology in a Baptist Way*, edited by Paul S. Fiddes, 6–18. Oxford: Whitley, 2000.

Fiddes, Paul S., Brian Haymes, and Richard Kidd. *Baptists and the Communion of Saints: A Theology of Covenanted Disciples.* Waco, TX: Baylor University Press, 2014.

Five Core Values for a Gospel People. Didcot, UK: Baptist Union, 1999.

Flett, John. *The Witness of God: The Trinity, Missio Dei, Karl Barth, and the Nature of Christian Community.* Grand Rapids: Eerdmans, 2010.

Foder, Jim. "Reading the Scriptures: Rehearsing Identity, Practicing Character." In *The Blackwell Companion to Christian Ethics*, edited by Stanley Hauerwas and Samuel Wells, 141–55. Oxford: Blackwell, 2004.

Frank, Arthur W. *The Wounded Storyteller: Body, Illness, and Ethics.* 2nd ed. Chicago: University of Chicago Press, 2013.

Gardiner, Craig. *How Can We Sing the Lord's Song? 2008 Whitley Lecture.* Oxford: Whitley, 2008.

Gathering Around the Table: Children and Communion. 2010. Reprint. Didcot, UK: Baptist Union, 2015.

Gay, Doug. *Honey from the Lion: Christianity and the Ethics of Nationalism*. London: SCM, 2013.

Gill, John. *Gill's Complete Body of Practical and Doctrinal Divinity: Being a System of Evangelical Truths Deduced from the Sacred Scriptures*. Philadelphia: Delaplaine and Hellings, 1810.

Gilmore, Alec. "Baptist Churches Today and Tomorrow." In *The Pattern of the Church: A Baptist View*, edited by Alec Gilmore, 114–56. London: Lutterworth, 1963.

Gilmore, Alec, Edward Smalley, and Michael Walker. *Praise God: A Collection of Resource Material for Christian Worship*. London: Baptist Union, 1980.

Goodliff, Andy. *"To Such as These": The Child in Baptist Thought*. Oxford: Regent's Park College, 2012.

———. "Why Baptist Ecclesiology is Non-Voluntary." *Baptistic Theologies* 6.2 (2014) 3–8.

Goodliff, Paul. *Care in a Confused Climate: Pastoral Care and Postmodern Culture*. London: Darton, Longman & Todd, 1998.

———. *Shaped for Service: Ministerial Formation and Virtue Ethics*. Eugene, OR: Pickwick, 2017.

Gouldbourne, Ruth. "Do Women Complement Men in Ministry?" In *Ministry Today: The Journal of the Richard Baxter Institute for Ministry* 17 (1999) 6–10.

———. "Encountering Christ: Zwingli, Signs and Baptists Around the Table." In *For the Sake of the Church: Essays in Honour of Paul S. Fiddes*, edited by Anthony J. Clarke, 78–90. Oxford: Regent's Park College, 2014.

Grebe, Matthias. *Election, Atonement, and the Holy Spirit: Through and Beyond Barth's Theological Interpretation of Scripture*. Princeton Theological Monograph Series. Eugene, OR: Pickwick, 2014.

Green, Bernard. *Crossing the Boundaries: A History of the European Baptist Federation*. Didcot, UK: Baptist Historical Society, 1999.

Grenz, Stanley. *Theology for the Community of God*. 2nd ed. Grand Rapids: Eerdmans, 2000.

Grey, Mary C. *The Outrageous Pursuit of Hope*. London: Darton, Longman & Todd, 2000.

Grundmann, Walter. "δόκιμος." In *Theological Dictionary of the New Testament*, Vol. 2. Grand Rapids: Eerdmans, 1964.

Harmon, Steven R. *Baptist Identity and the Ecumenical Future: Story, Tradition and the Recovery of Community*. Waco, TX: Baylor University Press, 2016.

———. *Towards Baptist Catholicity: Essays on Tradition and the Baptist Vision*. Milton Keynes, UK: Paternoster, 2006.

Harvey, Barry. "'This as That': Friendly Amendments to James McClendon's Theology." *Baptistic Theologies* 6.1 (2014) 36–52.

Hauerwas, Stanley. "Beyond the Boundaries: The Church is Mission." In *War and the American Difference*, 167–181. Grand Rapids: Baker, 2011.

———. *Performing the Faith: Bonhoeffer and the Practice of Nonviolence*. London: SPCK, 2004.

———. "Worship, Evangelism, Ethics: On Eliminating the 'And.'" In *A Better Hope*, 155–61. Grand Rapids: Brazos, 2000.

Hauerwas, Stanley, and L. Gregory Jones, eds. *Why Narrative? Readings in Narrative Theology*. 1989. Reprint. Eugene, OR: Wipf & Stock, 1997.
Hauerwas, Stanley, and Samuel Wells. "The Gift of the Church and the Gifts God Gives It." In *The Blackwell Companion to Christian Ethics*, edited by Stanley Hauerwas and Samuel Wells, 13–27. Oxford: Blackwell, 2004.
Haymes, Brian. "Baptism as a Political Act." In *Reflections on the Water: Understanding God and the World through the Baptism of Believers*, edited by Paul Fiddes, 69–83. Macon, GA: Smyth and Helwys, 1996.
———. *A Question of Identity: Reflections on Baptist Principles and Practice*. Leeds: Yorkshire Baptist Association, 1986.
———. "Still Blessing the Tie that Binds." In *For the Sake of the Church: Essays in Honour of Paul S. Fiddes*, edited by Anthony Clarke, 91–102. Oxford: Regent's Park College, 2014.
———. "Theology and Baptist Identity." In *Doing Theology in a Baptist Way*, edited by Paul S. Fiddes, 1–5. Oxford: Whitley, 2000.
Haymes, Brian, Ruth Gouldbourne, and Anthony R. Cross. *On Being the Church: Revisioning Baptist Identity*. Milton Keynes, UK: Paternoster, 2008.
Hedger, Violet. "Some Experiences of a Woman Minister." *Baptist Quarterly* 10.5 (1941) 243–53.
Heidebrecht, Doug. "James Wm. McClendon Jr.'s Practice of Communal Discernment and Conflicting Convictions among Mennonite Brethren." *Baptistic Theologies* 7:1 (2015) 45–68.
Helwys, Thomas. *A Short Declaration of the Mystery of Iniquity*, edited by Richard Groves. Macon, GA: Mercer University Press, 1998.
Hodge, Charles. *Systematic Theology*, Vol. III. London: James Clarke, 1960.
Holmes, Stephen. *Baptist Theology*. London: T. & T. Clark, 2012.
———. "Introduction: Theology in Context?" *Theology in Context* 1 (2000) 1–11.
———. "Knowing Together the Mind of Christ: Congregational Government and the Church Meeting." In *Questions of Identity: Studies in Honour of Brian Haymes*, edited by Anthony R. Cross and Ruth Gouldbourne, 172–88. Oxford: Regent's Park College, 2011.
———. "Trinitarian Missiology: Towards a Theology of God as Missionary." *International Journal of Systematic Theology* 8.1 (2006) 72–90.
———. *The Wondrous Cross*. Milton Keynes, UK: Paternoster, 2007.
Hooker, Morna. "Interchange and Atonement." In *From Adam to Christ: Essays on Paul*, 26–41. Cambridge: Cambridge University Press, 1990.
Hüffmaier, Wilhelm, and Tony Peck, eds. *Dialogue between the Community of Protestant Churches in Europe and the European Baptist Federation on the Doctrine and Practice of Baptism*. Frankfurt am Main: Limbeck, 2005.
Ignatius of Loyola. *Spiritual Exercises*. Translated by Louis J. Puhl. Chicago: Loyola University Press, 1951.
Iona Community Worship Book. Glasgow: Wild Goose, 1999.
Irwin, Kevin. *Context and Text: Method in Liturgical Theology*. Collegeville, MN: Liturgical, 1994.
Isasi-Diaz, Ada Maria. "Solidarity: Love of Neighbor in the 21st Century." In *Lift Every Voice: Constructing Christian Theologies from the Underside*, edited by Susan Brooks Thistlethwaite and Mary Potter Engel, 31–40. Mary Knoll, NY: Orbis, 1998.

Jennings, Theodore W. On Ritual Knowledge." *Journal of Religion* 62.2 (1982) 111–27.
Jenson, Robert W. *Systematic Theology, Vol. 1*. Oxford: Oxford University Press, 1997.
———. *The Triune Identity*. Philadelphia: Fortress, 1982.
Jewett, Robert. *Romans*. Hermeneia. Minneapolis: Fortress, 2007.
Jonathan, Stephen. *Grace Beyond the Grave: Is Salvation Possible in the Afterlife? A Biblical, Pastoral and Theological Evaluation*. Eugene, OR: Wipf and Stock, 2014.
Jones, Keith G. *The European Baptist Federation: A Case Study in Interdependency*. Milton Keynes, UK: Paternoster, 2009.
Jump, Phil. *Healthy Church Meetings: Discerning the Mind of Christ in a Christ-like Way*. Wigan, UK: North West Baptist Association 2007.
Kardong O. S. B. Terence G. "Benedict of Nursia." In *Encyclopaedia of Early Christianity*, edited by Everett Ferguson, 179–81. 2nd ed. New York: Garland, 1998.
Käsemann. Ernst. *Commentary on Romans*. Translated by Walter Bromiley. London: SCM, 1980.
Kavanagh, Aiden. *On Liturgical Theology*. Collegeville, MN: Liturgical, 1984.
Kay, William K. *Apostolic Networks in Britain: New Ways of Being Church*. Studies in Evangelical History and Thought. Milton Keynes, UK: Paternoster, 2007.
Kidd, Richard, ed. *On the Way of Trust*. Oxford: Whitley, 1997.
———. *Something to Declare: A Study of the Declaration of Principle*. Oxford: Whitley, 1996.
Kreider, Alan, and Eleanor Kreider. *Worship and Mission After Christendom*. Milton Keynes, UK: Paternoster, 2009.
Kreider, Eleanor. *Communion Shapes Character*. Scottdale, PA: Herald, 1997.
Kucová Lydie. "Pastors in the Dock: The Political Trial of Baptist Ministers in Czechoslovakia in the 1950s." In *Freedom and the Powers*, edited by Anthony R. Cross and John H. Y. Briggs, 127–45. Didcot, UK: Baptist Historical Society 2014.
Küng, Hans. *Christianity: Essence, History, Future*. Translated by John Bowden. New York: Continuum, 1995.
LaCugna, Catherine M. *God for Us. The Trinity and Christian Life*. San Francisco: Harper Collins, 1991.
Lalleman, Pieter J., ed. *Challenging to Change: Dialogues with a Radical Baptist Theologian. Essays presented to Nigel G. Wright*. London: Spurgeon's College, 2009.
Lathrop, Gordon. *Four Gospels on Sunday: The New Testament and the Reform of Christian Worship*. Minneapolis, MN: Fortress, 2011.
———. *Holy Things: A Liturgical Theology*. Minneapolis, MN: Fortress, 1993.
Lessing, Doris. *Under my Skin*. Fourth Estate, 1995.
Lomax, Tim. *Creating Missional Worship: Fusing Context and Tradition*. London: Church House, 2015.
Lumpkin, William L., ed. *Baptist Confessions of Faith*. Philadelphia: Judson, 1969.
The Leading Question? Women in Leadership in Churches and Ecumenical Organisations. Newmarket, UK: Inspire Services, 2011.
The Lydia Question—A Fresh Look at God's Calling. Didcot, UK: Baptist Union, 2014. http://www.baptist.org.uk/Publisher/File.aspx?ID=131592&view=browser
MacCulloch, Diarmaid. *Thomas Cranmer*. New Haven: Yale University Press, 1996.
MacDonald, Gregory. *The Evangelical Universalist*. 1st ed. Eugene, OR: Cascade, 2006.
Making Moral Choices in our Relationships. Didcot, UK: Baptist Union, 2000.
Manley, Ken R. *"Redeeming Love Proclaim": John Rippon and the Baptists*. Milton Keynes, UK: Paternoster, 2004.

Manning, Bernard L. *The Hymns of Wesley and Watts*. London: Epworth, 1942.
Martin, Gordon. *The Church: A Baptist View*. London: Baptist Union, 1976.
McBeath, Clare, and Tim Presswood. *Crumbs of Hope: Prayers from the City*. Peterborough: Inspire, n.d..
McClendon Jr., James W. *Biography as Theology: How Life Stories can Remake Today's Theology*. Rev. ed. Philadelphia, PA: Trinity, 1990.
———. *Doctrine*. Vol. 2 of *Systematic Theology*. Nashville: Abingdon, 1994.
———. *Ethics*. Rev. ed. Vol. 1 of *Systematic Theology*. Nashville: Abingdon, 2002.
McClendon Jr., James Wm., and James M. Smith, *Convictions: Defusing Religious Relativism*. Rev ed. Valley Forge, PA: Trinity, 1994.
McFague, Sallie. *Metaphorical Theology: Models of God in Religious Language*. London: SCM, 1982.
McFadyen, Alistair I. *The Call to Personhood: A Christian Theory of the Individual in Social Relationships*. Cambridge: Cambridge University Press, 1990.
Meyers, Ruth A. *Missional Worship Worshipful Mission: Gathering as God's People, Going Out in God's Name*. Grand Rapids: Eerdmans, 2014.
Migliore, Daniel L. *Faith Seeking Understanding: An Introduction to Christian Theology*. Grand Rapids: Eerdmans, 1991.
Miles, Sara. "Real Bread: Communion and Hospitality." *Mission Catalyst* 2 (2015) 3.
Mitchell, Nathan D. *Meeting Mystery: Liturgy, Worship, Sacraments*. New York: Orbis, 2006.
Moltmann, Jürgen, *The Trinity and the Kingdom of God. The Doctrine of God*. Translated by Margaret Kohl. London: SCM, 1981.
Moore, S. D. "Shepherding Movement." In *The New International Dictionary of Pentecostal and Charismatic Movements*, edited by Stanley M. Burgess, 1060–62. Rev ed. Grand Rapids: Zondervan, 2002.
Mullins, Edgar Y. *The Axioms of Religion: A New Interpretation of the Baptist Faith*. Philadelphia: American Baptist Publication Society, 1908.
Murray, Stuart. *Church After Christendom*. Milton Keynes, UK: Paternoster, 2004.
———. "Church Planting, Peace and the Ecclesial Minimum." In *Challenging to Change: Dialogues with a Radical Baptist Theologian. Essays presented to Dr Nigel G. Wright on his sixtieth birthday*, edited by Pieter J. Lalleman, 129–42. London: Spurgeon's College, 2009.
———. *Post-Christendom*. Carlisle, UK: Paternoster, 2004.
The Nature of Assembly of the Assembly and the Council of the Baptist Union of Great Britain. Didcot, UK: Baptist Union, 1994.
Nelson, Sally. *Confronting Meaningless Suffering*. PhD thesis, University of Manchester, 2011.
Niebuhr, H. Richard. "The Story of Our Life." In *Why Narrative? Readings in Narrative Theology*, edited by Stanley Hauerwas and L. Gregory Jones, 21–44. Eugene, OR: Wipf & Stock, 1997.
O'Murchu, Diarmuid. *Poverty, Celibacy and Obedience: A Radical Option for Life*. New York: Crossroad, 1998.
Orr, James *The Progress of Dogma*. London: Hodder and Stoughton, 1901.
Parker, G. Keith. *Baptists in Europe: History & Confessions of Faith*. Nashville: Broadman, 1982.
Parker, T. H. L. "Predestination." In *A Dictionary of Christian Theology*, edited by Alan Richardson, 264–72. London: SCM, 1969.

Patterns and Prayers for Christian Worship: A Guidebook for Worship Leaders. Oxford: Oxford University Press, 1991.

Payne, Ernest A. *The Fellowship of Believers: Baptists Thought and Practice Yesterday and Today.* 1944. Reprint. London: Carey Kingsgate, 1952.

Payne, Ernest A., and Stephen Winward. *Orders and Prayers for Church Worship: A Manual for Ministers.* London: Baptist Union of Great Britain, 1960.

Pexton, Mark. "A Theological Reflection on Approaches to Decision Making in Scottish Baptist Churches. Communal Discernment or Designated leadership Team." MTh diss., Spurgeon's College, 2011.

Phillips, Adam. *Houdini's Box.* London: Faber and Faber, 2001.

Phillips, Anne. *The Faith of Girls: Children's Spirituality and Transition to Adulthood.* Farnham, UK: Ashgate, 2011.

———. "Who Is the Problem? Reflecting on Leadership and Gender in English Church and Society." *Discussion Paper for the Women's Issues Committee,* 2002. Unpublished.

Pierce, Gregory F. Augustine. *The Mass Is Never Ended: Rediscovering Our Mission to Transform the World.* Notre Dame, IN: Ave Maria, 2007.

Pilli, Toivo. "Discipleship in Early Anabaptist Tradition." *Baptistic Theologies* 7.2 (2015) 44–56.

Piper, John, and Wayne Grudem. *Recovering Biblical Manhood and Womanhood.* Wheaton, IL: Crossway, 2012.

Pope, Robert. "The Nonconformist Conscience." In *The T. & T. Clark Companion to Nonconformity,* edited by Robert Pope, 437–58. London: Bloomsbury, 2013.

Porter, H. Boone. "Be Present, Be Present," *Studia Liturgica* 21 (1991) 158–59.

Porter, Mark. "The Developing Field of Christian Congregational Studies." *Ecclesial Practices* 1 (2014) 149–66.

Pushing at the Boundaries of Unity: Anglicans and Baptists in Conversation. London: Church House, 2005.

Rahner, Karl. *The Trinity.* Translated by Joseph Donceel. London: Burns and Oates, 1975.

Rand, Stephen. "Can Anyone Here Play the Piano Better Than My Wife?" *Talk: The Mainstream Magazine* 3.2 (2007) 21.

Randall, Ian M. "Counsel and Help: European Baptists and Wider Baptist Fellowship." *Journal of European Studies* 11:1 (2010) 25–35.

———. *The English Baptists of the 20th Century.* Didcot, UK: The Baptist Historical Society, 2005.

Ricoeur, Paul. "Creativity in language." *Philosophy Today* 17:2 (1973) 97–111.

———. *The Rule of Metaphor.* London: Routledge Classics, 2003.

———. *Time and Narrative.* Vol. 1. Translated by K. McLaughlin and D. Pellauer. Chicago: University of Chicago Press, 1984.

———. *Time and Narrative.* Vol. 2. Translated by K. McLaughlin and D. Pellauer. Chicago: University of Chicago Press, 1985.

———. *Time and Narrative.* Vol. 3. Translated by K. Blamey and D. Pellauer. Chicago: University of Chicago Press, 1988.

Robinson, John. *The Human Face of God.* London: SCM, 1973.

Rohr, Richard. *Everything Belongs.* New York: Crossroad, 1999.

Rollinson, Andrew R. "The Attentive Community: Recovering God's Gift of Communal Discernment." Unpublished Sabbatical studies, 2009.

Ruth, Lester. "Lex Agendi, Lex Orandi: Toward an Understanding of Seeker Services as a New Kind of Liturgy." *Worship* 70:5 (1996) 386–405.

Saliers, Don E. "Liturgy and Ethics: Some New Beginnings." In *Liturgy and the Moral Self: Humanity at Full Stretch Before God: Essays in Honor of Don E. Saliers,* edited by E. Byron Anderson and Bruce T. Morrill, 13–35. Collegeville, MN: Liturgical, 1998.

———. *Worship as Theology: Foretaste of Glory Divine.* Nashville, TN: Abingdon, 1994.

Scharen, Christian. *Public Worship and Public Work: Character & Commitment in Local Congregational Life.* Collegeville, MN: Liturgical, 2004.

Schelin, Christopher L. "Unbreaking the Circle: Conversational Hermeneutics and Intra-Congregational Difference." *Journal European Baptist Studies* 16:2 (2016) 19–32.

Schillebeeckx, Edward. "Towards a Rediscovery of the Christian Sacraments." In *Ordo: Bath, Word, Prayer, Table: A Liturgical Primer in Honor of Gordon Lathrop,* edited by G. Dirk, Dwight Lange, and W. Vogel, 6–34. Akron, OH: OSL, 2005.

Schlabach, Gerard W. "Breaking Bread: Peace and War." In *Blackwell Companion to Christian Ethics,* edited by Stanley Hauerwas and Samuel Wells, 360–74. Oxford: Blackwell, 2004.

Sell, Alan P. F. *The Great Debate: Calvinism, Arminianism and Salvation.* Worthing, UK: Walter, 1982.

Shaw, Michael. "True Worship Hurts," *Baptist Times,* 29th May 2015. http://www.baptist.org.uk/Articles/439677/How_true_worship.aspx

Sheldrake, Philip. *Befriending our Desires.* London: Darton, Longman and Todd, 1995.

Shepherd, Peter. *The Making of a Modern Denomination: John Howard Shakespeare and the English Baptists 1898–1924.* Milton Keynes, UK: Paternoster, 2001.

Shurden, Walter B. "Baptists and the Priesthood of All Believers: The Priesthood of All Believers and Pastoral Authority in Baptist History." In *Not An Easy Journey: Some Transitions in Baptist Life* by Walter B. Shurden, 64–87. Macon, GA: Mercer, 2005.

Slough, Rebecca. "'Let Every Tongue': An Exploration of Hymn Singing Events and Dimensions of Knowing." In *Religious and Social Ritual: Interdisciplinary Explorations,* edited Michael B. Aune et al., 175–208. Albany, NY: State University of New York Press, 1996.

Smith, James K. A. *Desiring the Kingdom Worship, Worldview and Cultural Formation.* Grand Rapids: Baker, 2009.

———. *Imagining the Kingdom: How Worship Works.* Grand Rapids: Baker, 2013.

Smith, Karen, and Simon Woodman, eds. *Prayers of the People.* Oxford: Regent's Park College, 2011.

Stackhouse, Ian. *The Gospel-Driven Church.* Milton Keynes, UK: Paternoster, 2004.

Standing, Roger. "Missional Church." In *As a Fire Burning: Mission as the Life of the Congregation,* edited by Roger Standing, 1–11. London: SCM, 2013.

Stanley, Brian. *A History of the Baptist Missionary Society, 1972–1992.* Edinburgh: T. & T. Clark, 1992.

Stassen, Glen. *A Thicker Jesus: Incarnational Discipleship in a Secular Age.* Louisville: Westminster John Knox, 2012.

Storkey, Elaine. *Created or Constructed? The Great Gender Debate.* Carlisle, UK: Paternoster, 2000.

Storrar, William. *Scottish Identity: A Christian Vision.* Edinburgh: Handsel, 1990.

Stott, John. *The Contemporary Christian.* Leicester, UK: IVP, 1992.

A Ten Year Plan Towards 2000 incorporating the National Mission Strategy. Didcot, UK: Baptist Union, 1992.

TeSelle, Sallie. *Speaking in Parables: A Study in Metaphor and Theology*. London: SCM, 1975.

Thatcher, Adrian. *God, Sex and Gender: An Introduction*. Chichester, UK: Wiley-Blackwell, 2011.

Tidball, Derek. "Mainstream: 'Far Greater Ambitions'—An Evaluation of Mainstream's Contribution to the Renewal of Denominational Life, 1979–1994." In *Grounded in Grace: Essays to Honour Ian Randall*, edited by Pieter J. Lalleman, Peter J. Morden and Anthony R. Cross, 202–22. London: Spurgeon's College/Baptist Historical Society, 2013.

Tidball, Derek and Dianne. *The Message of Women: Creation, Grace and Gender*. Nottingham, UK: IVP, 2012.

Tidball, Dianne, "Walking a Tight Rope: Women Training for Baptist Ministry." *Baptist Quarterly* 33.7 (1990), 388–95.

Took, Pat. "In his Image." *Baptist Minister's Journal* 300 (2008) 2–10.

———. "It Shall Not Be So Among You: Power and Love in the Community of Christ." *Signposts for New Century*. Hertfordshire Baptist Association, 2000.

Torrance, Thomas F. *Karl Barth: Biblical and Evangelical Theologian*. Edinburgh: T. & T. Clark, 1990.

Transforming Superintendency. The Report of the General Superintendency Review Group presented to the Baptist Union of Great Britain Council November 1996. Didcot, UK: Baptist Union, 1996.

Turner, Victor. *The Ritual Process*. Harmondsworth, UK: Penguin, 1969.

Updike, John Updike. *Couples*. London: Penguin, 1969.

Volf, Miroslav. *After Our Likeness: The Church as the Image of the Trinity*. Grand Rapids: Eerdmans, 1998.

Volpe, Medi Ann. *Rethinking Christian Identity. Doctrine and Discipleship*. Chichester, UK: Wiley-Blackwell, 2013.

Walker, Michael. "Baptist Worship in the 20th century." In *Baptists in the Twentieth Century*. Papers Presented at a Summer School. July 1982, edited by K. W. Clements, 21–30. London: Baptist Historical Society, 1983.

Warner, Rob. "Ageing Structures and Undying Convictions." *Mainstream Magazine* 58 (1997) 12–17.

Weaver, John. "Spirituality in Everyday Life: The View from the Table." In *Under the Rule of Christ: Dimensions of Baptist Spirituality*, edited by Paul S. Fiddes, 135–67. Regent's Study Guides 14; Macon, GA: Smyth & Helwys, 2008.

Webber, Esther. "Scottish Independence: Can Anything Be Learnt from the Scotland Debate?" 12 September 2014. http://www.bbc.com/news/uk-29044563.

Webber, Robert E. *Common Roots: The Original Call for an Ancient-Future Faith*. Grand Rapids: Zondervan, 2009.

Wells, Samuel. *God's Companions: Reimagining Christian Ethics*. Oxford: Blackwell, 2006.

———. *Improvisation: The Drama of Christian Ethics*. SPCK, 2004.

West, W. M. S. *Baptist Principles*. 1960. Reprint. London: Baptist Union, 1986.

What Are Baptists? On the Way to Expressing Baptist Identity in a Changing Europe. Study Paper issued by the Division for Theology and Education of the European Baptist Federation. Hamburg: EBF, 1993.

White, B. R. *The English Baptists of the Seventeenth Century*. Didcot, UK: The Baptist Historical Society, 1996.

White, Dave. "Depth a Close Friend But Not a Lover." In *Curating Worship*, edited Jonny Baker, 80–86. London: SPCK, 2010.

White, James F. *Introduction to Christian Worship*. Rev. ed. Nashville: Abingdon, 1990.

———. *Sacraments as God's Self Giving*. 2nd ed. Nashville, TN: Abingdon Press, 2001.

White, Rob. "Mr. and Mrs." *Talk: The Mainstream Magazine* 7.2 (2007) 5.

Wild Goose Resource Group. *A Wee Worship Book*. Glasgow: Wild Goose, 1999.

Williams, Glen Garfield. "European Baptists and the Conference of European Churches." *Baptist Quarterly* 28 (1979) 52–58.

Williams, Rowan. *The Wound of Knowledge*. London: Darton, Longman & Todd, 1990.

Wink, Walter. *Engaging the Powers: Discernment and Resistance in a World of Domination*. Minneapolis: Fortress, 1992.

———. *Naming the Powers: the Language of Power in the New Testament*. Philadelphia: Fortress, 1984.

———. *The Powers That Be: Theology for a New Millennium*. New York: Doubleday, 1999.

———. *Unmasking the Powers: The Invisible Forces That Determine Human Existence*. Philadelphia: Fortress, 1986.

———. *When the Powers Fall: Reconciliation in the Healing of the Nations*. Minneapolis: Fortress, 1998.

Winter, Sean. "God's Inclusive Story." *Talk: The Mainstream Magazine* 7.2 (2007) 6–7.

Winward, Stephen. *The Reformation of our Worship*. London: Carey Kingsgate, 1964.

Women, Baptists and Ordination. Didcot, UK: Baptist Union, 2006.

Women in Ministry: A Reader Exploring the Story of Women in Leadership and Ministry within the Baptist Union of Great Britain. Didcot, UK: Baptist Union, 2011.

Woodhead, Linda. "Introduction." In *Religion and Change in Modern Britain*, edited by Linda Woodhead and Rebecca Catto, 1–33. Abingdon: Routledge, 2012.

Woodman, Simon. "A Biblical Basis for Affirming Women in Ministry—Part 1." *Baptist Ministers' Journal* 296 (October 2006) 8–13.

———. "A Biblical Basis for Affirming Women in Ministry—Part 2." *Baptist Ministers' Journal* 297 (January 2007) 10–15.

———. "Presentation to Baptist Union Council on the Difficult Passages." March 2010. Unpublished.

"The Word of God in the Life of the Church: A Report of International Conversations between the Catholic Church and the Baptist World Alliance, 2006–2010." *American Baptist Quarterly* XXXI.1 (2012) 28–122.

WCC et al. *Christian Witness in a Multi-Religious World: Recommendations for Conduct*. 2011. https://www.oikoumene.org/en/resources/documents/wcc-programmes/interreligious-dialogue-and-cooperation/christian-identity-in-pluralistic-societies/christian-witness-in-a-multi-religious-world/@@download/file/ChristianWitness_recommendations.pdf

Wright, Nigel G. *Challenge to Change*. Eastbourne, UK: Kingsway, 1991.

———. *Disavowing Constantine*. Carlisle, UK: Paternoster, 2000.

———. "Election and Predestination in Baptist Confessions of the Seventeenth Century." In *Grounded in Grace: Essays to Honour Ian Randall*, edited by Pieter J. Lalleman, Peter J. Morden, and Anthony R. Cross, 16–32. London: Spurgeon's College/Baptist Historical Society, 2013.

———. *Free Church, Free State: A Positive Baptist Vision.* Milton Keynes, UK: Paternoster, 2005.

———. *New Baptists, New Agenda.* Carlisle, UK: Paternoster, 2002.

———. *The Radical Evangelical: Seeking a Place to Stand.* London: SPCK, 1996.

———. "Spirituality as Discipleship: The Anabaptist Heritage." In *Under the Rule of Christ: Dimensions of Baptist Spirituality*, edited by Paul S. Fiddes, 79–101. Regent's Study Guides 14, Macon, GA: Smyth & Helwys, 2008.

———, ed. *Truth That Never Dies. The Dr. G. R. Beasley-Murray Memorial Lectures 2002–2012.* Eugene, OR: Pickwick, 2014.

———. *Vital Truth: The Convictions of the Christian Community.* Eugene, OR: Cascade, 2015.

Wright, N. T. *New Heavens, New Earth: The Biblical Picture of Hope.* Cambridge: Grove Books, 1992.

———. *The New Testament and the People of God.* London: SPCK, 1993.

Yoder, John Howard. *Body Politics: Five Practices of the Christian Community before the Watching World.* Scottdale, PA: Herald, 1992.

———. "The Hermeneutics of Peoplehood: A Protestant Perspective on Practical Moral Reasoning." *Journal of Religious Ethics* 10.1 (1982) 40–67.

Zizioulas, John D. *Being as Communion.* London: Darton, Longman and Todd, 1984.

Lightning Source UK Ltd.
Milton Keynes UK
UKOW05f1032160217
294554UK00001B/232/P